WORLD BANK INDEPENDENT EVALUATION GROUP

IEG

Assessing World Bank Support for Trade, 1987–2004

An IEG Evaluation

2006
The World Bank
Washington, D.C.

http://www.worldbank.org/ieg

1818 H Street, NW
Washington, DC 20433
Telephone 202-473-1000
Internet www.worldbank.org
E-mail feedback@worldbank.org

Photo credits: Maputo harbor cranes, workers offloading rice imports, Mozambique, by Eric Miller, World Bank Photo Library; television manufacturing plant, Tajikistan, by Gennadiy Ratushenko, World Bank Photo Library; Cocoa farmer lays out beans to dry, Ghana, by Karen Robinson, courtesy of Panos Pictures; laborers from Myanmar with Chinese goods ready for loading onto trucks for export, China, Jiegao border, by Mark Henley, courtesy of Panos Pictures.

ISBN-10 0-8213-6591-6
ISBN-13: 978-0-8213-6591-5
e-ISBN 0-8213-6592-4
DOI: 10.1596/978-0-8213-6591-5

Library of Congress Cataloging-in-Publication Data has been applied for.

World Bank InfoShop
E-mail: pic@worldbank.org
Telephone: 202-458-5454
Facsimile: 202-522-1500

Independent Evaluation Group
Knowledge Programs and Evaluation Capacity Development (IEGKE)
E-mail: eline@worldbank.org
Telephone: 202-458-4497
Facsimile: 202-522-3125

Printed on Recycled Paper

Contents

- **Import-related:** Policies such as eliminating or reducing quantitative restrictions and other nontariff barriers, reducing import tariff levels and dispersion, making tariff regimes more uniform and transparent, reducing import surcharges, improving import procedures, and eliminating official reference prices.
- **Export-related:** Policies related to making imports available for exporting; reducing export bans, taxes, and licenses; reducing the anti-export bias; export credit and financing; and other export incentives.
- **Exchange rate and foreign exchange management:** Moving toward market-determined exchange rates, exchange rate devaluation, or step adjustment, and away from the administrative allocation of foreign exchange.
- **Industrial and other supporting policies:** Pricing reform, investment promotion, competition policy, marketing, privatization, labor markets, and safety nets.

Bank support for trade reform was generally consistent with the 1987 WDR on trade, Operational Directive 8.60, and the literature on trade policy reforms. Eliminating quantitative restrictions (QRs) and addressing exchange rate disequilibria were often the first actions the Bank recommended, in line with the literature. Most trade loans initially contained measures to address both import liberalization and to reduce disincentives for exporting. But in 14 countries that together received 55 loans, the Bank focused only on import-related measures. Over time, the Bank has paid increased attention to export-related measures relative to import liberalization.

More generally, overall conditionality associated with trade has declined across Regions and greater reliance is being placed on floating or single tranche conditions, rather than on prior actions, as was previously the case. The decline in conditionality reflects the move toward more open regimes, a shift in the Bank's focus toward longer-term institutional and structural policies, a concurrent rise in IMF trade conditionality, and a rise in trade liberalization through regional trading arrangements (RTAs). In more recent years, the shift also likely reflects the evolution of the Bank's approach toward greater country-owned conditionality and less prescription, as outlined in Operational Policy 8.60 on development policy lending.

Four areas of concern emerge, however. First, the literature suggests the importance of macroeconomic stabilization to complement trade reforms. But the Bank sometimes supported trade reforms in the presence of serious macroeconomic instability. Second, it is crucial that complementary measures such as removing marketing and price distortions as well as competition policy, reducing labor market rigidities, and improving the regulatory environment (currently more commonly thought of as "investment climate" issues) accompany trade reforms. While this was the case sometimes, compliance with these conditions tended to be the lowest of all conditions, underscoring the political and other difficulties associated with their implementation. Third, trade-related projects did not adequately attend to the poverty and distributional outcomes, including labor market dynamics, and this continues to be a major weakness in project design. Fourth, the Bank did not take the external environment into account sufficiently, and thus did not distinguish the impact of external trade policies and shocks on trade outcomes for different groups of developing countries.

A common criticism of the Bank's trade policy advice is that it has followed a "one-size-fits-all" approach. The Independent Evaluation Group (IEG) examined all adjustment loans approved between 1987 and 2004 that contained trade policy components. While the loans followed sequencing that was broadly in line with the 1987 WDR and the economic literature, IEG found little evidence of a generic (or one-size-fits-all) approach to trade reform in the Bank's client countries. Countries varied in the extent of macroeconomic stabilization they had achieved before the reform was introduced, and in how and when they chose to use export-related policies to stimulate trade promotion. Moreover, countries were heterogeneous in how deeply they reformed and in the range of complementary policies they introduced to support the trade reform.

Given the concerns raised above, and in light of the evolving circumstances, it can be seen that Bank trade advice and support during the 1980s and 1990s was too narrow in focus. Specifically, it underestimated the complexity and sequencing of complementary policies; the role of the external environment (taking that environment as largely given); the interaction among trade, growth, and distributional outcomes; and the country-specific context (such as initial conditions and institutions) in which these policies interacted. Consequently, Bank advice was too optimistic about the benefits of trade liberalization for growth in the short run.

Project-level Outcomes

Trade-related projects have improved in performance over time. In general, trade adjustment loans have performed better than other adjustment loans in terms of project outcomes (86 versus 78 percent satisfactory), while trade investment loans performed slightly worse than other investment loans (69 versus 72 percent satisfactory, respectively). At an aggregate level, positive project outcomes were more likely to be associated with middle-income countries, low conditionality, good institutional frameworks, and prior ESW. Project design, unrealistic assumptions, and unstable macroeconomic environments contributed most frequently to unsatisfactory outcomes for individual projects.

Outputs

The project data and aggregate data from 45 sample countries show that Bank advice and lending contributed to systematic reductions in protection and to making trade regimes more open, though the pace differed across countries. Many developing countries sharply reduced the level and dispersion of their import tariffs and their use of quantitative restrictions, with the greatest reductions in Latin America. Developing countries also largely eliminated export taxes, licenses, and bans. Black market premiums also disappeared as countries moved their exchange rate regimes toward market-based systems and foreign exchange availability improved, notably in African countries. The Bank was less successful in helping countries reduce other nontariff barriers, notably in the Middle East and North Africa.

Outcomes

The export supply response was often variable. While export diversification occurred in most Regions, the low base from which nontraditional exports grew in Africa meant even rapid growth rates were inadequate to dramatically change the composition of Africa's export baskets. Moreover, many African countries experienced an erosion of competitiveness in their export baskets, contributing to increased marginalization in global trade. Imports responded to the reforms undertaken, growing rapidly in all Regions and easing input constraints for importers. However, the speed of import liberalization increased competitive pressures in countries that were unable to generate dynamic and sustained manufacturing growth. For countries where data are available, total factor productivity growth gains are apparent.

Impact

Employing a "difference-in-differences" approach that corrects for potential sample selection bias by using a Heckman selection procedure, a counterfactual was constructed to compare countries that reformed their trade regimes with a Bank loan, and those that reformed without such Bank support. Bank clients that obtained loans to support trade reform experienced higher economic growth rates in the medium term (3–6 years) following trade reform, and their growth rates exceeded those independent reformers that reformed without the financial support of the Bank.

Both groups of reformers also experienced dramatic increases in import demand, although this effect lasted longer for Bank-supported reformers. However, Bank-supported reformers exhibited a modest supply response, suggesting that trade liberalization alone was not sufficient—a finding supported by recent research in this area. The gains in economic growth were often driven by domestic demand arising from improved resource allocation, rather than just export expansion. The employment and poverty outcomes associated with trade reforms were mixed, and the Bank did not conduct sufficient analysis to inform its policy advice and lending on this issue or systematically measure the outcomes.

While the initial impetus for trade reform was often an economic crisis, sustaining the reform required broad support and ownership. Conditionality was generally not conducive to achieving that ownership, and the Bank was more judicious in using it in countries where it had less leverage. Bank advice and analytical work were often instrumental in supporting reform; its value, however, was reduced where it was perceived to be dogmatically based. External factors (market access, regional integration), coherent macroeconomic policies, exogenous shocks (droughts, commodity prices), and timely implementation of complementary policies were critical in determining whether or not individual countries reaped the full benefits of trade reform.

Bank Trade Activities: 2001–04

The Bank's recent trade program, which was revamped in 2001, has two objectives: (1) make the world trading system more "friendly to development" or reciprocally open; and (2) make trade an important part of country development strategies. The Bank employed research, participation in global policy discussions and advocacy, trade capacity building, and mainstreaming of trade as tools to achieve these objectives. The assessment of developments during this period has to be considered in the context of the relatively brief period under review. This is especially likely to be a factor in the mainstreaming agenda , which necessarily requires greater commitment and action by operational units.

The resurgence in the Bank's attention to trade is not primarily characterized by greater trade lending or conditionality. Instead, it is reflected in a higher profile in global advocacy, an increased volume of trade-related analysis, and greater attention to the institution's capacity to respond to trade-related analytical needs and operational support.

This evaluation finds the Bank's objectives between 2001 and 2004 to be relevant, timely, and largely responsive to the rapidly changing global environment on trade issues. However, given the inherent limitations of the Bank's role in global negotiations and the importance of country-specific policy dialogue, the evaluation finds that more attention should have been given to strengthening the analytical tools, processes, and systematic interactions between the Trade Department and operational colleagues. Moreover, the dependency on trust funds in research and capacity building potentially poses serious challenges to the Bank in determining an independent work program.

Progress toward a More Development-Friendly Trading System

Much of the Bank's research between 2001 and 2004 was of consequence (published in respected journals), and in some cases innovative (for example, in new fields such as services, agricultural standards, transport costs, and other behind-the-border issues). Research on some issues related to the multilateral trading system was often timely. For example, in the run-up to the Doha Trade Ministerial, the Bank released the *2002 Global Economic Prospects Report: Making Trade Work for the World's Poor* and produced a paper about the global trade architecture (Hoekman 2002). The *2004 Global Economic Prospects Report: Realizing the Development Promise of the Doha Agenda* was published in the run-up to the Cancun Trade Ministerial meeting.

Research on regionalism has been forward-looking and has moved toward a pragmatic view of RTA membership. However, several areas identified in the trade agenda have been slow to yield significant insights (agricultural trade and policies) or have not been adequately researched (adjustments costs and distributional outcomes associated with trade, microlevel adjustment to trade, and export processing zones).

The Bank has positioned itself more effectively as an advocate for the developing countries on global trade issues and, given the wide reach of its publications, has contributed to increasing awareness of the issues. Given the plethora of other actors in the advocacy field (nongovernmental organizations such as Oxfam and Third World Network, as well as development partners such as the U.K. Department for International Development) and the Bank's limited direct role in WTO talks, the Bank could be seen most accurately as an indirect participant—contributing ideas and adding to the pressure to influence changes, rather than directly influencing outcomes. Staff indicate that the Bank's global advocacy role is useful in positioning the Bank among client countries, especially those in whom the institution might otherwise be less engaged on trade issues (such as in Latin America).

The Bank is meeting its trade-related capacity building (TCB) objectives unevenly and it appears that, as currently stated, the objectives may not adequately capture the scope and priorities of Bank activities. Specifically, the Bank is meeting its commitment to advise countries on trade policy through a dramatically increased volume of trade-related analytical work that is the basis for country policy dialogue, as well as through capacity building components in lending operations.

The Bank has also increased its dialogue with regional trade institutions. This is especially notable in the Africa Region. Analysis has been conducted on common external tariffs, revenue implications, and possible trade diversion for several RTAs (such as the East Africa Community, the Economic Community of West African States, and Union Economique et Monetaire Ouest Africaine), as well as on Economic Partnership Agreements with the European Union. In Latin America, work on Central America Free Trade Agreement (CAFTA) with Latin American officials was timely.

The Bank is doing less well helping countries to meet its stated objectives of adopting appropriate regional policies and participating more effectively in negotiations. It has been least effective in helping countries manage external shocks and adjustment costs related to trade liberalization.

The most high-profile initiative in the Bank's TCB work is the Integrated Framework for Trade-Related Technical Assistance (the IF), a multidonor, multiagency collaboration originally set up in 1997 to provide trade-related technical assistance to the 49 least-developed countries (LDCs). While diagnostic needs assessments have been carried out for almost half of eligible LDCs, follow-up and implementation have been slow.

Concrete proposals and approvals for trade capacity projects are finally emerging. As of May 30, 2005, 23 activities ($8.1 million) had been approved. A review of the proposed activities suggests overlap with other donor activities in some cases, defeating the purpose of donor harmonization. More generally, the pace is slow relative to the Doha negotiations and the needs identified in the Diagnostic Trade Integration Study (DTIS), and there is no mechanism to ensure that the most critical priorities are funded first.

Two independent evaluations of the IF were undertaken, in 2003 and 2004. Among the main evaluative findings are that despite a 2001 restructuring, weaknesses from the original program remain, including insufficient focus on improved trade outcomes, rather than the process alone, and a shortage of funds (financial and administrative) to meet the identified demands for technical assistance in developing countries. More generally, IEG's review of 26 global public programs provides some useful lessons (OED 2004a). The most relevant for the IF are the need to link financing to priorities in a systematic fashion, to strengthen and streamline the governance and management of programs, and to develop a results-based management framework.

Progress toward Mainstreaming Trade

Mainstreaming trade in Bank operations has several dimensions (ESW, trade in assistance strategies, knowledge management, and incorporation of relevant trade issues in sector activities and strategies); the Bank is doing better along some dimensions than others. It has responded quickly to keep up with the WTO negotiations and other global trade issues, and to catalyze a rapid increase in trade-related analytical work. Trade Department staff members have been an important part of this improvement—sharing their expertise through mission participation, contributions to and leadership of reports, and as peer reviewers.

After sustained decline from the mid-1990s following the conclusion of the Uruguay Round, ESW on trade issues has risen in recent years in every Region except Latin America and the Caribbean, which started at a high level. In the past three years, strategic Regional flagships on trade have been carried out in every Region except Africa (where one is under way) and have been well focused on the particular concerns of the Regions they cover.

Underpinning this reversal is the greater interest of client countries in trade issues as they grapple with more complex integration into the global economy, greater commitment and interest of donors leading to additional trust funds, and development of a new trade-focused economic report—the DTIS, which was an important initial catalyst in spurring analytical trade work in low-income countries by the Bank.

The focus of trade ESW broadened over time from changes in incentives and general trade performance in the 1980s to encompass a broader definition of competitiveness (labor costs and infrastructure) and external environment considerations (such as the impact of Regional arrangements or market access issues). Increasing attention has been given to the analysis of Regional trade integration issues with analysis and advice to Regional organizations, notably in Africa (Economic Partnership Agreement and common external tariffs for several African RTAs) and Latin America (such as the US-CAFTA agreement). However, reports have only rarely presented an in-depth analysis of the welfare implications of trade policies, analyzed the institutional framework for trade, or incorporated political economy factors that could influence trade reform and outcomes. Also largely missing is microeconomic analysis on the response of firms to changes in incentives.

Despite the overall increase in operational trade ESW, the Bank has done less well in systematically mainstreaming trade in Country Assistance Strategies and in sector activities and policies, although the trend is improving. Regional trade coordinators (RTCs) in each of the Bank's six operational Regions are expected to facilitate the information flow between country management units (CMUs) and the PREM Network and to provide strategic direction on trade issues. However, it appears that achieving full effectiveness in their interventions is limited by budgetary, staffing, organizational and leadership issues. With the exception of Africa, the RTC role remains largely an unfunded mandate. The role of the coordinator varies across Regions, with sector leaders, lead economists, and sector managers variously being assigned the role. However, in most Regions it is unclear whether the RTC has the necessary authority to play a strategic role that cuts across sectors, or even lead discussions with CMUs. In addition, the absence of tangible budget support and links to annual performance evaluation reduces incentives. To enhance the role of Bank Regional vice presidential units (VPUs) in making trade linkages, it would be useful to clarify responsibilities, establish clear terms of reference and accountabilities, and for Regional management to indicate the modalities for integrating trade into the country dialogue and growth agenda.

After a slow start, knowledge management activities are picking up. A series of *Trade Notes* was initiated in 2003 and the trade thematic group is being revived. But a gap still exists between these activities and the needs of country economists. A survey of Bank country economists indicated a need for more knowledge about transitional costs associated with trade reform, greater empirical and comparative analysis, and practical research on global supply chains.

The current trade agenda goes beyond the traditional concern with border regimes of tariffs, nontariff barriers, and other impediments to trade. The gross distortions in trade regimes endemic in the 1980s have been reduced significantly. For this reason, greater attention is now focused on behind-the-border barriers (internal constraints) that adversely affect a country's investment climate, along with the constraints and opportunities associated with the global trading system.

Within the Bank, global advocacy to redress imbalances in the global trading system can be handled by senior management and the Trade Department alone. However, all the other impediments to global integration have to be addressed in conjunction with other sector groups and require strengthened implementation by operational VPUs (as highlighted above) and country management units.

In areas where the other sector groups worked with the Trade Department or where the Trade Department provided intellectual leadership—such as sanitary and phytosanitary standards and trade facilitation—the Bank has been successful in ensuring the operational relevance of its activities. In other areas where the Bank might have made an impact—agricultural trade and policies, trade and poverty linkages—inadequate investment and less intellectual leadership has led to less success. In an important area of focus in the ongoing WTO negotiations—services liberalization—the Bank lacks a critical mass of staff with the necessary skills to underpin country dialogue and operations.

To enhance the effectiveness of its trade activities, the Bank will have to face more squarely the multisectoral nature of the current trade agenda. Over half of the trade-related projects approved in the past 10 years were assigned to a non-PREM network. Specifically, the Bank will have to improve links between the various sectors and the Trade Department on trade issues (research, trade-related capacity building, knowledge management, and development of tools and templates). The Trade Department can bring the global perspective to sector issues. However, implementation rests squarely in the hands of the operational VPUs and the country management units. Success on this multisectoral front will be the difference between individually competent pieces of analytical pieces and a more synergistic approach.

Recommendations

Recommendation 1: Address Poverty-Distributional Outcomes and External Shocks in a Balanced Approach

This evaluation found that despite the increasing volume of research on poverty issues in the Trade Department and of poverty and social impact analysis more generally, trade-related projects do not consistently or systematically address poverty and distributional outcomes. While much import liberalization has already occurred, further liberalization appears possible for some developing countries, notably within agriculture. With that in mind, three actions are critical:

- First, IEG recommends that, at the country level, all new projects with trade policy components include a discussion of this issue that, at a minimum, draws on the cross-sectoral expertise of economic policy, poverty, gender, private sector development, and (as appropriate) agricultural and rural development units, as well as existing research in the country. Identification of possible transitional costs and an assessment of the existing institutional framework for cushioning shocks and actions to mitigate or minimize shocks would be important considerations in the discussion. Placing trade in a broader discussion of the determinants of poverty will help ensure that this is not a mechanical exercise, but one rooted in its expected importance.
- Second, at the institutionwide level, and following the Bank's statement at the Cancun Ministerial in 2003, IEG recommends that a concrete program of adjustment assistance be developed more rapidly to respond to the trade-related shocks that developing countries may face. To the extent that such a program is no longer deemed relevant, it would be helpful for management to clarify this.
- Third, IEG recommends a more systematic program of research on micro-level adjust-

ment to trade policies, looking at firms, individuals, and households.

Recommendation 2: Revisit the Balance between Global and Country Agendas and Strengthen Operational Links on Trade Issues

IEG recommends that management revisit the balance between its activities at the global level on the one hand, and on the Regional and country agenda on the other. Given the multisectoral nature of trade issues, a participatory process that involves operational sector colleagues, other networks, and the Trade Department is likely to yield the greatest benefits. Operational linkages need to be strengthened among different units of the Bank and greater emphasis placed on country and field operations. Three actions are necessary:

- First, greater strategic and intellectual guidance is needed from the Trade Department with respect to the conceptual framework within which country teams should consider trade issues. The design of a guidance note and upstream support on a pilot basis to country teams planning country assistance strategies would be practical first steps and would help distinguish cases where trade is logically a priority element in the country dialogue.
- Second, in three thematic areas of focus, a more formal set of arrangements between operations, networks, and the Trade Department is needed to maximize synergies—agricultural trade and policies, services liberalization, and distributional outcomes associated with trade policies.
- Third, as has been done between the Transport and Agriculture Units on the one hand, and the Trade Department on the other, IEG recommends that working arrangements with the Private Sector Department Vice-Presidency be established to highlight the interface between the two areas and bring the global dimension to bear more precisely. This cross-fertilization of trade and the need for better integration of trade and the finance, private sector, and infrastructure (FPSI) work program is especially evident in the work on trade in services. Greater interaction between the Trade Department staff specialists in trade in services and the subsectoral expertise in transport, power, finance, telecoms, and so on located in FPSI is needed.

Recommendation 3: Strengthen Knowledge Management Efforts

Two actions are important in this area:

- First, a concerted effort to bring all country economists up to date on the main features and applications of the World Integrated Trade Solution (WITS) software would enhance their awareness of the global trade issues and their implications for the countries they work on. It would also enable them to supervise research assistants and consultants and to seek further training if and when needed.
- Second, knowledge management efforts could reflect greater cross-fertilization with other networks and better integrate trade work done in the center with country-level work on agriculture, economic policy, labor markets, and private sector development. As part of these efforts, the possibility of joint thematic groups with other networks should be explored. More generally, IEG recommends a more effective use of knowledge management tools tailored to key target groups—across sectors. A mechanism to obtain regular systematic feedback from operational staff on the most immediate and relevant trade-related topics would be helpful, as the survey identified gaps, despite the canvassing conducted by regional trade coordinators during the year. Finally, greater sharing of country experience in particular areas, much as was done with the work in agricultural standards, is needed. This will require greater support from the center to ensure quality at entry for project design, as well as economic and sector work.

ACRONYMS AND ABBREVIATIONS

AAA	Analytical and advisory activities
AERC	African Economic Research Consortium
AFR	Africa Region (Sub-Saharan Africa)
CAFTA	Central America Free Trade Agreement
CAS	Country Assistance Strategy
COMESA	Common Market for Eastern and Southern Africa
CPI	Consumer price index
CPIA	Country Policy and Institutional Assessment
DEC	Development Economics
DECRG	Development Research Group
DFID	Department for International Development (U.K.)
DTIS	Diagnostic Trade Integration Study
EAP	East Asia and Pacific Region
ECA	Europe and Central Asia Region
EPZ	Export Processing Zone
ESAF	Enhanced Structural Adjustment Facility
ESSD	Environmentally and Socially Sustainable Development
ESW	Economic and sector work
FDI	Foreign direct investment
FPSI	Finance, Private Sector, and Infrastructure
FY	Fiscal year
GDP	Gross domestic product
GEP	Global economic prospects
IBRD	International Bank for Reconstruction and Development
IDA	International Development Association
IEG	Independent Evaluation Group
IF	Integrated Framework for Trade-related Technical Assistance
IMF	International Monetary Fund
LAC	Latin America and the Caribbean Region
LDC	Least developed country
MERCOSUR	Southern Common Market
MFA	Multi-Fibre Arrangement
MIT	Massachusetts Institute of Technology
MNA	Middle East and North Africa Region
NAFTA	North American Free Trade Agreement
NGO	Nongovernmental organization
NTB	Nontariff barrier
OECD	Organisation for Economic Co-operation and Development
OED	Operations Evaluation Department of the World Bank*
PREM	Poverty Reduction and Economic Management

PRSP	Poverty Reduction Strategy Paper
PSD	Private sector development
QR	Quantitative restriction
RTA	Regional trading arrangement
SAL	Structural adjustment loan
SAR	South Asia Region
SECAL	Sector adjustment loan
SIL	Sector Investment Loan
SME	Small and medium-size enterprise
SPS	Sanitary and phytosanitary standards
TA	Technical assistance
TAE	Trade Assistance Evaluation
TCB	Trade-related capacity building
TNC	Trade Negotiation Committee
UNCTAD	United Nations Conference on Trade and Development
UNDP	United Nations Development Programme
WBI	World Bank Institute
WDR	World Development Report
WITS	World Integrated Trade Solution
WTO	World Trade Organization
ZCCM	Zambia Consolidated Copper Mines

*OED has changed its official name to Independent Evaluation Group (IEG). The new designation "IEG" will be inserted in all of IEG's publications, review forms, databases and Web sites in the next few weeks.

Chapter 1: Evaluation Highlights

- While trade has helped expand the global economy, the gains have been uneven.
- The Bank has contributed to trade both intellectually and financially, stressing its potential contribution to economic development.
- The evaluation assesses the effectiveness of Bank trade assistance between fiscal years 1987 and 2004.

Introduction

Economists have long viewed international trade as an engine of overall economic growth. Greater volumes of trade among countries have partly fuelled the expansion of the global economy and increased wealth for many of its members, although the distribution of the gains has been unequal.

The Bank has supported the reform of trade policies and the strengthening of trade-related institutions and infrastructure in its client countries. Between fiscal years 1987 and 2004, about 8.1 percent of total Bank commitments (or $38 billion) went to 117 countries to help them better integrate into the global economy.[1] This financing has been accompanied by a large volume of analytical work in the form of operational economic and sector work, numerous research publications on trade, and working papers on trade-related topics.

This period also coincides with a worldwide expansion of trade and trade liberalization in developing countries. Export growth has outpaced growth in gross domestic product (GDP) over the past three decades, and average tariffs have fallen steadily globally (figure 1.1). The Bank has both influenced and been influenced by these developments. Appendix A1 highlights key developments in international trade both inside and outside the Bank over the past two decades.

Rationale for Bank Involvement

The Bank has strongly supported trade-related policies, institutions, and infrastructure.

The Bank's interest in trade has gone through three phases. During the first phase (starting in the 1980s and extending to the mid-1990s), the Bank based its involvement on the perceived importance of trade for economic growth and on the role of openness in enhancing a country's economic efficiency. Important channels between trade and growth were assumed to include improved resource allocation from changes in relative prices, stronger incentives for adaptation and innovation, cheaper capital goods, and higher foreign direct investment flows associated with new trade opportunities. By increasing incentives and the profitability of exporting, Bank support for trade reform was expected to help expand and diversify exports by improving what was then known as the *enabling environment* (now commonly referred to as the *investment climate*).[2]

Figure 1.1: Declining Import Tariffs, But Some Regions Still Significantly Protected

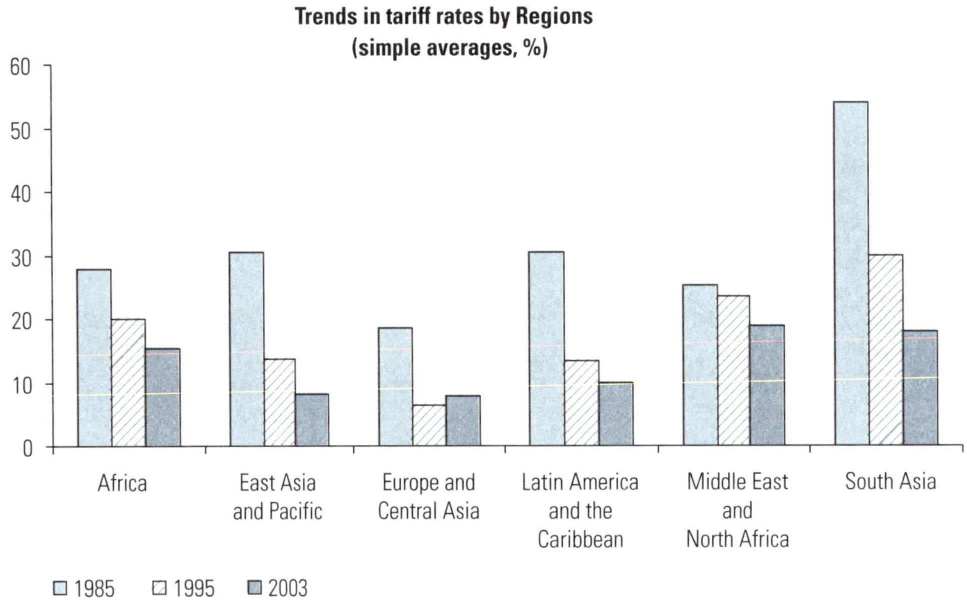

Sources: WTO, IDB CD ROM database and Trade Policy Review — Country Report, various issues, 1990-2003, and IMF Global Monitoring Tariff Data.

During the second phase, from the mid to late 1990s, the Bank's focus on trade diminished. Analytical work and (to a lesser extent) lending were reduced from the first phase. The most evident aspect of the diminished attention to trade was the merging of two trade units and an accompanying reduction in the number of staff working on trade issues. The concurrent elimination of the old technical units under the reorganization of 1996 dispersed trade experts throughout the institution, and several subsequently moved on to work on non-trade issues.

Following this lull in Bank trade activities during the second half of the 1990s, when trade lending slowed considerably, the Bank expanded its trade work following the Doha Trade Ministerial in 2001—through research, advocacy, capacity building, and operational activities. The Bank established a Trade Department in July 2002, comprising units from the Development Economics (DEC) Vice-Presidency, Poverty Reduction and Economic Management (PREM) Vice-Presidency, and World Bank Institute (WBI) to help further the trade agenda.

Since 2001, the Bank has viewed the multilateral trading system as a framework for clients to achieve greater economic integration.

In this third phase, the Bank's increased interest in and support for the current multilateral trade liberalization talks rests on several assumptions. First is the idea, as outlined in a 2001 trade development report, that progress on important issues such as agriculture and services liberalization is most likely to occur in a multilateral framework. Second, smaller countries would have greater bargaining power and protection in the multilateral system. Third, larger developing countries would benefit from the dispute settlement mechanism. The fourth assumption is that developing country participation in the World Trade Organization (WTO) would help lock in domestic trade reforms, and thereby boost investor confidence. Above all, there was an implicit assumption that the Bank's client countries would benefit from having the institution act as an "honest broker"—a counterweight to the interests of the developed world.

Despite the importance of trade in the Bank's corporate agenda over the past three decades, the institution did not have a formal strategy until recently. During the 1980s, however, some influential research appears to have guided operational policies on trade liberalization (and indeed, the intellectual environment within the Bank for trade reform). The Bank-sponsored work of Balassa, Choksi, Krueger, Michaely, Papageorgiou, and others outside the Bank played an important role. These earlier studies noted the complexity of trade reform and emphasized sequencing (with stabilization preceding other reforms in the presence of high inflation). They also highlighted the need to consider the fiscal implications of trade liberalization, and noted the importance of complementary policies (elimination of price controls and regulations, financial policy reforms, labor market liberalization, infrastructure improvements, and institutional reforms) to improve the payoff to trade reform.

While there was no formal trade strategy prior to 2001, three key documents provided strategic and technical guidance on Bank trade policy advice. These are the *1987 World Development Report* (*Industrialization and Foreign Trade*), a 1989 report on strengthening trade policy, and the section on trade adjustment lending in Operational Directive 8.60.[3]

The main policy reforms embedded in these documents included replacing quantitative restrictions with tariffs as a useful first stage of trade liberalization, maintaining low and relatively uniform tariffs for reasons of efficiency and political economy, realistic exchange rates requiring low inflation, studies of the economic costs of existing policies and evaluations of the expected benefits of reform, improved data on indicators and measures of nominal and effective protection, and strengthened capacity of reforming countries to assess their own policies. The *World Development Report* (WDR) also supported the increased use of conditionality in structural adjustment lending as a catalyst for trade reform. Operational Directive 8.60 contained additional guidance that eventual tariff levels were to range between 5 and 20 percent.[4]

Current Bank objectives in trade (first articulated in a 2002 trade progress report) are twofold. At the global level, the Bank assumes a much more proactive role. Specifically, it aims to promote changes in the world trading system to make it supportive of development—especially of the poorest of the developing countries and of the poor across the developing world. At the country level, the Bank aims to promote integration through trade as a core aspect of country development strategies.

No formal strategy guided the Bank's trade work in the 1980s and 1990s.

Objective of the Evaluation

This evaluation assesses the effectiveness of the Bank's assistance to client countries for trade between fiscal years 1987 and 2004, based on the Bank's strategies and objectives embedded in the 1987 WDR (and later codified in OD 8.60) and the 2002 trade progress report. Trade assistance in this context refers to lending operations, analytical work (research as well as economic and sector work [ESW]), advocacy, and capacity building activities that are intended to enhance the environment and capabilities of Bank clients to produce and trade goods and services in the global economy.[5]

Instead, several Bank documents provided guidance for reforms.

Capturing the effectiveness of the Bank's trade work is challenging for at least three reasons. First, country conditions influence the effectiveness of trade reforms and assistance, including macroeconomic environment, endowments, non-trade investment climate factors (notably institutions), governance and political economy dynamics, and institutional capacity. It is often difficult to disentangle trade's contribution from these other determinants.

Second, international external factors also influence government attitudes toward trade and government's ability to implement policies supportive of trade. Especially relevant are commodity price shocks; market access; and the country's participation

This study evaluates lending and nonlending assistance for trade between fiscal years 1987 and 2004.

in regional, bilateral, or multilateral trading arrangements.

Third, other actors, such as the private sector, bilateral and multilateral development agencies, and nongovernmental organizations (NGOs), influence the pace and nature of reforms.

The broad evaluative question relates to the development effectiveness of the Bank's assistance on trade, specifically, growth and poverty reduction. In addition, the evaluation addresses the following two questions:

Evaluative questions examine the relevance and effectiveness of Bank trade assistance and its impact on growth and poverty reduction.

- **Relevance of Bank assistance:** *Was the Bank's trade-related assistance relevant to promoting improved trade and economic outcomes? Did the Bank "do the right things"?* Specific examples include whether the advised speed and sequencing of trade reforms and associated conditionality were appropriate, and to what extent these inputs were grounded in adequate research and analytical work. To what extent did Bank trade advice and support take key external factors (such as multilateral trade liberalization, multilateral institutions/rules, industrial country policies, and the rise of regionalism) into account? Was the Bank's trade support accompanied by appropriate and relevant complementary policy and institutional reforms in the countries? To what extent did the Bank's assistance on trade focus on poverty and distributional outcomes?
- **Effectiveness of Bank assistance:** *Were Bank-supported interventions effective and efficient in achieving their stated objectives? Did the Bank "do things right"?* Specific questions include whether Bank-supported interventions facilitated trade reforms. What was the impact of Bank trade assistance on specific outcomes such as protection, import liberalization, export supply response, and economic growth? What were the distributional outcomes? In the more recent period, did the Bank succeed in integrating trade in Country Assistance Strategies?

A logical framework linking Bank inputs to outcomes underpins the evaluation.

This report is timely for two reasons. One is that no comprehensive and independent evaluation of Bank assistance on trade has been done since the early 1990s.[6] The second reason is the recent resurgence in Bank attention to trade issues; the evaluation is intended to shed some light on where to go from here.

Conceptual Framework and Methodology

The conceptual framework underpinning the evaluation builds on a logical framework of the links between Bank actions (inputs), desired objectives, outputs, outcomes, and impacts (figure 1.2 and Appendix A2 provide illustrative indicators).[7] The main desired immediate outcome of the Bank's support for trade (based on an analysis of project documents) is improved trade performance: higher export volumes, faster export growth rates, a more diversified basket of exports, cheaper and more readily available imports, and greater integration in the global economy. The underlying assumption behind these objectives (often explicitly stated) is that expanded trade will contribute to achieving the Bank's overarching goal of poverty reduction in two ways—by contributing to economic growth and by creating jobs (Wood 1997, 1995). The study's analysis takes place at the project, country, and global levels.

The evidence on which this evaluation rests includes an Independent Evaluation Group (IEG) portfolio review, background papers, interviews with key stakeholders, surveys, and country case studies and desk reviews.[8] In addition, it draws from the extensive literature on trade issues published inside and outside the Bank. Finally, as appropriate, it draws on related IEG reviews such as those of Global Public Goods (IEG 2004a), the Investment Climate (IEG 2004b), and Lines of Credit (IEG 2005).

The study has six chapters in line with the results-based approach outlined above. Chapter 1 comprises an introduction to the scope, objective, and organization of the report,

Figure 1.2: Conceptual Framework for the Evaluation

Inputs

Trade adjustment and investment lending
Economic and sector work (ESW) and policy advice
Technical assistance—for example, for trade negotiations
Research and advocacy
Country Assistance Strategies

Objectives

Competitiveness	**Institutional Capacity**
Transparent incentives	Policy makers
Neutral to importers/exporters	Exporting firms
Access to inputs at world prices	Trade promotion institutions
Allocative efficiency gains	(customs, standards)

Outputs

Tariffs: Lower levels, narrower ranges, less dispersion
Shorter customs clearance times
Increased trade financing

Outcomes

Improved Trade Performance
Increase in exports and faster growth rates
Greater export diversification
Increased market shares
Higher firm-level productivity
Reduced rent-seeking and greater import competition

Impact

Economic growth
Poverty reduction

while Chapter 2 briefly reviews the literature. The next three chapters focus on inputs, outputs, and outcomes. Specifically, Chapter 3 examines the inputs, trends, and evolution of Bank assistance in trade, while Chapter 4 reviews the main economic outcomes and impacts. Chapter 5 analyzes the resurgence of Bank trade activities since 2001, while Chapter 6 concludes with the main findings and presents specific recommendations.

Chapter 2: Evaluation Highlights

- Despite long-term benefits from trade, trade liberalization is often controversial.
- The literature has extended the factors that help maximize the benefits from trade liberalization.
- Design of trade reform, complementary policies, geography, and institutions matter to differing degrees in each country.

Lessons from the Literature

The literature generated by the debate on the effect of trade and related policies on country economic performance concludes that although trade offers long-term benefits for developing countries, trade liberalization alone is not sufficient for economic growth.

Rather, it has become clear that maximizing trade and welfare outcomes depends on the underlying macroeconomic environment, policies for export development, the design and sequencing of trade policies, external constraints and opportunities, and complementary policies that contribute to the overall investment climate. These factors in the outcome of trade liberalization, together with a summary of the lessons from previous IEG assessments, are the subject of this chapter. The objective is to provide context for the evaluation of the Bank's approach to trade.[1] The chapter partly draws on Oyejide (2004) and the literature survey in Appendix B1.

Trade Policy Reform and Economic Growth

The first multi-country studies of developing countries' trade regimes (Little, Scitovsky, and Scott 1970; Balassa and Associates 1982; and an influential study done by the NBER and summarized in Bhagwati 1978 and Krueger 1978) systematically detailed the inefficiencies of the import-substituting development strategies that prevailed throughout the developing world. The studies were influential in promoting export orientation as a path to more rapid economic growth.[2]

Early multicountry studies promoted outward orientation as a path to more rapid growth.

Despite the potential benefits from trade, policies related to trade liberalization remain controversial in some circles.[3] First, critics assert that these policies led to instances of liberalization that proceeded too rapidly, resulting in severe transitional costs of adjustment reflected in increased poverty, deindustrialization, and job loss.

A second criticism revolves around design issues. Critics argue that the Bank recommends the same programs for all countries, taking too little account of differing country circumstances. They also assert that the Bank emphasizes "import liberalization" at the expense of "export promotion," despite evidence from the East Asian countries that promoted export growth before general import

Despite the expected benefits, trade liberalization is often controversial.

Process may differ from textbook theory.

liberalization by using duty drawbacks and preferential exchange rate schemes.

Third, in contrast to the "first best" world that underpins trade theory, the "real" world has several deviations that are likely to influence the outcome of unilateral trade liberalization. Protectionism in industrial and other developing countries, the rise of regionalism, and unanticipated political events are just three factors that can result in unanticipated outcomes. Therefore, some observers have criticized the Bank for not taking these factors into account.

The expected benefits from trade may not be fully realized in the short run for several reasons:

- Inappropriate macroeconomic policies, such as incomplete stabilization, resulting in contractionary fiscal or monetary policies that squeeze out credit from the private sector and reduce the entry of new firms, or lead to appreciation of the real exchange rate, thereby reducing competitiveness
- Missing complementary (so-called "behind-the-border") policies and institutions to support faster export growth, such as customs, rule of law, quality and standards, and trade logistics[4]
- Insufficient or inadequate skills and capital to take advantage of emerging opportunities that arise from the liberalization
- External constraints such as market access.

Beyond these points on imperfect trade liberalizations, there are questions about the link between trade reform and economic growth. The econometric evidence on the links between trade reform, economic growth, and trade performance remains mixed.[5] It has proven difficult to use the cross-sectional approach to establish causality and to identify the role of other intervening factors such as geography and institutional elements. In particular, the verdict is still out on the relative importance of each factor.

The econometric links between trade reform and growth are often inconclusive.

Researchers continue to extend existing methodologies to explore the links between trade reform and growth. They have focused on refining the measurement of "openness" and on incorporating additional economic variables that influence whether trade liberalization results in accelerated economic growth, and, if so, the extent of this influence. By identifying the years when non-reversed trade liberalization programs were launched and using panel regression techniques, Wacziarg and Welch (2003) find that, on average, growth, investment, and openness increase after trade liberalization.

Others have focused on the role of additional country-specific factors, such as institutions (Rodrik, Subramanian, and Trebbi 2004; Freund and Bolaky 2004) and complementary factors (Chang, Kaltani, and Loayza 2005).

The new growth theory predicts that openness to trade (and investment) increases access to new technology; enhances efficiency by making market structures more competitive, allowing the exploitation of economies of scale; and by spurring innovation. In a study of 93 countries, Edwards (1998) finds that total factor productivity growth is faster in more open economies. Subsequent work in this area has supported this finding (Tybout 2003; Choi and Harrigan 2003; Amiti and Konings 2005). De Melo (2005) documents how the Bank's research in this area has contributed to establishing the microeconomic channels at the firm and sector levels through which trade openness contributes to economic growth.

Building on enterprise and census surveys in manufacturing, Bank research contributed to establishing the beneficial impact of "import discipline" on pricing and productivity gains. More recently, De Melo notes that Bank industry studies have complemented firm-level studies by establishing the links among a variety of factors (research and development embodied in trade, foreign direct investment [FDI], and product variety) and productivity growth.

Despite differences of opinion among econometricians on the causal relationship between trade reform and economic growth, there are areas of common ground. Few, if any, countries have grown rapidly and reduced poverty by following a long-term autarkic approach. As noted in Panagariya (2004), neither Rodrik (1999) nor Stiglitz (2002), critics of the Bank's approach to trade liberalization, dispute the benefits countries can gain by opening up their economies. Researchers on both sides of the issue also increasingly agree on the importance of country specificity and of institutions in disentangling the policies that affect trade and growth.

Table 2.1 (and Appendix B1) summarizes the main lessons from the literature on the impact of the underlying macroeconomic environment, policies for export development, the design and sequencing of trade policies, external constraints and opportunities, and complementary policies on trade outcomes.

Lessons from Past IEG Evaluations

Previous IEG trade-related evaluations focused on agriculture (IEG 1996a), industrial sector and policies (IEG 1991b, 1995), aspects of trade adjustment lending (IEG 1991a, 1992a), social impact of lending (IEG 1997, 1999), and trade infrastructure (IEG 1996b).[6] These are summarized in Appendix B2.

The main trade-related conclusions and recommendations of those studies were:

- The Bank paid inadequate attention to the role of selective promotion in export development. It would be useful to increase support for technology development, improved information about market opportunities for exports, and labor training.
- Reduce trade conditionality to a few key variables that would be easy to monitor.
- Achieve macroeconomic stabilization before trade liberalization and better coordinate tax and trade reforms (stronger conclusion than the literature).
- Greater internal competition is needed to prevent deregulation from becoming anti-competitive.
- Identify population groups negatively affected by trade reforms and use well-targeted relief measures for losers.
- Strengthen the links between poverty and macroeconomic policies, such as trade and exchange rate policy, in poverty assessments.

With respect to design, there is consensus on the role of macro, exchange rate, and complementary policies, but less agreement on the role of selective and industrial policies.

Findings from previous OED ratings of trade-related activities are largely consistent with the literature, but place stronger emphasis on macro stabilization as a prerequisite.

Table 2.1: Summary of Policy Design Issues

Policy / issue	Literature
Macroeconomic Environment and Trade Policy Reform	
Macro stabilization	Necessary to have significant effects on resource allocation. Literature less clear on whether trade policy reform should be implemented after macroeconomic stability has been achieved or whether it should proceed simultaneously (Dean, Desai, and Riedel 1994).
Real exchange rate	Strong consensus on relevance; perhaps single most important variable (Williamson 1997). Considerable empirical evidence shows real exchange rate misalignment detrimental to export growth, and that real exchange rate variability and uncertainty associated with negative effects on export performance (Diaz-Alejandro 1984; Paredes 1988; Caballero and Corbo 1989).
Timing of foreign exchange liberalization	For countries with overvalued currencies, the first step in the adjustment process has typically been a sustained real devaluation, which enables the real exchange rate to be held stable before implementing any trade liberalization.
Policies for Export Development	
Compensatory measures designed to offset any inherent anti-export bias in a trade regime Additional incentives meant to address specific problems that exports face	Effectiveness of these incentives—and other industrial policy measures—continues to be debated (Pack 2000). Successes noted in East Asia; export processing zones have been effective in Madagascar, Mauritius, and Mexico; temporary subsidies stimulated the growth of nontraditional exports in Chile. Changes in the economic environment and in the international "rules of the game" mean more constraints using these compensatory measures (Lall 2004). These constraints not necessarily overwhelming (Amsden and Hikino 2000; Chang 2004).
Design, Sequence, and Duration of Trade Policy Reform	
Components of the trade reform package and the sequence in which the various elements should be reformed	The literature is relatively clear on the components and sequence of actions on the import and export sides. Imports: eliminate quantitative restrictions first. Exports: Remove export licensing and bans at the same time as restrictions on imported inputs used by exporters. Next, export taxes and other export incentives.
How long it should take to complete trade reform?	Evidence on the intensity of reform (strong or moderated) and its speed (sudden or gradual) is less conclusive, with more recent literature discounting political economy benefits of speed (credibility, signaling) in favor of gradualism to reduce adjustment costs (Winters 2000), from competing interest groups (Collier, Greenaway, and Gunning 1997).
External Constraints and Opportunities	
Role of multilateral negotiations/system	Mixed; in theory more equal playing field but empirical evidence scant and mixed (Rose 2004; Subramanian and Wei 2003) and rising bilateralism poses a challenge.
Market access in Organisation for Economic Co-operation and Development countries	External market constraints may cause problems for developing countries that adopt outward-oriented trade strategies (Cline 1989; Ghosh 1992). Preferential market access has helped some developing countries to take advantage of export opportunities in preference-giving countries. But the schemes have not fully eliminated the trade barriers faced. Remedies include duty-free and quota-free market access to all exports of low-income and small countries (Hoekman and others 2003). Poorest countries must first be assisted to address their export supply capacity constraints through increased investment in infrastructure and skills (Helleiner 2002a).
Complementary and mitigating measures	Limited empirical evidence is inconclusive and it is difficult to make broad generalizations. Papageorgiou and others (1991) and Matusz and Tarr (1999) suggest that the costs of trade policy reforms are small, even in the short term. More recent studies that focus on least-developed countries (such as Oyejide, Ndulu, and Gunning 1999) show that short-term costs constitute realistic concerns. Winters (2000) concludes: More protected sectors likely to have greater transitional costs, may also offer the largest long-run returns to reform; if labor market is exposed to large shocks emanating from policy reforms that render it dysfunctional, transitional unemployment may be larger in volume and longer in duration; and rapid or concentrated reforms more likely to generate transitional losses through unemployment than more diffuse reforms.

Source: Appendix B1.

Chapter 3: Evaluation Highlights

- Lending for trade varies but shows a secular decline.
- Trade conditionality and trade lending have fallen.
- Trade facilitation, largely customs, is most frequent area of support.
- Trade economic and sector work is on the rise, and it is paying more attention to institutional and welfare issues.

Inputs, Trends, and Evolution of World Bank Trade Assistance

This chapter reviews the scope, trends, and evolution of World Bank assistance on trade to its client countries from fiscal year 1987 through 2004.

Until the 1980s, the Bank was project-focused, but in the 1980s and 1990s it became increasingly involved in policy reform using noninvestment loans. Lending for trade adjustment through Structural and Sector Adjustment Loans (SALs and SECALs) to address balance of payments problems accounted for 25 percent of all adjustment lending during the 1980s. Bank analytical work was also important in the policy dialogue with client countries.

Lending Inputs to Trade

IEG carried out a comprehensive review of the Bank's portfolio to identify trade-related projects. Bank trade-related support can be classified into six main areas: trade liberalization, institutional trade facilitation (for example, customs), infrastructure-related trade facilitation (for example, air freight, ports), private trade financing, public trade financing, and technical assistance for trade negotiations and the WTO accession processes (Appendix C1).[1]

Magnitude, Relative Importance, and Trends

Bank lending for trade was substantial during the period under review. Between 1987 and 2004, the Bank supported more than 500 lending operations that were partly or fully focused on trade in 117 countries.[2] This assistance of about $38 billion supported free-standing trade loans and loans with trade-related components—about 8.1 percent of total Bank commitments during this period.

Despite the common perception that trade was a large part of the Bank's portfolio, the share of trade-focused lending operations[3] in the Bank's total commitments was comparable to that for the Bank's major sectors of assistance such as education, health, and public governance.

Lending for trade has fluctuated, but shows a long-term decline.

Since reaching just over $3 billion annually in 1993, Bank lending for trade has varied, but continues a long-term pattern of decline (figure 3.1). Several concurrent events may be linked to this trend. To begin with, as discussed in the next chapter, many countries liberalized their trade regimes in the 1980s, so that trade-related lending adjustment became less necessary, and it is not surprising that trade lending would decline. Liberalization was further deepened through regional agreements.

In addition, over this period, the International Monetary Fund (IMF) became more prominent in trade policy advice and incorporated trade conditionality in its stand-by arrangements. The share of Fund programs with formal trade conditionality rose from 55 percent in the years before 1995 to 70 percent between 1998 and 2001, though this has dropped in the four years since (IMF 2005). The decline in Bank lending would have been even more dramatic if not for the East Asia crisis in 1999 and the emergence of new clients in Europe and Central Asia (ECA) during the 1990s. Several of these clients undertook trade-related operations, including a large multi-country trade facilitation project in 2001.

In the past four years, a modest resurgence in trade-related lending has occurred in tandem with renewed interest in trade by the Bank and its clients. This lending is limited to a few countries and focuses on trade facilitation initiatives, which comprise two-thirds of all new lending. Given the significant volume of previous adjustment lending, it is unclear whether that lending will recover to the levels of the early to mid-1990s.

Thematic Focus: From Trade Liberalization to Trade Facilitation

The overall figures conceal a shift in the composition and emphasis of trade lending over the past two decades. While Bank assistance in the early 1980s focused on direct lending to development banks through lines of credit for trade finance, by the beginning of 1987 lending was concentrated on trade liberalization and more direct trade promotion activities, such as supporting trade-related institutions and exporters (figure 3.2). Together these two categories accounted for 70 percent of all lending for trade between 1987 and 1994. In part, this was linked to the export-led growth messages of the *1987 World Development Report*. But it was also attributable to reform-minded policy makers (notably in Latin America) who believed in the benefits of trade liberalization.

Figure 3.1: Trade-Related Bank Lending Has Varied But Trended Downward Overall

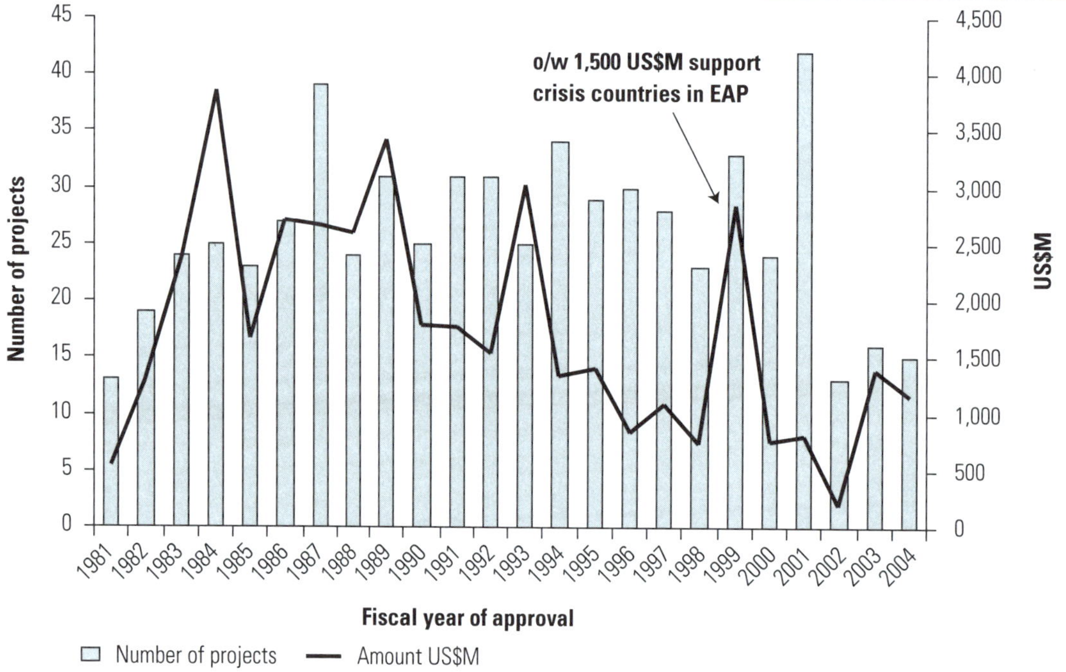

Source: Trade Assistance Evaluation Project Database.

Note: Excludes oil, gas, and electricity export projects. EAP = East Asia and Pacific Region.

Figure 3.2: The Thematic Focus of Bank Lending for Trade: Trade Liberalization and Direct Lending to Exporters Gave Way to Trade Facilitation

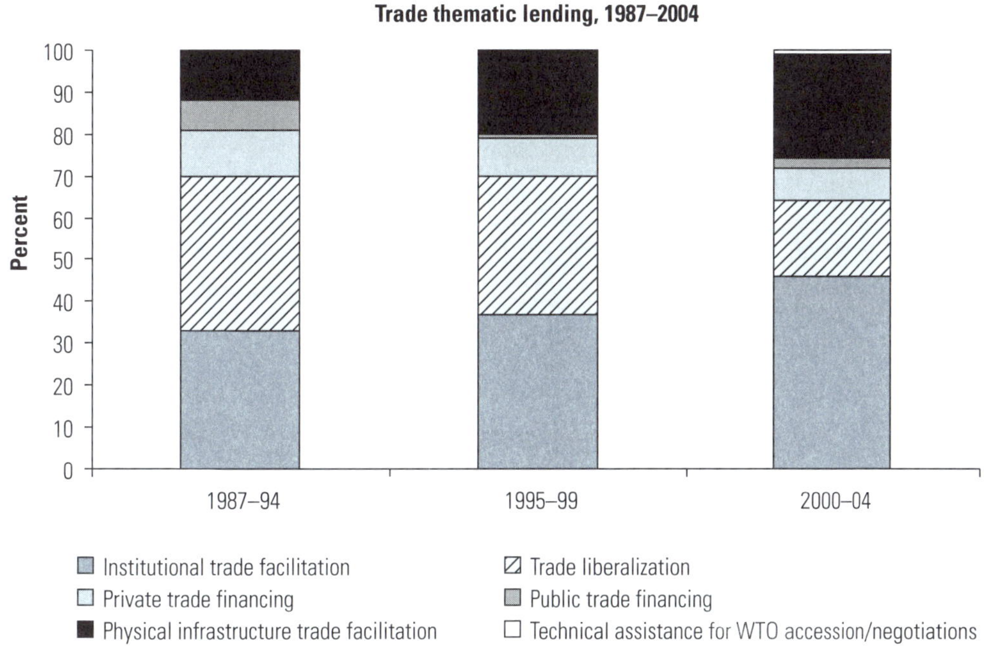

Source: Trade Assistance Evaluation Project Database.

Note: Total lending - 1987-94 = $22.1 billion; 1995-99 = $10.2 billion; 2000-04 = $5.1 billion.

During the mid-1990s, while trade liberalization remained an important component of Bank lending for trade (33 percent), the focus on trade facilitation activities intensified as attention shifted to broader investment climate issues such as the importance of trade logistics in competitiveness and the global value supply chain. On the infrastructure side, greater emphasis on the trade benefits from infrastructure improvements was evident in major commitments supporting international road corridors and ports. The number of loans devoted to trade-related institutions (primarily customs) accounted for 37 percent of trade-related lending between 1995 and 1999, making this the single largest thematic area supported.

Lending for trade liberalization has moved in waves across Regions over time, suggesting a "neighborhood" effect. Large amounts initially supported a set of early reforms in the Latin America and Caribbean Region (LAC). The emphasis then shifted to Sub-Saharan Africa. Over time, the Bank moved to support Middle East and North African countries, and then most recently to Eastern Europe and Central Asia (Appendix C2). Lending to East Asia was concentrated during the crises in the late 1990s.

The composition and emphasis of trade lending has shifted over two decades from trade liberalization to trade facilitation.

In the past four years, lending for the institutional and infrastructure aspects of trade facilitation has increased further as a share of trade-related lending. Institutions-related trade facilitation accounted for almost half of all trade-related lending between 2000 and 2004, while lending for trade liberalization declined noticeably.[4] While lending and advice related to the multilateral trading system continues to be minuscule, the number of Bank lending operations including such support during the 3 most recent years was double the number during the preceding 13 years.

Much of the Bank's earlier work on trade-related capacity building was embedded in lending operations and is more properly defined as technical assistance.[5] Between fiscal years 1987 and 2000, there were 29 trade-related technical assistance projects, of which 20 are closed and 9 are still active. The overwhelming majority of these interventions (20 out of 29) focused on support for customs reform and modernization, or on analysis related to trade policy reform.

What Was Recommended? The Design of Trade Adjustment Loans

At the height of adjustment lending in the 1980s, trade policy accounted for a quarter of all structural adjustment conditionality. Trade conditionality offers a useful and systematic way to identify actions that the Bank assumed were most critical. This section draws on a trade conditionality database (built from information in the Bank's Adjustment Lending and Conditionality Implementation Database and an IEG desk review of loan agreements) to analyze the design of trade adjustment loans between fiscal years 1987 and 2004.[6]

The sample characteristics are presented in table 3.1. These 152 loans include all adjustment loans with trade components exceeding 10 percent.[7] The sample constitutes 65 percent of all non-emergency rehabilitation adjustment loans with trade components (regardless of size) that were approved and closed between 1987 and 2004, and 89 percent in value. Of the 65 countries, 25 received three or more trade-related adjustment loans. The average number of trade-related adjustment loans received by the countries was 2.3; the median was 2.

Focus of Lending Conditions

The focus of Bank trade conditionality has varied over time and across Regions, but some general patterns can be discerned. Trade-related conditionality is classified into four areas: import-related, export-related, exchange rate and foreign exchange–related, and industrial or supporting policies (box 3.1).[8]

Trade conditions have focused on imports, exports, exchange rates, and supporting policies.

Between 1987 and 1990, import-related policies comprised almost half of all conditions (or 6.4 conditions on average per loan) in all Regions except South Asia (figure 3.3 and Appendix C3).[9] With the exception of South Asia, the emphasis on industrial policies was greater between 1991 and 1999 compared with the earlier period. Conditionality in this period reflected the importance the Bank placed on increasing enterprise efficiency and the Europe and Central Asia effect, resulting in continuing and expanding privatization.

Very few supporting policy conditions involved labor market and safety net issues or non-customs trade-related institutions. The lack of attention to labor market rigidities was an oversight. While the literature does not yield strong evidence of employment losses from greater openness (see, for example Papageorgiou and others 1991; Revenga 1995 on Mexico; Currie and Harrison 1997 on Morocco; Bourguignon and Goh 2004 on East Asia), distortions in the labor markets can influence the extent to which trade liberalization is associated with gains in employment and lower poverty.

In the five most recent years, trade-related conditions have been quite diverse across Regions. This may be because of the relatively small size of the sample during this period (20 lending operations), which renders Regional breakdowns less informative. Over time, export promotion has risen in importance in almost every Region.

Conditions related to the exchange rate and to foreign exchange rate management were the least frequently represented condition (7 percent) between 1987 and 2004. They were most heavily emphasized at the beginning of reforms, consistent with the advice from the literature, and these conditions were normally met (reflected in reduced black market premiums for the countries with available data). In addition, the "Concordat" with the IMF meant that the latter was more likely to be giving and "conditioning" exchange rate policy advice.[10]

Sequencing of Conditions: Did the Bank Follow a "One-Size-Fits-All" Approach?

A common criticism of the Bank's trade advice

Table 3.1: Trade Adjustment Loans—Sample Characteristics, 1987–2004

	Sample[a]	
	Loans	**Countries**
Geographic Region		
Africa	69	26
East Asia and Pacific	12	6
Europe and Central Asia	13	8
Latin America and the Caribbean	32	15
Middle East and North Africa	14	5
South Asia	12	5
Total	**152**	**65**
By income		
IDA		34
IBRD		31
Time periods (number of loans)		
1987–90	44	
1991–99	88	
2000–04	20	

Sources: Tsikata (2005) based on calculations from the IEG Trade Policy Conditionality Database; Adjustment Lending Conditionality and Implementation Database (ALCID).

Note: Sample also includes 29 loans with trade component < 10%. Of the 29 loans, the following countries have other loans within the larger sample of 152 loans: Bulgaria, Cameroon, Malawi, Mexico, Morocco (2), Mozambique, Niger (2 loans with trade component <10%), Romania, Sierra Leone, Tanzania, Tunisia, Vietnam, and Zambia (4). The remaining 11 loans went to countries that did not have any other loans during the review period and were thus included for completeness.

a. All adjustment loans with ≥10% of trade-related components, excluding Emergency Rehabilitation Loans.

is that it has followed a "one-size-fits-all" approach. This section examines that criticism. In terms of sequencing, on the import side, policies aimed at reducing or eliminating quantitative restrictions (QRs) and other forms of nontariff barriers were typically the starting point, consistent with the literature. In two-thirds of the countries (42 out of 65), QRs were

Box 3.1: Elements of Trade Policy Reform Are Varied and Diverse

Trade reform in developing countries typically involves a range of changes in the use of trade policy instruments on both the export and import sides. The typical trade policy reform package consists of the following four components:

Import-related: Policies such as eliminating or reducing quantitative restrictions (and converting them to tariffs) as well as other types of nontariff barriers, reducing import tariff levels and dispersion, making tariff regimes more uniform and transparent, reducing import surcharges, improving import procedures, and eliminating official reference prices.

Export-related: Policies related to making imports available for export (such as duty drawback and temporary admission schemes), reducing export bans, taxes and licenses, reducing the anti-export bias, export credit and financing, and other export incentives.

Exchange rate and foreign exchange management: Moving toward market-determined exchange rates, exchange rate devaluation or step adjustment, and moving away from the administrative allocation of foreign exchange.

Industrial/supporting policies: Pricing reform, investment promotion, competition policy, marketing, regulatory, privatization, labor markets, and safety nets.

Source: Tsikata (2005).

Figure 3.3: Focus of Trade Conditions in Adjustment Loans Shifted over 1987–2004 (average number of conditions per loan)

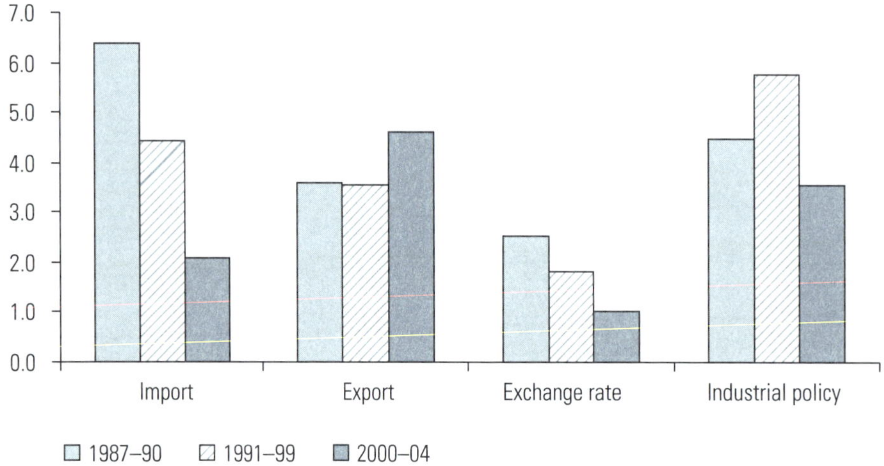

Source: IEG Trade Assistance Evaluation Project Database.

a first step of trade reform. Fifteen of the remaining 23 countries had previously reduced such restrictions or had a simultaneous loan that addressed their elimination. Of the remaining eight countries, six had a low incidence of QRs, in some cases having previously reduced them (but without a Bank loan). The QR reforms were often introduced simultaneously with supporting policies aimed at reducing price distortions and at creating a complementary competitive environment.

While the projects described above followed sequencing that was broadly in line with the 1987 WDR and the literature as outlined in Chapter 2, IEG found little evidence of a generic (or "one-size-fits-all") approach to trade reform in the Bank's client countries. Countries varied in the extent of macroeconomic stabilization that they had achieved before the reform was introduced, and in how and when they chose to use export-related policies to stimulate trade promotion. Moreover, countries were heterogeneous in how deeply they reformed and in the range of complementary policies they introduced to support the trade reform.

The actual path of trade reform was less frequently prescriptive than is commonly perceived.

The actual path of trade reform was less frequently prescriptive than is commonly perceived. For example, only about 40 percent of import tariff conditions specifically recommended quantitative targets for tariffs (minimum, maximum, or average levels, ranges) and fewer than 10 percent of conditions gave specific targets for the number of tariff bands.

By contrast, about half of all import tariff conditions provided general guidance (for example, simplify and reform tariff regime, reduce dispersion).[11] The magnitude of tariff reductions also varied widely across countries. Figure 3.4, which shows the distribution of maximum tariffs recommended by the Bank in loan agreements, illustrates a wide range, reflecting the varying initial conditions and the context-specificity of the political economy of trade reform. More generally, it suggests that the tariff guidance in OD 8.60 and Thomas and Nash (1991) were not "hard" targets to be met instantaneously, and that there were several paths to the recommended tariff ranges.

Another criticism of Bank trade advice has been that it has emphasized "import liberalization" over "export promotion," despite the evidence from East Asia that suggests that policies to promote exports in advance of import liberalization may be more effective and

Figure 3.4: Maximum Tariff Recommendations Covered a Wide Range (frequency of tariff ranges recommended)

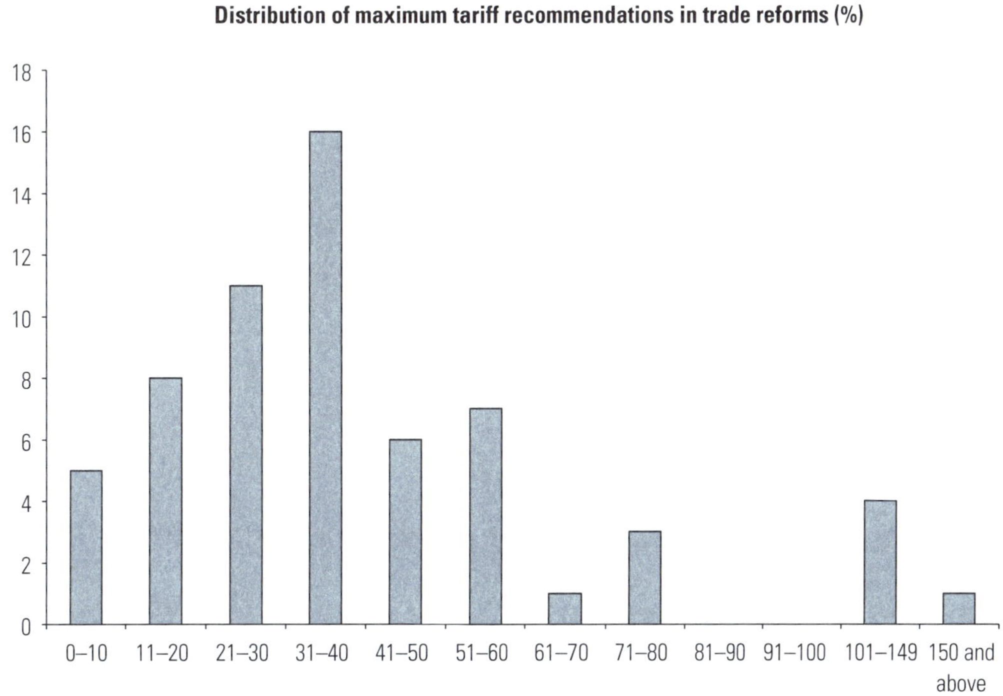

Source: Staff calculations from IEG Trade Assistance Evaluation Project Database.

reduce the likelihood of deindustrialization.[12] All 152 trade adjustment loans were reviewed to assess the sequencing and distribution of recommendations. The results presented in table 3.2, summarized by Region, show that in most Regions, loans that had conditions focusing solely on imports exceeded those focusing exclusively on exports. The exception was Europe and Central Asia. However, in all Regions except Europe and Central Asia and the Middle East and North Africa, loans were more likely to feature a combination of import and export actions.

Another way of examining this hypothesis is to analyze the trade reforms supported by the Bank in each country over time, particularly the focus of the conditions. In 51 of the 65 countries where the Bank supported trade reforms, it advised a combination of import liberalization and export promotion (defined as the export-related conditions above), or export promotion first. Of the 65 countries, 5 started out solely with import liberalization before moving on later to export promotion (Honduras, Madagascar, Mexico, Pakistan, and Panama). In another 9 (Armenia, Cape Verde, Congo, Georgia, Guatemala, Mauritania, Niger, Sri Lanka, and Yugoslavia), the focus of conditionality was primarily import liberalization, with no later export promotion. Thus, while the evidence suggests that the Bank largely supported export promotion, in 14 countries that received 55 loans (between a quarter and a third of the sample), the Bank focused only on import-related measures.

Evidence suggests that while the Bank did not follow a "one-size-fits-all" approach for all countries, a sizable number of projects focused on import liberalization over export promotion.

Recommendation Implementation and Outcome

Knowledge of the policies recommended to countries is not sufficient to make a link with outcomes unless one assumes *a priori* that the

Table 3.2: Trade Loan Conditions Most Often Addressed Both Imports and Exports, But a Third of Loans Focused Solely on Imports

	Total loans	Focus of loan conditions[a]		
		Import only	Export promotion only	Both
Africa	69	24	7	29
East Asia and Pacific	12	4	2	6
Europe and Central Asia	13	3	4	2
Latin America and the Caribbean	32	12	5	14
Middle East and North Africa	14	7	2	3
South Asia	12	5	0	5
Total	152	55	20	59

Source: IEG staff calculations.

a. May not add to total because some loans had neither import-related nor export-promoting conditions.

policies were implemented exactly as designed. In this section, compliance with trade conditionality or (in other words) policy reform implementation (PRI) is compared with actual results.[13] The review of the experience with implementing trade conditionality at the level of individual loans draws on project supervision reports, tranche-release reports, project implementation completion reports and their IEG reviews, and (where available) project performance assessment reports.

Countries largely met trade conditions, which were better implemented than other adjustment loans.

Policy implementation was rated from 1 (highest, or strong implementation, with all conditions met on time) to 3 (lowest, or weak implementation, with conditions only partially met and significant delay). Moderate implementation was assigned a 2 and reflected cases in which conditions were largely met, but with delays. An overall index of PRI for each country was calculated as a simple average of all the country's loans (Appendix C4).[14]

The PRI shows that about 73 percent of countries exhibited strong implementation on trade issues. This share is higher than IEG (1997) found for overall adjustment lending, but is in line with that report's specific findings for trade. If moderate implementation is included, the figure rises to 84 percent. Particularly strong compliers on trade included Mexico, Mozambique, Panama, and Pakistan. Papua New Guinea and Venezuela were weak compliers. There did not appear to be a pattern between income or Region and the rate of compliance.

Table 3.3: Trade Adjustment Loans Featured Strong Implementation

	Total loans (US$ billion)	Number of loans	Average number of tranches
Strong compliers (39 countries)	15.1	84	1.7
Moderate compliers (9 countries)	2.2	13	1.7
Poor compliers (9 countries)	3.8	18	2.2
Total (57 countries)	21.1	115	1.8

Source: IEG staff calculations.

Note: Thirty-seven loans (for 8 countries) could not be evaluated either because there were no legally binding conditions (6 loans), or because project documents did not contain enough information to assess compliance (31 loans).

Despite this relatively strong compliance record, economic outcomes were mixed for this group (table 3.4). Countries with a strong compliance record experienced only average improvements in growth (12 out of 26) and investment (14 out of 26), but fewer than half experienced an improvement in exports. This is partly explained by the heterogeneity in initial conditions across countries; it also illustrates that trade liberalization by itself is not sufficient to generate improved economic performance. Some poor compliers had very good outcomes in exports and poor investment outcomes. This seems largely to be the product of unusual circumstances: in two poor compliers (Nigeria and Venezuela), oil-related exports account for the good performance. The existence of oil, however, may have meant less incentive to liberalize.

Specific areas of weak implementation have varied over time. During the late 1980s, countries had greater difficulty in complying with core trade issues. Since the early 1990s, however, this has changed. Recent difficulties with compliance appear to be linked to domestic supporting policies, particularly in privatization and regulatory reform. Waivers of conditionality were sought most frequently in these areas. Fourteen of the 33 waivers for the 93 adjustment loans with trade conditions approved since fiscal year 1992 were sought for privatization-related conditions.

Reflecting the progress with meeting trade conditions, the average number per loan and the percentage of loans with trade conditions have fallen significantly since 1987 (figure 3.5).[15] This pattern of decline is generally consistent across Regions and also across International Development Association (IDA) and International Bank for Reconstruction and Development (IBRD) countries, except in the Middle East and North Africa Region, where the average of 10 trade-related conditions per loan remains the same as in the 1980s.

Despite above-average project implementation, economic outcomes were mixed.

In addition to the three factors mentioned earlier in the chapter (the move toward more open regimes, a shift in the Bank's focus toward longer-term reforms in institutional and structural policies and a concurrent rise in IMF trade conditionality, and a rise in trade liberalization through regional arrangements such as free trade areas), it is possible that conditionality has declined because of increasing skepticism about the efficacy of conditionality, more generally, in motivating policy reform (box 3.2). However, the causality of these various factors is difficult to disentangle. In more recent years, the shift also likely reflects the evolution of the Bank's approach to conditionality toward greater country-owned

The most difficult recent areas of compliance concern the regulatory framework.

The average number of trade-related conditions per loan and the incidence of trade conditionality have fallen significantly since 1987.

Table 3.4: Meeting Lending Conditions Did Not Necessarily Improve Economic Performance

	Number of countries with data	Number of countries with improvement in		
		Growth rates	Export	Investment
Strong compliers (63 loans)	38 (12)	6	7	10
Moderate compliers (17 loans)	16 (8)	6	3	4
Poor compliers (16 loans)	14 (4)	2	4	2

Source: IEG staff calculations.

Note: Thirty-seven loans could not be evaluated either because there were no legally binding conditions, or because project documents did not contain enough information to assess compliance.

Figure 3.5: Number of Lending Conditions Declined over 1987–2004

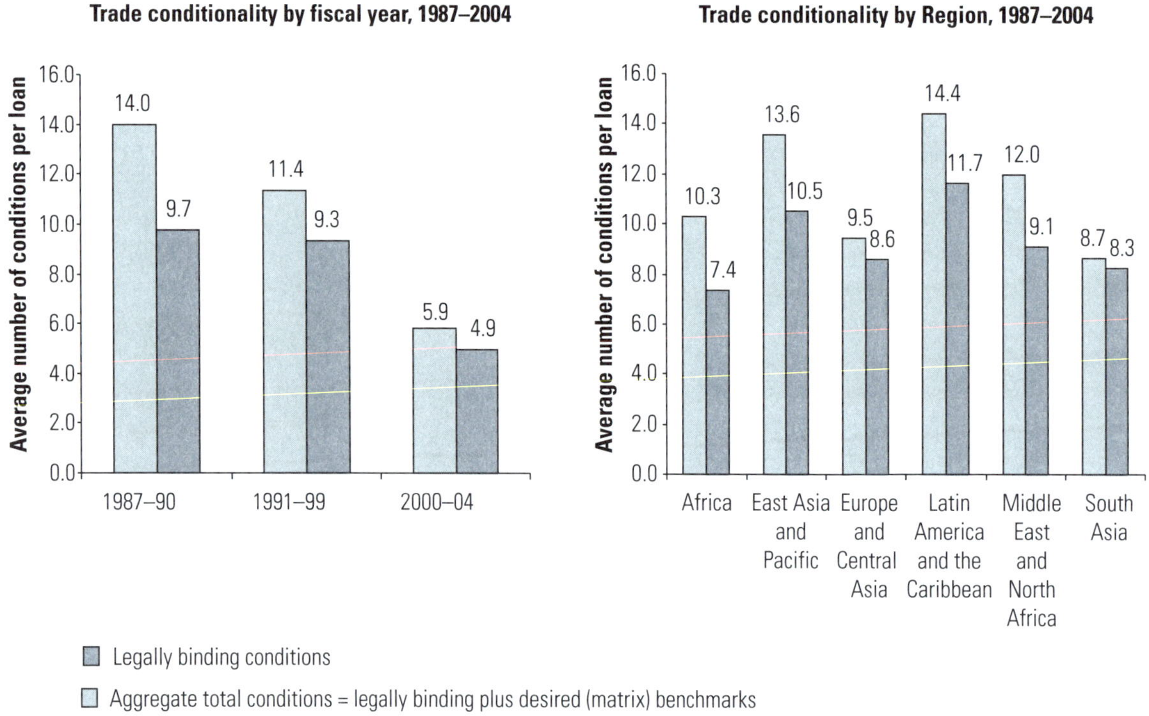

Source: Tsikata (2005).

conditionality and less prescriptiveness, as outlined in Operational Policy 8.60 on development policy lending.[16]

Nonlending Inputs

In addition to the substantial lending portfolio, Bank activities in trade have included important nonlending inputs—notably economic and sector work (ESW) carried out in the operational Regions of the Bank.[17] The discussion of nonlending inputs below focuses on ESW; Chapter 5 analyzes the Bank's trade-related activities, advocacy, research, and trade-related capacity building, mainly focusing on the period since 2001.

Early ESW focused on incentives and trade performance; less attention was paid to politics, institutions, and welfare outcomes.

The focus of trade-related ESW has broadened over time, but insufficient attention is given to the political, institutional, and welfare dimensions. Between 1987 and 2001, ESW focused on the change in incentives, and on general trade performance. The next-most important areas of focus, though far less frequently addressed, were assessing the regulatory framework and the impact of the external environment.

Since 2002, while trade-related ESW continues to review progress in trade performance and incentives, more reports now focus on a broader definition of competitiveness (labor costs, infrastructure), include external environment considerations (such as the impact of regional arrangements or market access issues), and analyze microeconomic issues. In both periods, however, reports have only rarely presented an in-depth analysis of the welfare implications of trade policies, analyzed the institutional framework for trade, or incorporated political economy factors that could influence trade reform and outcomes. Also largely missing is microeconomic analysis on the response of firms (exit/entry) to changes in incentives.

Evidence from the country case studies suggests that high-quality analytical work can

Box 3.2: Conditionality May Be Neither Necessary nor Sufficient

The record of the appropriateness of Bank conditionality on core trade issues is mixed. In some cases, the conditionality was light, flexible, and adaptable. For example, in **India**, conditionality was light, except for the 1991 Structural Adjustment Loan. Yet even then, the authorities had some leeway, as noted earlier.

In a few other cases, the country failed to meet the condition—in part because it felt it could not act because of political constraints—and received a waiver. In **Indonesia**, four trade policy loans implemented between 1987 and 1996 were devoid of legally binding conditionality. They were given by the Bank in general support of Indonesia's ongoing trade and investment reform program, reflected the Bank's confidence in the credibility of the authorities, and were informal precursors of what is now known as "ex-post conditionality."

In other cases the Bank continued to introduce conditionality even when it was ineffective or when the authorities had serious concerns. In **Zambia**, despite conditions repeated in three successive loans, the government procrastinated on the privatization of the mining parastatal, the Zambia Consolidated Copper Mines (ZCCM), because of political concerns. The phenomenon of Zambia continuing to receive high levels of assistance in the absence of reform has been dubbed "the nonreform" paradox: more and more conditions lead to less and less effective conditionality (Rakner and others 1999).[a] First highlighted as an agricultural structural adjustment condition in 1995, the privatization of SONACOS was a key performance indicator in the Private Investment Promotion Project (fiscal 2003) almost a decade later.

In **Indonesia**, the 1997 financial crisis was associated with diminished credibility of the authorities, and the Bank introduced conditions that had been on its agenda for several years. Notwithstanding the relatively small role of trade issues in the crisis, the Bank introduced legally binding trade-related conditionality.[b] These conditions, related to export taxes and controls and regulatory issues, were eventually satisfied. As noted in the case study, however, it is difficult to argue that any of these issues were critical to resolving Indonesia's financial crisis. They appear to have been at best excessive, and possibly inappropriate.[c] At the same time, two reasons could explain the decision to include them. First, by taking on some of the core interests of the president and his associates, the conditions were intended to send a strong signal to investors about the government's commitment to reform.[d] Second, the World Bank (and IMF) used the opportunity of the crisis to include the most critical trade-related reforms. Regardless of the reason they were introduced, the resulting strained relationship with the Indonesian authorities suggests that in countries where the Bank may not ordinarily have much leverage, the institution needs to be careful to attach only critical conditions during times of crisis.

Sources: Country Case Studies for IEG Trade Assistance Evaluation.

a. The authors argue that that the underlying problem was a defensive government agenda to maximize donor inflows, rather than a properly articulated strategy for medium-term growth and development. Rakner argues that one of the key elements of the defensive agenda is in "in the area of trade reforms, the Movement for Multiparty Democracy (MMD) government is seen as having overcommitted and carried out reforms too rapidly" (p. 574). Given the government's willingness, it perhaps is not surprising that the Bank undertook so little analytical work—there was less need to convince than in other cases. However, this does not excuse the need for the Bank to have identified the implications of such reforms to the authorities.

b. The three trade-related conditions in the First Policy Reform Support (PRS) 1 were: (i) replace all existing quantitative export controls on crude and processed palm oil, olein, and stearin with an export tax not exceeding 40 percent ad valorem; (ii) introduce a system of resource use royalties for forestry, reduce export taxes on logs, sawn timber, and rattan to a maximum of 30 percent ad valorem, and adopt and announce a program for lowering this progressively over time; and (iii) ensure that all traders, including foreign direct investors, continue to be free to compete with Bulog (the government-owned rice procurement agency) by importing, wholesaling, or retailing any commodity other than rice, and ensure that private traders and Bulog have access to foreign exchange at the same rate when importing goods other than rice. PRS 2 reiterated the condition on maximum export tax rates on logs, rattan, and minerals (Indonesia Project Performance Assessment Report for PRS1 & PRS2).

c. Feldstein 1998 as cited in the Indonesia Country Case Study for IEG Trade Evaluation.

d. Hofman and others (2004) as cited in the Indonesia Country Case Study for IEG Trade Evaluation.

improve policy dialogue and the quality of lending (box 3.3 and Appendix D7). But the case studies also highlight that these benefits may sometimes emerge only in the medium term, years after the research was first carried out (India, Morocco). By contrast, disputed technical analysis (Mozambique) or the absence of sustained analytical work underpinning trade reforms, as in Zambia, can strengthen the perception of a Bank caught up in dogmatic prescriptions.

Evidence from country studies suggests high-quality analytical work can significantly improve policy dialogue and quality of lending.

In terms of trends, after sustained decline from the mid-1990s following the

Box 3.3: High-Quality ESW Supports Policy Dialogue

The Bank's trade-related analytic work in **Senegal** has supported the development of adjustment lending over a long period. In the early 1990s, Bank studies of industrial and agricultural prices and incentives identified state interventions and the associated economic costs. These analyses helped prioritize sector adjustment reforms.

While the Bank was precluded from active and open involvement in the devaluation debate in the early 1990s, it worked behind the scenes with a small group of policy makers on macroeconomic and competitiveness issues. Simulation of the fiscal impacts of devaluation-cum-tariff reform were undertaken by the Ministry of Finance's Policy Options Group in 1994 with Bank guidance, and was acknowledged by Senegalese policy makers to have been crucial in convincing them that the risks of the devaluation could be managed.

In **Morocco**, a major contribution of trade ESW has been the quantification of the costs and benefits of freer trade and a generally high emphasis on empirical analysis. During the 1980s, Bank research focused on the potential aggregate gains from trade. The Bank also seconded an economist to the Ministry of Commerce and Industry who, working with staff, helped provide real-time analyses of potential trade policy effects and became a trusted interlocutor for those interested in pursuing trade reform.

By the time the authorities decided to reform in response to crisis in the mid-1980s, the government technocrats were convinced of the value of reform and had a blueprint for its introduction. The benefits of the ESW and advice were not limited to the earlier period. While the pace of reform slowed in the second half of the 1980s, the consistent proponents of reform include those staff first convinced in the early 1980s. Alavi (1993) is another example of analytical work making an impact on policy dialogue and reform.

Source: Country Case Studies prepared for the Trade Assistance Evaluation.

ESW on trade issues has risen in recent years, catalyzed by donor support.

conclusion of the Uruguay Round, ESW on trade issues has risen in recent years.[18] Underpinning this reversal is greater interest in trade issues by client countries as they grapple with more complex integration into the global economy, greater commitment and interest by donors leading to additional trust fund resources, and development of a new trade-focused economic report—the Diagnostic Trade Integration Study (DTIS), which was an important initial catalyst (figure 3.6).[19] Whether funded though the multi-agency Integrated Framework initiative (for the least-developed countries) or bilateral donors (for other developing countries), the DTIS spurred analytical work in trade within the Bank.

While it is too soon to tell with the more recent analytical work, early trade-related ESW was associated with trade-related lending. Between 1987 and 1990, 65 percent of trade ESW was followed by trade-related lending within two years. This figure has fallen slightly since then—between 1990 and 2001, 60 percent of trade ESW was followed by lending. The discussion of the links between ESW and project outcomes is taken up in Chapter 4.

But it is too early to tell its impact on lending.

The share of countries in which trade-related ESW has been conducted has risen in each Region since 1994, except Latin America and the Caribbean, which started at a high level. The most dramatic rise occurred in the Africa and South Asia Regions. In Latin America, trade-focused ESW at the country level has declined, but a number of major trade-related Regional studies have been done, and given the stock of existing trade research on those countries, they do not appear to have been underserved. More generally, in the past three years, strategic Regional trade studies have been done in every Region except Africa and have been well focused on the particular concerns of the Regions they cover (box 3.4).[20]

To place the analysis on Regional trade issues in perspective, the Bank has carried out much research and analytical work on regionalism. Research has been published in established journals. Among the contributions, several deal with the political economy aspects of regional trading arrangements (RTAs) (Cadot, de Melo, and Olarreaga 2003;

Figure 3.6: New Diagnostic Studies and Trust Funds Catalyzed Increased Economic and Sector Work (number of trade-focused reports)

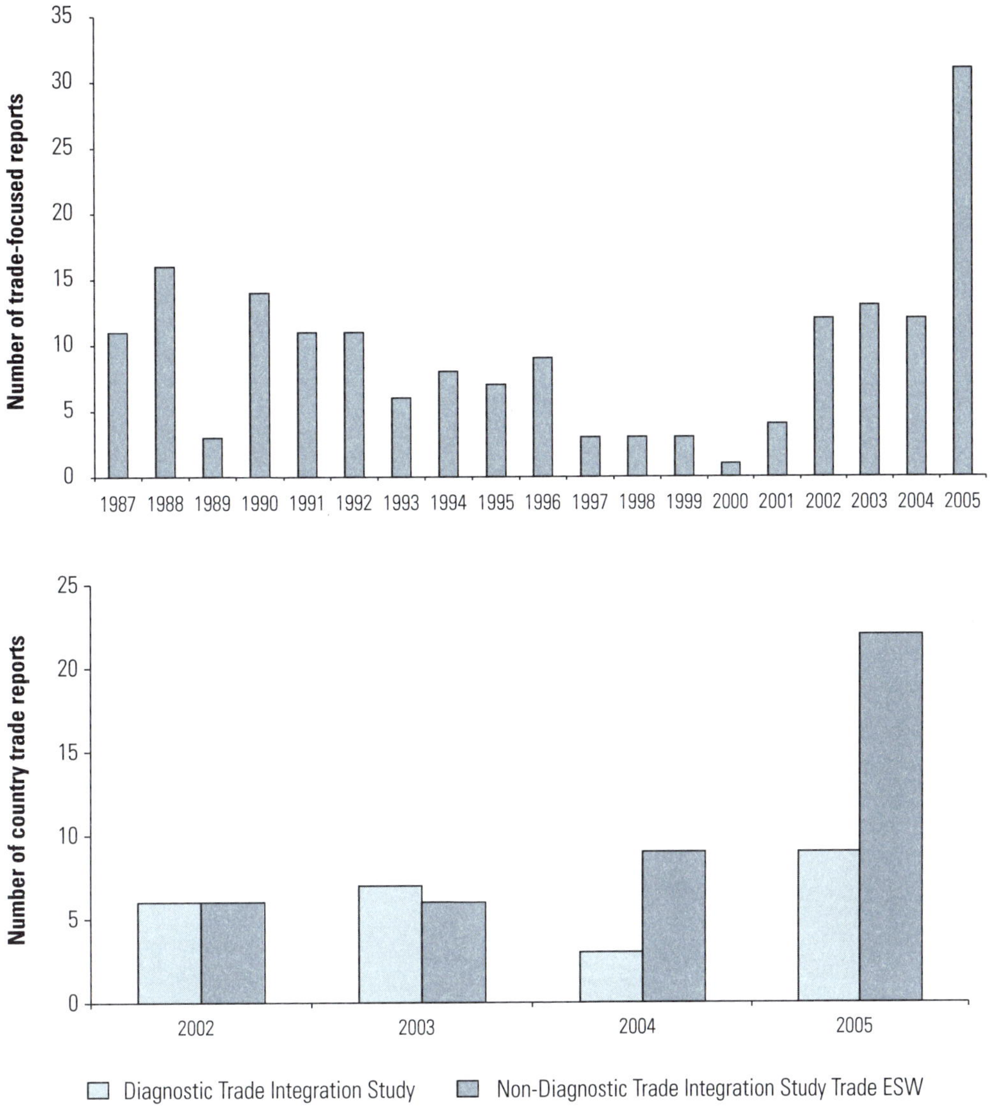

Source: IEG Trade Assistance Evaluation Database.

Note: Trade-related ESW was selected using two approaches. For 1987–2001, trade-related ESW was identified by searching the ESW database for key trade words, followed by manually checking the depth and relevance of the trade content of the report in question. For 2002–05, the study benefited from the OPCS revamping of sector and thematic codes. The relevant list was obtained by selecting sector codes (45-50 in the OPCS coding system) that correspond to trade and integration. Code 48 (technology diffusion) was excluded because, while trade-related, it is beyond the scope of this study. A number of trade-related studies identified by the Regions were still not captured by the OPCS classification, including most of the trade diagnostic studies. Diagnostic Trade Integration Studies (DTIS)=Trade Study that follows specific template and funded by one of the following: (a) Integrated Framework Initiative; (b) U.K. DFID trust funds; (c) Dutch trust funds.

Olarreaga, Soloaga, and Winters 1999). Among the issues explored is why it is easier to 'exchange market access' by reducing trade barriers bilaterally than to reduce trade barriers unilaterally, even though most of the efficiency gains from trade reforms come from unilateral reduction in trade barriers. The research shows that bilateral rather than multilateral (or unilateral) trade liberalization is most likely to occur if negotiators reflect mostly producers' preferences. The research also established systemic externality effects of RTAs through terms-of-

Box 3.4: Regional Reports on Trade—Strategic and Nontraditional

In De Ferranti and others (2002), the Latin America and the Caribbean Region's experience is used to argue that a substantial natural resource base is not necessarily detrimental to economic growth and income equality. Econometric analysis is used to argue that comparative advantage in the Region has been as variable as in countries and Regions with a weaker natural resource base; thus, policy makers have greater control over outcomes.

Drawing on the Chilean success with rapid agricultural productivity growth following trade reforms in the late 1970s, the report shows that similar trends in labor productivity growth have been achieved in countries following a similar path. Case studies of successful export processing zones in Central America (Costa Rica and El Salvador) are developed to show that policy incentives can generate rewards. The report is complemented by insightful historical lessons from nineteenth century industrialization patterns in natural resource–based economies.

The Middle East and North Africa Region offers an interesting contrast as the only Region that failed to reduce its protection during the 1990s. It is also notable as the Region with countries that are the furthest away from predicted trade volumes. With a labor force growing at twice the average of other countries, the Region faces a significant job-creation challenge.

Dasgupta and Nabli (2003) review the Region's disappointing performance and use comparative analysis to highlight— based on country characteristics—that the Region holds the possibility for accelerated growth through faster trade and investment integration. The report emphasizes that both the resource-rich and resource-poor countries in the Region face poorly functioning labor markets (wage rigidities, skill mismatches, and institutional factors such as expatriate worker quotas that raise employment costs for expatriates). The report argues that incentives to liberalize trade have been weak economically and politically because a coalition of powerful constituents benefits from rents (such as public sector agencies, public sector enterprises, and private enterprises in import-substituting activities) that would be lost under a more liberal trade and investment regime.

Both of these reports are well-focused and draw on research conducted within the Bank as well as externally. While they draw on research themes emphasized by the Trade Department, they also develop areas that have not figured prominently in the research at the center. Examples include the role of labor markets (including education policies and technological absorption through trade) in Latin America and the Caribbean and on labor market institutions and adjustment costs to trade reforms in the Middle East and North Africa. More extensive empirical work on the political economy of reform, emphasizing the differences between resource-rich and resource-poor countries, would have been welcome for both reports.

Source: De Melo (2005).

trade effects on third countries (Winters and Chang 2000, 2002), giving support to the concerns of excluded countries facing such trade arrangements.

The research on regionalism has been forward-looking (starting early on) and consequential in its impact in refereed journals and in the overall debate on the relation between regionalism and multilateralism. At the same time, countries enter into regional agreements for many reasons (politics, security, insurance, and so on) that are often beyond the scope of reasonable quantification by economists. Thus, for much of the 1980s and 1990s, the Bank focused on the suboptimality of RTAs.

After highlighting the second-best nature of preferential trading arrangements during much of the 1990s (in favor of unilateral or multilateral trade liberalization), reflecting some ambivalence toward RTAs, the Bank has taken a pragmatic approach in recent years, and has had an active dialogue with regional trade institutions in some Regions. This is especially notable in the Africa Region, where analysis has been conducted on the common external tariff for several RTAs (EAC, ECOWAS, UMOEA),[21] revenue implications and possible trade diversion, the Environmental Protection Agencies (EPAs) with the European Union (Hinkle and Schiff 2004), and Latin America (work on CAFTA and the Free Trade Area of the Americas [FTAA]). The Europe and Central Asia Region, which has always conducted Regional trade analysis, has continued to do so.

Chapter 4: Evaluation Highlights

- The trade portfolio performed as well as the rest of the Bank portfolio.
- Trade adjustment loans were most likely to meet their objectives, while institutional-related investment lending was least likely to do so.
- Nominal tariffs were significantly reduced and overall growth often improved.
- But the export supply response has been uneven and diversification limited, particularly in Africa.

Outcomes and Results

This chapter first analyzes outcomes at the **project** level, assessing the extent to which project objectives were met.

Then, using a broader set of trade and macroeconomic outcomes at the **cross-country** level, it compares countries that borrowed from the Bank to a control group of countries that reformed without the financial assistance of the Bank, to capture outcomes such as trade performance, export diversification, and greater integration into the global economy. Finally, the chapter examines results at the **country** level, drawing on case studies commissioned by IEG.

Project Outcomes

What Were the Objectives?

Figure 4.1 shows that improving incentives for tradables and achieving macroeconomic stabilization and economic growth were almost equally important objectives for adjustment loans with trade components. Promoting and diversifying exports was the most important objective of investment loans and the third most important for adjustment loans.

How Did the Projects Perform?

Of the 215 operations with trade-related components exceeding 50 percent that the Bank approved between fiscal years 1987 and 2004, 132 had closed and been rated by IEG (about 57 percent of all projects, or 59 percent in terms of value) as of April 2005.

Trade loans focused on improving incentives for tradables, diversifying exports, macroeconomic stabilization, and economic growth.

Core trade lending operations (in which trade components accounted for more than 80 percent of project costs) performed about the same as the rest of the Bank portfolio over the period on outcome and sustainability, but worse on institutional development impact. They yielded a *satisfactory* outcome rating 70 percent of the time,[1] slightly lower than the percentage of overall Bank lending operations rated satisfactory between 1987 and 2004. In general, trade adjustment loans performed better than other adjustment loans (86 versus 78 percent), while trade investment loans performed slightly worse than other investment loans (69 versus 72

Trade lending performed as well as the rest of the Bank portfolio on outcomes and sustainability, but worse on institutional development impact.

Figure 4.1: Stated Objectives of Trade-Related Projects, 1987–2004 (frequency cited)

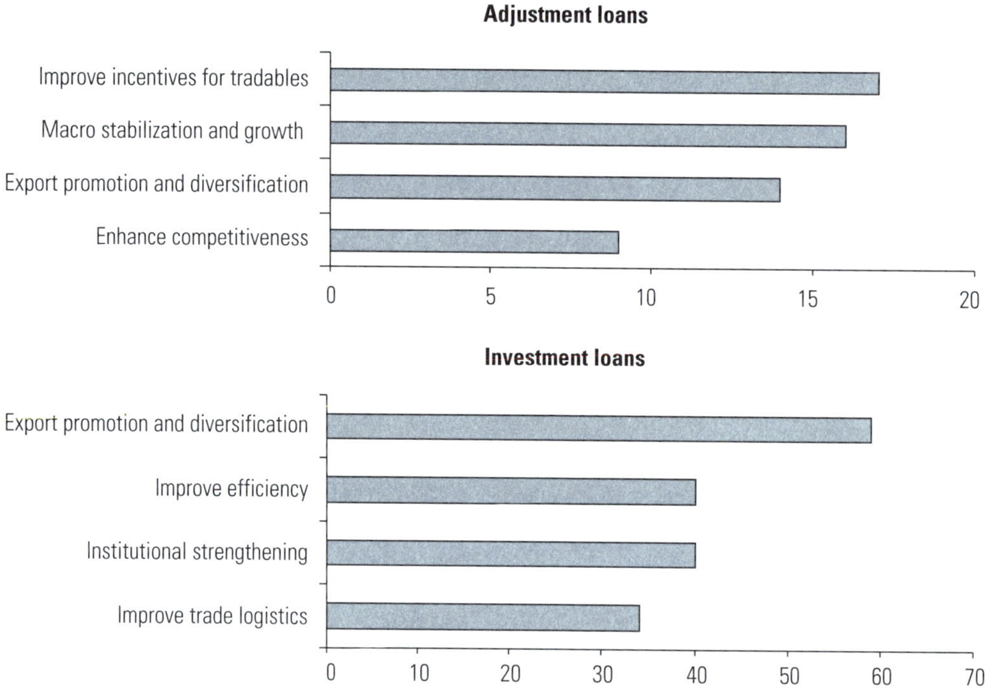

Source: IEG staff calculations.

Note: Only loans approved between 1987 and 2004 in which more than half the components focused on trade were considered. Adjustment loans = 42; Investment Loans = 173. Because loans frequently have more than one objective, the frequency with which objectives appear exceeds number of loans.

percent, respectively). The trade portfolio had a *likely* sustainability rating 64 percent of the time, slightly higher than the average for all Bank operations.

In contrast, trade operations achieved a *substantial* institutional impact only 29 percent of the time over the review period. This is significantly lower than the Bank average of 42 percent over the same period, but is driven by extremely poor performance in the late 1980s and early 1990s. Trade adjustment and investment loans each performed worse than the Bank portfolio. In line with Bank lending operations in other sectors, all evaluated dimensions of trade-related operations have improved steadily over time.

Projects focused on different thematic areas in trade have performed differently, but overall performance has improved over time.

The relative importance of trade in any project did not generally make an appreciable difference in its performance (Appendix D1). The overall ratings were comparable in all dimensions for projects with smaller trade components (between 50 and 80 percent trade component share), with the notable exception of the institutional development rating, which was substantially lower for core trade projects (29 percent as against 71 percent).[2]

Components that focused primarily on trade liberalization achieved the best performance outcome ratings: 85 percent were rated satisfactory (Appendix D2). Components related to private financing (such as export finance guarantees and export reinsurance) were the least successful, with only 56 percent rated as satisfactory.

The superior performance of projects focusing on trade liberalization reflects the relative legislative ease (the so-called "stroke of the pen" actions)[3] of putting in place the associated actions (such as the reform of tariff regimes, reduction and elimination of import and export licenses or bans).

By contrast, the thematic areas that make greater demands on institutional and administrative capacity are more difficult to implement. Failure to address key supply-side constraints can ultimately short-circuit export expansion, even if trade liberalization is accomplished.

Appendix D3 summarizes the performance of three key groups of trade-related investment projects: customs, export processing zones (EPZs), and matching grant schemes. Transport-related trade facilitation projects are the subject of two ongoing IEG evaluations of Regional integration and transport.

An econometric estimation of the determinants of project outcomes at an aggregate level suggested that country and loan characteristics were important. Middle-income countries and those with low conditionality had a higher probability of having better-performing loans. The probit estimation also confirmed that project implementation had improved over time (Appendix D4).[4]

In addition to per capita income, other country characteristics were important determinants of trade project outcomes. The Country Policy and Institutional Assessment (CPIA) index was used as a proxy for a country's institutional and policy capabilities.[5] In the trade portfolio, unsatisfactory lending operations were more likely to be associated with countries with lower CPIAs than were satisfactory lending operations. This holds true for both core trade and other trade-related projects. Performance in projects that focused exclusively on trade did not differ as much between countries with low and high CPIAs. This suggests that these projects made relatively lower demands on the client countries. In contrast, multisector loans with trade components were more complex, required greater capacity, and were thus more likely to pose a greater challenge for countries with low CPIAs. Projects implemented in the transition countries were also likely to have poorer performance, driven by exceptionally poor performance of trade finance loans.

Country income and policy characteristics were important determinants of trade project outcomes.

The existence of economic and sector work (ESW) underpinning a trade lending operation appeared to have positively affected the outcome. Lending operations that

ESW affected project outcomes positively.

Box 4.1: Trade Finance—A Continued Struggle to Be Effective for Some

The overall outcome of a variety of trade financing loans (lines of credit, pre- and post-shipment credits, export credit and guarantee schemes) was unsatisfactory in a range of countries (Bangladesh, Bolivia, Guinea, India, Romania, Tunisia, and Turkey). Based on project evaluation documents, the most common reason for their relative lack of success was an over-estimation of demand. This may have arisen partly because the projects failed to consider competition from other, cheaper (often subsidized) sources that created a distorted market for term finance. Reform of the financial system is a prerequisite for provision of these lines of credit and, more generally, other sources of finance (such as multilateral or bilateral donors) should be considered. Two other factors that help explain the performance of the trade financing loans were cumbersome implementation arrangements and macroeconomic conditions that were not supportive (such as high and variable inflation and overvalued exchange rates).

These lessons, which were captured in guidelines introduced in the Bank's Operational Directive for Financial Sector operations in 1992, were not embedded in subsequent trade finance projects, though lower inflation rates in the mid- to late 1990s did improve the environment. These projects continue to exhibit mixed performance, however. Several of these loans went to transition clients where there was weak capacity in the implementing banks and where more unstable macroeconomic conditions skew the results—operations with non-transition clients have performed much better.[a]

Source: Lindahl 2004.

a. IEG 2005 points out that while lines of credit were approved in relatively stable macroeconomic conditions, 20 of the 29 approved lines of credit that did not meet this criterion were in the Europe and Central Asia Region.

were rated unsatisfactory were more likely to lack any preceding ESW in the years before the operation. By contrast, projects that were rated as satisfactory were much more likely to have benefited from recent ESW (up to two years preceding the operation). Conducting ESW in advance of the trade reforms may have offered an opportunity to sensitize country officials to the need for reform and to provide the Bank with a greater awareness of potential political difficulties. Prior ESW also often addressed the fiscal implications of trade reform, perhaps enabling the Bank to better discuss alternatives to generate revenue-neutral outcomes and to minimize a common source of country reluctance to liberalize. This point is further detailed in the case study discussion.

A review of trade operations that were rated unsatisfactory or highly unsatisfactory showed some common causes of failure. Poor project design, unrealistic assumptions (related to targets and projections), and unfavorable macroeconomic environments were most frequently cited as the cause of unsatisfactory outcomes (table 4.1). Unsatisfactory loans were more likely to be associated with investment loans, with the likelihood of this rising after 1995. No Regional patterns emerged.

Conclusions. Projects that focus primarily on trade perform about the same as the rest of the Bank portfolio on outcome (70 versus 73 percent) and sustainability (64 compared to 61 percent), but worse on institutional development (29 percent of core trade projects compared with 42 percent for the Bank).

The performance of the trade portfolio has improved over time, in line with the rest of the Bank. The degree to which a project contains trade does not make an appreciable difference to outcomes.

Projects that focused on thematic areas that make greater demands on institutional and administrative capacity, such as trade financing, performed the worst, making it more difficult for the Bank to achieve its institutional-strengthening objectives.

At an aggregate level, positive project outcomes were associated with middle-income countries, low conditionality and good institutional frameworks, and prior ESW.

At a project level, poor project design, unrealistic assumptions, and unstable macroeconomic environments contributed most frequently to unsatisfactory outcomes.

Did Trade Loans Pay Attention to Poverty and Distributional Issues?

As noted in Chapter 2, critics of the Bank have been particularly concerned about the adjustment costs associated with trade liberalization. IEG's review of project design found that trade-related adjustment loans have not paid sufficient attention to potential adjustment costs from trade liberalization or to the

Table 4.1: Factors Underlying Poorly Performing Projects

Thematic focus	Closed (before 1995)	Closed (after 1995)
Unrealistic assumptions	2	8
Project design	0	9
Macroeconomic conditions	4	8
Borrower administrative capacity	2	5
Weak borrower ownership	2	4
Political developments	2	2
Memo:		
Number of unsatisfactory projects[a]	10	20
Total projects > 50% trade	43	172

Source: IEG staff calculations from project documents.

a. Unsatisfactory or highly unsatisfactory trade loans with trade component exceeding 50 percent of total project costs.

functioning of labor markets, despite heavy emphasis on poverty in the 1990 and 2000–01 *World Development Reports*.[6] The latter WDR acknowledged trade liberalization had yielded ambiguous results for the poor over the past 15 years, and that the initial push for trade liberalization as an instrument for poverty reduction had been influenced by a "narrow reading of predictions from trade theory: that removing trade barriers in developing countries would increase demand for their abundant low-skilled labor and expand unskilled employment and earnings"(World Bank 2001b, p. 70).

Between 1987 and 1995, 31 percent of trade adjustment loans included compensation or mitigation measures to cushion the social and economic effects of trade reform on the poor. Since then, 38 percent—a slight increase—of trade adjustment loans have done so. The nature of the measures ranged from targeted subsidy programs to supplement the caloric intake of the poor in Mexico[7] to the introduction of social safety net measures to protect the unemployed during the period of transition.

The Bank also supported some safety nets through separate adjustment credits, such as in India's National Renewal Fund, which provides a social safety net to cover the labor costs of restructuring and to mitigate its employment effects. The failure of trade-related ESW to analyze the links was also a contributory factor, given the importance of quality analysis for well-performing lending.

IEG finds little evidence that more recently approved trade-related lending operations are doing a much better job of identifying potential winners and losers or of integrating adjustment assistance strategies. Even in cases where projects build on analysis of poverty considerations, implementation is sometimes unsuccessful in mitigating the associated adjustment costs.

Economic Outcomes for the Sample Countries

The cross-country sample analyzed in this section comprises 45 developing countries that had a complete set of trade and macroeconomic data for a period of 10 years (2 years before the trade reform and 8 years afterward). The date of reform was ascertained based on a review of Bank reports and outside research, as well as discussions with country economists where necessary. The sample excludes countries that were in conflict during the period, as well as the republics of Eastern Europe and the former Soviet Union that were in transition.

Trade-related adjustment loans have not sufficiently attended to poverty and distributional outcomes.

The 45 countries include 2 groups: 35 countries that undertook trade reform with the support of a Bank loan, and 10 countries that undertook trade reform without a Bank loan during this period. The countries are additionally classified according to several dimensions: (i) whether they were gradual or fast reformers; (ii) whether they were intensive reformers undertaking deep reforms in several areas or less intensive; (iii) Bank geographical Region; (iv) export structure; and (v) per capita income. Appendix D5 and Jinjarak and others (2005) provide additional detail and description.

A sample of 45 countries that undertook trade reform provides a cross-country view of economic outcomes.

Initial Conditions

The conditions prevailing at the time of trade reforms in the 35 liberalizing countries supported by the Bank often constituted a bias against trade and reflected unstable macroeconomic conditions. The introduction of trade reform in the presence of macro instability was consistent with the consensus from the literature, but differed from previous IEG analysis, which views stabilization as a prerequisite (IEG 1992a).

With average tariffs on goods above 30 percent and nontariff barrier (NTB) frequency ratios[8] above 50 percent, the 45 countries in the sample would be considered highly protected by any standard. Their import duty regimes were also characterized

Bank clients tended to have more unstable initial macro conditions and greater anti-export bias.

by various forms of restrictive import licensing arrangements, and "cascading" tariff structures, all contributing to high effective protection and a wide dispersion in protection.

On the export side, these 45 countries frequently applied restrictions to export activities (export bans, export licenses) and introduced repatriation requirements related to export profits. Particularly in Africa, major export commodities were governed by government marketing monopolies. Exchange rates were often fixed at official rates and overvalued, resulting in the emergence of black market premiums in some countries as foreign exchange shortages arose. These policies constituted a major bias against exports.

The 35 reformers supported by the Bank had slightly higher initial import tariff levels (31.9 versus 27.6 percent, on average, for unweighted tariffs, and 21.6 versus 25.8 percent for weighted tariffs reflecting exemptions) than non-Bank-supported or independent trade reformers. However, even this figure is misleading as it masks their much greater use of nontariff barriers—almost 70 percent of tariff lines compared with 23.9 percent for the 10 independent reformers.[9]

Changes in Target Variables and Economic Activity

Impact of policy reforms on target variables (tariffs and protection)

On average, countries that borrowed from the Bank for trade reform tended to have larger initial fiscal deficits when compared with countries that undertook reforms on their own, and they relied slightly more on import duties as a source of tax revenues (table 4.3).[10] Bank borrowers had lower investment and economic growth rates. Bank clients also faced greater precariousness in their foreign trade regimes, reflected in higher external debt-to-GDP ratios and lower foreign exchange reserves. The economic imbalances of the Bank's clients were often associated with balance of payments difficulties, presaging their tendency to borrow from the Bank.[11]

This section examines the performance of developing countries at an aggregate level to assess the achievement of objectives. Specifically, it examines the impact of the policy actions discussed above on the directly targeted policy variables (such as tariffs), on economic incentives, and on economic activity in the real sector—major objectives of the Bank's assistance on trade such as exports and growth. In addition, we attempt to delineate the role of the Bank in this process by using a "difference-in-differences" approach to correct for any potential sample selection bias. Given the pervasive trend toward trade liberalization among developing countries during the review period, a second counterfactual (comparing trade reformers to non–trade reformers) was not explored.[12]

A word about attribution: while other actors were important in influencing trade policies in developing countries (such as the IMF, and more recently the WTO and regional trading arrangements), for the period during which most of the sample countries liberalized with support from the Bank (mid-1980s to early 1990s), the Bank was the predominant advisor on trade policies. This is borne out by a review of the trends in IMF trade conditionality and an examination of the nature of Bank trade conditionality during this period.

Another dimension that is more difficult to capture is the impact of the existence of a Fund program. While econometrically this did not generate additional results, to the extent that a Fund program contributed to good macroeconomic outcomes or to the perception of good macroeconomic management, this is likely to have contributed to greater support by development partners, helping to ease macroeconomic imbalances.

All groups of countries in the sample of 45 reformers generally showed a trend toward more openness in terms of lower tariffs (table 4.2), although the pace differed, with notably slow liberalization by countries that started out with a larger manufacturing base. Trade reform was significant across all Regions, although significant NTBs remain in Africa, East Asia and the Pacific, and the Middle East and North

Table 4.2: Indicators of Protection

Region	Simple unweighted tariff (%)			Weighted tariff (%)[a]			Nontariff barriers (% of lines)		
	t = 0	t = 1	t = 2	t = 0	t = 1	t = 2	t = 0	t = 1	t = 2
All reformers	30.4	27.9	20.8	24.6	12.7	7.0	59.1	42.1	17.2
Bank-supported	31.9	29.1	23.1	21.6	10.9	10.2	69.9	44.1	17.4
Independent	27.6	21.0	14.7	25.8	13.4	5.7	23.9	14.6	5.1
By Region									
Africa	18.2	24.7	18.1	16.9	12.2	6.4	57.0	36.1	41.3
East Asia and Pacific	32.8	23.1	21.4	17.9	12.5	11.9	38.0	42.2	25.6
Europe and Central Asia	22.7	9.5	8.3	..	..	3.9	96.4	96.4	9.4
Latin America and the Caribbean	25.9	13.5	12.5	35.6	12.4	6.4	33.6	18.6	6.6
Middle East and North Africa	26.0	25.0	26.8	..	14.9	10.0	63.7	63.7	27.6
South Asia	66.0	48.0	31.6	49.8	14.7		74.3	48.8	21.5
By income									
Low-income	34.5	29.2	24.7	31.0	12.3	5.4	66.1	40.3	9.2
Middle-income	28.7	27.1	18.2	19.8	13.0	8.0	45.6	37.3	17.5
Reform intensity									
Intensive	30.7	21.7	21.7	21.1	15.1	8.4	57.3	62.6	24.8
Non-intensive	30.6	29.4	20.7	25.1	12.1	6.4	56.0	33.8	12.9
Reform pace									
Gradual	27.6	27.1	23.2	32.1	12.7	8.6	56.9	45.8	15.3
Fast	34.3	28.8	18.9	14.5	12.7	5.0	55.3	31.2	15.0
Initial exports structure									
Fuel	28.5	21.7	14.8	..	10.8	4.5	79.1	53.7	5.6
Manufacture	41.9	41.0	34.8	33.4	15.1	5.7	72.8	52.5	26.7
Other	29.1	24.5	19.9	18.0	12.3	7.9	52.4	35.9	14.5

Source: Jinjarak, Salinas, and Tsikata (2005).

Note: t = 0 is initial period of 0 to 2 years before trade reform; t = 1 is 0 to 2 years after reform; t = 2 is 3 to 5 years after reform.

a. This underestimates the extent of protection in earlier years because it does not include import surcharges, which were quite prevalent.

Africa.[13] While some countries in South Asia were still protected after the reforms, they made progress, actually reducing average tariffs by half and reducing NTB coverage by more than that.

While nominal tariffs are readily available and an easily comparable source of data to try and ascertain changes in protection, they can be deceptive. In particular, if countries substitute other instruments of protection, such as surcharges, overall protection may rise. While the study could not examine this for all countries, evidence from country reviews suggests instrument substitution was not uncommon (Indonesia, Morocco, Peru, Senegal).

Much like the findings from project-level data, the whole-sample data on the evolution of tariffs and nontariff barriers do not support the common criticism that the Bank followed a "one-size-fits-all" approach to trade liberalization. The pattern of trade reform was heterogeneous across countries, differing widely in magnitude.[14] Some countries in the sample (Tunisia, Vietnam) implemented a dual-scheme approach to reform, maintaining high protection of domestic industries, but providing liberal trade regimes in free trade or export processing zones.

The assertions that Bank-supported reforms were consistently more rapid and that the speed of reform was inappropriate are difficult to evaluate. There was no correlation between the presence of Bank support and the speed of reform. Independent reformers were as likely to be fast reformers as were Bank-supported reformers. Almost half (44 percent) of all liberalization episodes were rapidly implemented—that is, with most of the reform completed within three years—with the other half taking anywhere from 4 to 11 years. But by historical standards, all these liberalizations were implemented rapidly. For example, after World War II, the average U.S. tariff was slightly below 50 percent, and it took 50 years for this figure to decline to 6–8 percent.

Trade reform led to lower tariffs, and was accompanied by higher import demand and faster economic growth, but only modest export supply response.

Real sector

Independent and Bank-supported countries shared common trends (table 4.4 and Appendix D5) for the main macroeconomic and trade indicators. Both groups of countries were successful in bringing down inflation, reducing their fiscal deficits, and broadening their tax revenue bases. The introduction of trade reforms was accompanied by a significant increase in import demand, in part because these reformers had been experiencing more import compression before the reform, brought about by foreign exchange shortages and quantitative restrictions. Export growth was modest for both groups—it stayed relatively stable for Bank-supported liberalizers but slowed down for independent trade liberalizers. The current account balance increased slightly for the Bank's clients and

Table 4.3: Bank Trade Clients Differed from Other Developing Countries

	Sample countries excluding those under hyperinflation		
Trade reformers	**All**	**Bank-supported**	**Non-Bank-supported**
Macroeconomic indicators			
Real effective exchange rates (1980 = 100)	96.4	96.4	96.0
Consumer price index inflation (%)	21.7	21.0	20.4
Fiscal balance/GDP (%)	–4.1	–4.7	–2.2[a]
Tax revenue/GDP (%)	13.8	13.4	15.5
Investment to GDP (%)	19.7	18.3	24.3[a]
Per capita GDP growth (%)	0.8	0.4	1.8
External indicators			
Export growth (%)	6.1	5.3	6.5
Import growth (%)	2.3	2.4	0.6
Trade to GDP (%)	54.7	52.6	64.5
Current account balance to GDP (%)	–3.8	–4.4	–2.1
Terms of trade (1980 = 100)	99.2	98.2	102.7
Total external debt of GDP (%)	80.5	92.3	41.1[a]
Reserves in months of imports	2.5	2.3	3.1
Memo: Number of countries	45	35	10

Source: Authors' calculation from World Development Indicators (WDI) 2004 and data provided by country economists. Figures are an average of the two years prior to reform.

a. 10% statistical significance.

turned into a small surplus for the independent reformers.

There were some differences as well between the two groups of countries in other macroeconomic indicators. The investment performance of the Bank-supported reformers was positive, but not remarkable; after an initial boost immediately following the reform, the investment rate slowed. In the independent reformers group, the investment rate rose more rapidly. In both sets of countries, per capita GDP growth rose—from 0.4 percent before the reform for the Bank-supported reformers to 2 percent three-to-five years after the reform, and from 1.8 to 3.1 percent for the independent reformers.

While the combined before-and-after trade reform and with-and-without Bank assistance approach used above presents an easily understood statistical analysis, it has been criticized as a poor estimator of the counterfactual (what would have happened in the absence of the Bank-supported trade program?) because the approach tends to yield biased and unsystematic results of the effects of borrowing from the Bank.[15] To address these concerns, two econometric approaches were used.

Bank borrowers experienced larger import flows and GDP growth after liberalization, but export supply response was modest.

First, the significance of the differences discussed above was tested. The results, presented in table 4.4, show that the differences were statistically significant for the following variables: per capita GDP growth, imports, the current account balance, terms of trade, and the external debt-to-GDP ratio. Second, an econometric analysis was conducted that corrects for the potential sample selection bias that could potentially arise if Bank clients were to systematically differ (in characteristics) from non-Bank clients.[16]

The results from the second exercise, discussed in detail in Jinjarak, Salinas, and

Table 4.4: Economic Indicators: With and without Bank Assistance and Before and After Trade Reform

			Trade reformers			
	All		Bank-supported		Non-Bank-supported	
Before trade reform	t = 0	t = 2	t = 0	t = 2	t = 0	t = 2
Macroeconomic indicators						
Real effective exchange rate	96.4	80.7	96.4	77.7	96.0	87.4
Consumer price index inflation (1995 = 100)	21.7	18.9	21.0	17.7	20.4	16.6
Fiscal balance as share of GDP (%)	–4.1	–2.6	–4.7	–2.6	–2.2	–2.2
Tax revenue as share of GDP (%)	13.8	15.6	13.4	15.3	15.5	16.8
Investment as share of GDP (%)	19.7	22.7	18.3	21.8	24.3	26.1
Per capita GDP growth (%)	0.8	2.2	0.4	2.0[a]	1.8	3.1
External indicators						
Exports as share of GDP (% growth)	6.1	7.4	5.3	7.8	6.5	5.7
Imports as share of GDP (% growth)	2.3	7.5	2.4	7.5[a]	0.6	7.7[a]
Trade as share of GDP (%)	54.7	64.2	52.6	64.8	64.5	65.3
Current account balance to GDP (%)	–3.8	–2.7	–4.4	–3.9[a]	–2.1	1.2[a]
Terms of trade	99.2	96.2	98.2	94.3[a]	102.7	101.7[a]
Total external debt as share of GDP (%)	80.5	74.8	92.3	85.9[a]	41.1	38.1[a]
Reserves in months of imports	2.5	3.0	2.3	2.7	3.1	3.9

Source: Jinjarak, Salinas, and Tsikata (2005).

Note: t = 0 is 0 to 2 years before reform; t = 1 is 0 to 2 years after reform; t = 2 is 3 to 5 years after reform.

a. 10% statistical significance.

Tsikata (2005) and summarized in Appendix D5, suggest that trade liberalization has a strong and often statistically significant positive impact on economic growth and imports for both the Bank's clients and other independent reformers, and that these impacts persist beyond the short term. With respect to exports, the impact of trade liberalization is more mixed. Bank-supported reformers exhibit rather modest export supply responses, while reformers not supported by the Bank fare slightly worse. So, while the existence of a Bank trade loan freed up imports and was associated with faster economic growth compared with reformers not supported by the Bank, this growth could not be attributed to faster exports growth.

Contribution of trade to growth

Following Chenery (1979), variations in output growth were disaggregated into demand factors—domestic demand, import substitution, and export expansion—for the periods before and after the year of reform for the 45 countries in the sample.[17] Appendix D6 presents the results. Three points can be made:

Relatively speaking, import demand made a larger contribution to economic growth.

- First, domestic demand is a major source of growth for the developing countries in the sample. In all but six countries for which the calculation was done, domestic demand was by far the largest contributor to output growth, explaining more of the increase in growth than either export expansion or import substitution.
- Second, before reform, the reverse of import substitution—import penetration—was more prevalent. After reform, while the degree of import penetration increased in a few countries, the more common pattern was declining import penetration, which was sufficient to reverse the pattern to one of import substitution in some countries.
- Third, the importance of export expansion was uneven across countries following trade liberalization. In half of the countries it increased, while in the other half it declined in importance.

Export diversification was modest, especially for the Region with the highest initial concentration—Sub-Saharan Africa.

Diversification of exports

Diversifying the export basket has been an important objective of the Bank's assistance. Table 4.5 provides three measures of progress in export diversification: the number of products exported, an export concentration index, and the share of a country's top three exports in the overall export basket. Two points emerge. First, all three measures suggest a reduction in export concentration for developing countries as a group and across the major groupings of income, Bank trade loan or not, and regardless of the intensity of reform. Second, despite the overall progress, the Africa and the Middle East and North Africa Regions continue to have extremely concentrated export baskets, and Africa lags well behind the other Regions.

Another way of examining progress in diversification is through an "exports prospects index." Developed in Ng and Yeats (2003), this index helps gauge how favorable (or not) prospects are for a country's exports baskets. An index above one suggests above-average growth prospects, while a value below one suggests the converse. In an estimate of the index for 26 African countries, the authors find only one African country (Mauritius) whose export basket currently suggests that it has the potential to grow at about the same rate as world trade.[18] Given the well-documented (see, for example, Page and Hewitt 2001) continuing secular decline and volatility of commodity prices relative to manufactures and services, there is an urgent need for African countries to reduce their commodity dependence in the long term with the help of transitional assistance.

Both supply and demand factors can influence trade performance. Export growth in the sample of 45 countries between 1982 and 2003 was decomposed into demand, competitiveness, and diversification changes.[19] The results for the analysis at the three-digit Standard International Trade Classification

Table 4.5: Changes in Export Concentration—Half-Full or Half-Empty?

Group	Number of products exported[a]		Export concentration index[b]		Share of three largest exports in total exports (%)	
	Pre-reform	Post-reform	Pre-reform	Post-reform	Pre-reform	Post-reform
All	137	142	0.32	0.31	44.3	38.5
Africa	92	92	0.40	0.41	59.6	54.4
East Asia and Pacific	195	193	0.19	0.20	18.3	14.3
Europe and Central Asia	205	212	0.12	0.12	6.2[c]	4.5[c]
Latin America and the Caribbean	144	154	0.33	0.31	34.4	30.6
Middle East and North Africa	156	156	0.24	0.21	24.4	24.0
South Asia	137	134	0.30	0.27	8.5	11.5
By income						
Low-income	152	160	0.29	0.27	31.6	27.8
Middle-income	110	109	0.37	0.36	56.3	49.6
Reformers						
Bank-supported	137	143	0.35	0.34	57.3	51.8
Independent	136	141	0.31	0.30	41.8	36.0

Source: IEG estimates based on UNCTAD 2004.

a. Number of products exported at three-digit SITC, revision 2 level; this figure includes only products that are greater than $100,000 or more than 0.3 percent of the country's total exports.

b. The Herfindahl-Hirschmann index is a measure of the degree of market concentration. It has been normalized to obtain values ranking from 0 (least) to 1 (maximum concentration).

c. Turkey only.

(SITC) level are presented in table 4.6. The table suggests that the overall diversification contribution to export expansion was minimal across different groups of developing countries, with China dominating the results when included in a group. The table shows that experience varied significantly across Regions and groups of countries. East Asia was the only geographic Region in which gains in competitive position underpinned export performance. Competitive gains were notably low in Africa, and in over half of the African countries the competitive position actually deteriorated. Aggressive and more rapid reformers were more likely to experience greater competitive gains relative to demand.

Did deindustrialization occur?

As discussed in Chapter 2, a criticism of Bank advice on trade liberalization is that it has led to deindustrialization. Table 4.7 and Appendix D5, table D5.2d, present summary statistics on export performance and manufacturing value added (the latter used as a proxy to measure deindustrialization between 1983 and 2003).

The tables suggest that in 11 countries with the highest overall export growth (averaging 12.8 percent), manufacturing value added grew at the respectable rate of almost 7 percent. In contrast, 23 countries with medium export growth rates (about 7 percent) experienced modest growth in manufacturing value added and overall GDP growth, despite growth in manufacturing exports; indeed, manufacturing value added fell over time. This suggests that the gains in manufacturing exports in this group represented a diversion from domestic markets and that some degree of deindustrialization had occurred. Exceptions to this pattern were Chile, Indonesia, and Mauritius.

Internal efficiency gains and productivity

The evaluation conducted a literature review of country experiences with trade and productivity

Table 4.6: Factors behind Change in Exports: By Country Groups (US$ million)

All countries	Exports (annual average) 1982–85	2000–03	Change	Factors underlying change: Overall demand	Competitive factor
All countries	126,768	680,980	554,212	220,313	333,899
Region					
Africa	19,060	37,316	18,256	17,790	466
East Asia and Pacific	34,894	391,832	356,938	91,655	265,283
East Asia and Pacific, excluding China	27,936	208,105	180,169	79,595	100,573
Europe and Central Asia	4,494	18,272	13,778	9,667	4,112
Latin America and the Caribbean	56,940	186,965	130,025	76,221	53,804
Middle East and North Africa	3,314	10,682	7,368	6,291	1,077
South Asia	8,066	35,913	27,847	18,689	9,157
Intensity of reforms					
Low-intensity reformers	112,986	455,556	342,571	195,438	148,584
High-intensity reformers	13,782	225,424	211,641	24,876	186,766
High-intensity reformers excluding China	6,825	41,697	34,872	12,816	22,056
Pace of reforms					
Gradual reformers	61,504	385,007	323,503	99,861	223,642
Gradual reformers excluding China	54,547	201,281	146,734	87,801	58,933
Fast reformers	65,264	295,973	230,709	120,452	110,257

Source: IEG estimates based on United Nations COMTRADE Database.

Note: The demand factor isolates the effect of the increase or decrease in global demand for sample country exports. It shows the percentage increase or decrease in exports that would have occurred had there been no change in the countries' import market shares from the 1982–85 base period. The competitive factor shows the percentage change in exports over or under that associated with demand changes that is brought about solely by the introduction of new products. Any differences between changes in a country's total exports and the sum of these "demand" and "competitive" changes are the result of product diversification.

gains. Because of data constraints, this issue is not well researched for all developing countries, especially less-developed countries. However, countries that have been studied overwhelmingly experienced positive gains in productivity growth following trade liberalization, either as a result of reductions in output tariffs or tariffs on intermediate goods.[20]

Liberalizing countries experience productivity gains.

Lessons at the Country Level

Six country case studies were conducted for this evaluation—of India, Indonesia, Morocco, Mozambique, Senegal, and Zambia. The studies covered fiscal years 1987 through 2003 and 47 lending operations. This section summarizes the lessons that can be generalized to the Bank's trade activities (Appendix D7 summarizes the case studies).

In all case study countries, tariffs were lowered in the medium term, and foreign exchange reserves positions improved (although aid often played a part). Economic outcomes were mixed. India, Indonesia, Morocco, and Mozambique enjoyed higher GDP growth, as well as revenue gains. Nontraditional exports were diversified in some countries (Indonesia, Senegal, Zambia), but export growth was often uneven. In general, results with respect to the sustainability of reforms, the implementation pace, investment response, and productivity gains differed widely. Employment losses occurred in the

Table 4.7: Export Growth and Increased Value Added, 1983–2003 (annual increase, percent)

	Manufactured exports adjusted for purchasing power	Total exports adjusted by purchasing power	Value added by manufacture	Total value added
By growth				
High export growth	11.9	12.8	6.6	5.5
Medium export growth	11.4	7.3	3.0	3.2
Low export growth	7.2	3.0	2.1	1.9
By income				
Low-income	10.6	7.6	3.8	3.3
Middle-income	10.5	7.2	3.5	3.4
By speed of reform				
Gradual	9.5	7.2	4.1	3.7
Fast	11.6	7.4	2.8	2.8

Source: IEG staff calculations from 3-digit SITC data.

cashew industry in Mozambique and in manufacturing in Senegal and Zambia. A closer look at the main lessons helps explain the varying outcomes.

Crises Can Precipitate Reform, but Broad Ownership Sustains It

In the six case study countries, macroeconomic or financial crises precipitated the initial trade reform, whether supported financially by the Bank or not.

In **Zambia**, a crisis was compounded by political change. Subsequent reform was often driven by a move toward regional harmonization, notably as countries joined various regional trading arrangements (**Morocco, Senegal**) or by multilateral WTO obligations (**India**).

India, Indonesia, and **Morocco** exhibited a high degree of ownership. This manifested itself in trade policy reforms that sometimes did not follow exactly the Bank's analytical advice or loan design to better adapt them to the country's political economy. Strong ownership was also characterized by a willingness to go beyond the Bank's recommendations in some aspects.

In **Zambia**, the early days of the reform were marked by strong ownership from a new political party eager to make a break with the socialist past and to signal donors and investors that the business environment had improved. Thus, a broad range of reforms were undertaken from the start. But over time, ownership of the reforms became diluted and reforms took longer to implement.

Country case studies and desk reviews of selected programs provide additional insight into Bank support for trade.

In **Senegal**, despite a history of policy reversal, a coalition of pro-reform elements in the public and private sectors was instrumental in keeping the reform agenda going. One lesson for advising on a reform program during crisis is that it pays to have in-depth knowledge of the economy from earlier ESW (as in India, Indonesia, and Morocco).

Crisis can precipitate reform, but broad ownership sustains it.

Sequencing of Macroeconomic Policies

While the Bank's initial diagnosis of the issues constraining trade development in the case study countries was generally correct, in some cases the sequencing of macroeconomic, trade, and other structural policies was suboptimal. In particular, some countries kept one foot firmly on the accelerator (liberalizing trade), and one foot on

Poor policy advice and poor implementation sabotaged trade reform in some cases.

the brake (overvaluing their currency).[21]

In **Senegal**, the persistent overvaluation of the currency in the late 1980s and early 1990s meant that Bank recommendations to liberalize trade were premature. In **Morocco**, failure to consider alternative sources of revenue to replace losses from lowering tariffs led to fiscal distress and a reversal of trade liberalization. Subsequently, the real appreciation of the Moroccan dinar during the 1990s made it more difficult for the country to compete.

Failure to conquer fiscal constraints also proved to be a stumbling block for India and Senegal by making those countries more cautious about the pace of reform. In **Zambia**, the 1990s were characterized by adverse macroeconomic conditions (high real interest rates, a tendency toward a volatile and overvalued exchange rate), general instability, and a banking sector that financed government deficits rather than private investment.

The Enhanced Structural Adjustment Facility (ESAF) review by the IMF (Botchwey and others 1998) highlights the finding that the sequencing of macroeconomic policies recommended by the IMF and the Bank contributed to the poor macroeconomic outcomes in Zambia. With rising inflation and liberalized interest rates, there was a liquidity squeeze that drove real interest rates up to high levels. This, in turn, caused real exchange rate appreciation that, in conjunction with the rapid trade liberalization, placed Zambian firms under intense competitive pressure. The failure to achieve macro stabilization proved costly.

The Need for Complementary Policies Was Underestimated

The Bank was generally aware of the importance of complementary policies on the regulatory side, often incorporating them in its lending to the countries. Yet implementation in these areas was often weaker than those actions linked directly to trade policy. The evidence from the country case studies suggests that the Bank may initially have underestimated the complexity of the regulatory reforms and the political constraints associated with carrying them out. The failure to complete these reforms in a timely fashion affected the outcomes from trade reform negatively in some cases. Moreover, the most critical complementary policy varied across countries, suggesting the need for in-depth analytical work.

The complexity of complementary policies was underestimated.

In other cases where the authorities were interested in introducing reforms, the Bank was able to craft a comprehensive program of assistance to complement trade reform. In **Morocco**, the Bank adapted to its reduced role in trade policy and was able to use its ESW to identify the most pressing supply-side issues and make a convincing case for reform (for example, in customs). In **India**, Bank staff saw industrial deregulation and trade liberalization as mutually reinforcing; thus, its analytical work and lending operations tackled both.[22] In **Indonesia**, the Bank financed a cluster of projects that complemented trade reform and addressed supply-side issues. These included a manpower and training development project, two export development loans, an industrial restructuring loan, and a loan for private sector development.

Apart from regulatory reforms, the studies on **Senegal** and **Zambia** identified skills shortages, notably at the technical and managerial levels, as important constraints to improved global competitiveness. The potential positive role of high-quality economic and sector work was also addressed in all case studies (see box 4.2 and Appendix D7).

Institutions Matter and Underpin Sustainability

Institutions that facilitate trade policy and development and ensure implementation are important in carrying out the strategic vision of countries. In **Morocco**, Bank lending and technical assistance to a variety of institutions (Ministry of Commerce and Industry, Port Authority of Morocco, customs administration) is widely viewed as having been highly effective—having led to strengthened strategic and regulatory capacity. The Moroccans

Box 4.2: Failure to Implement Complementary Policies Can Be Costly

In **Zambia,** the privatization of the mining parastatal Zambia Consolidated Copper Mines (ZCCM) was an important element in the trade reform program. When Zambia initiated its reforms in 1991, it was still dependent on copper for over 90 percent of merchandise export revenues. ZCCM was an inefficient producer and a drain on the national budget. Although the new reformist party had advocated the reorganization of ZCCM, including the options of "divesture, joint ventures and privatization" in the New Economic Recovery Programme (1992), the formal decision to privatize was only announced in 1995.

By 1996–99, ZCCM was suffering catastrophic losses, equivalent to 6-10 percent of GDP yearly (Zambia Country Assistance Evaluation). Yet privatization dragged on and conditionality was ineffective. Apart from the economic costs, Zambia's slowness in implementing the recommended policies jeopardized the trade reform program and its outcomes by reducing the credibility of the government's commitment to reform. Other interventions intended to complement the trade reform probably came too late—they included an agricultural sector investment project (approved three years after the liberalization) and an enterprise development project (approved six years after the reform) or were ineffective (for example, the duty drawback scheme remained inefficient despite being the subject of conditionality in two different loans).

Source: Zambia Country Case Study for IEG Trade Assistance Evaluation.

emphasized that Bank success came about in part because (i) the government was convinced that those institutions had become a drag on the economy and (ii) each of the reforms took place at a time of crisis. Each of these institutions has been critical in Morocco's path toward global competitiveness.

In **Mozambique**, the government signed a contract with a pre-shipment inspection agency while it strengthened its own customs administration. The inspection agency was successful in tightening and improving import duty collection.

In **Indonesia**, the interdepartmental team known as Team Tariff (not financed by the Bank) was an important mechanism for reviewing all changes in import taxes and regulations. It helped put limits on the ability of particular ministers or government officials to make arbitrary changes for the benefit of particular groups.

In countries with weaker capacity, such as **Senegal** and **Zambia**, the plethora of trade issues on the negotiating agenda at the regional and global levels overwhelms under-resourced and under-staffed technocrats. Countries are unable to present positions unique to their countries. The consequence is often failure to keep up with policies and agreements that have implications for exporters, leading to resistance when the costs of the agreements are felt.

The private sector also sometimes lacks capacity. Efforts to nurture public-private partnerships as well as private sector associations can pay off in broadening the support for reform (**India**, **Senegal**), but the Bank has only infrequently supported private exporter groups (it has more frequently supported individual exporters through matching grant facilities).

Both private and public trade-related institutions matter in carrying out reforms.

External Factors Were Largely Understudied

In general, Bank country assistance strategies and country economic reports did not take adequate account of external factors such as the multilateral trade negotiations under the Uruguay and Doha Rounds or multilateral trade institutions, agreements, and rules emanating from the various WTO agreements.

In **Senegal**, according to policy makers, special conditions that apply to developing countries (such as more lenient tariff reduction schedules or flexibility in food security–related trade areas) were infrequently discussed. Despite the enormous amount of Bank research on these topics and significant advice and technical assistance from other development partners, these issues passed largely unnoticed in the Bank's

External factors were largely understudied.

country-level dialogue until 2003, when tariff and nontariff barriers in foreign markets (horticulture, fisheries), standards information and compliance, and low world cotton prices were systematically analyzed to assess their impact on Senegal.[23]

In **India**, Bank reports on the country in the late 1980s and early 1990s rarely analyzed foreign investment in depth, although the China experience had already underscored the importance of foreign investment liberalization, and even though liberalization in services trade was a major emerging issue in the Uruguay Round and necessarily required some easing of the rules on foreign investment.

In **Zambia**, the Bank failed to consider the country's complex trading environment, which arose in part from overlapping preferential trading arrangements. Zambia had to grant preferential access to final products from Common Market for Eastern and Southern Africa (COMESA) trading partners such as Zimbabwe. At the same time, Zambian manufacturers had to try to compete while importing inputs from non-COMESA sources. The result was very low—or even negative—effective rates of protection.

Distributional outcomes get too little attention.

In another example, at the time of its democratization in 1994, South Africa (a new member of Southern Africa Development Community [SADC], but not COMESA) maintained high import barriers, while subsidizing its exports through its general Export Incentive Scheme.

Although it cannot be determined precisely how serious these regional problems were, strategically Zambian policy makers felt they would have been better placed if they had "more" to bargain with (in terms of tariff reductions) when it came to subsequent free trade arrangements with COMESA and SADC. Zambia, however, had already liberalized significantly in the context of Bank projects.

Until recently, Bank advice on particular products was given in isolation from the global industry. In **Mozambique**, the controversial liberalization of the cashew nut industry did not lead to the intended beneficiaries (the farmers) receiving as great a share of the export price as anticipated. The Bank's analytic work did not systematically examine the cashew's global value chain, yet the entire thrust of the proposed reforms was to raise the international competitiveness of the industry and, with it, the farmers' share in the export earnings. Increasingly, however, the Bank's Private Sector Development Vice-Presidency is encouraging and broadening the inclusion of value chain analysis; the integrated trade logistics work in **Morocco**, for example, includes value chain analysis.

Distributional Outcomes Get Too Little Attention

A review of project documents, ESW, and assistance strategies generally found little evidence of consistent or widespread attention to the distributional outcomes arising from trade liberalization in the case study countries. Even where the Bank incorporated distributional concerns, it was hampered by poor implementation. In **Senegal**, the Bank was sensitive to authorities' concerns about the social costs of adjustment in the run-up to the devaluation and included a component in the 1994 post-devaluation Economic Recovery Credit. The IEG assessment of the credit, however, found that a well-planned safety net was missing, and that targeting was not refined enough to reach the people who most needed assistance.

Conclusions. While the initial impetus for trade reform is often an economic crisis, sustaining the reform requires broad support and ownership. Conditionality was generally not conducive to achieving that ownership, and the Bank was more judicious in using it in larger countries. Bank advice and analytical work were often instrumental in supporting reform. Its value, however, was reduced in cases where it was perceived to be dogmatically based.

Bank advice and lending contributed to systematic reductions in protection and in opening up economies, although the pace differed across countries. The long-term outcome in poorer countries' export supply response was less than expected, even when there were short-term gains in economic growth. As discussed earlier, the impact on employment and poverty was less than expected, and the Bank did not conduct sufficient analysis to inform its policy advice and lending on this issue.

Less than satisfactory outcomes were explained by inappropriate macroeconomic conditions (notably currency overvaluation or instability) or incomplete trade reform. In addition, the Bank needs to ensure adequate analysis of the distributional consequences of trade reform, complementary policies (regulatory reforms, infrastructure requirements, and skills needs), and external factors (such as the lack of knowledge by governments and entrepreneurs of global value chain links for the country's existing and potential exports, and market access restrictions). Weaknesses in these areas contributed to the inability of some countries to take advantage of the opportunities offered by trade reforms.

Chapter 5: Evaluation Highlights

- The Bank has increased its presence and work on trade issues following the failed Seattle trade meeting.
- Research is of high quality and advocacy has raised the Bank's profile.
- The Bank is meeting its trade capacity building objectives unevenly, and more effort is needed to mainstream trade.

Trade Returns to the Agenda, 2001–04

Difficulties at the 1999 Seattle trade ministerial meeting of the World Trade Organization (WTO) and growing pressure to deliver on the Millennium Development Goals led the World Bank to reappraise its trade activities, which had diminished during the 1990s.

After the discussion in April 2001 of a Development Committee paper, *Leveraging Trade for Development*, the Bank expanded its work on trade issues considerably[1] (Appendix A1).[2]

The Bank trade program, as revamped in 2001, has two objectives:

(1) Make the world trading system "friendlier" to development—that is, make it a reciprocally open trading system.
(2) Make trade an important part of country development strategies (World Bank 2002d).

Following the recommendations laid out in the Development Committee paper, the trade-for-development agenda was to be pursued by the Bank at three levels: global, Regional, and national.[3]

In early 2001, the Bank began collaborating with other agencies on how best to help the least-developed countries. By July 2002, a new sector unit dedicated to trade had been established. In addition, the Bank formally created a virtual Trade Department (TD) made up of staff working on trade issues from the Development Economics Vice-Presidency (DEC), the Poverty Reduction and Economic Management Network (PREM), and the World Bank Institute (WBI) (Appendix E1).[4]

Since 2001 the Bank has expanded its focus on trade issues considerably.

Anticipating that trade-related work would decline after the conclusion of the Doha Development Round (initiated in 2001 and originally expected to conclude in 2005), a sunset clause was established for July 2005, with the virtual Trade Department to be subjected to "major review" at that time (Appendix E2). *This evaluation does not evaluate the Trade Department, though its findings are expected to contribute to this review and to the work of the department and other Bank units working on trade-related issues.*

This chapter draws in part on an evaluation of the Bank's revamped trade program between 2001 and 2004 commissioned by IEG (De Melo 2005). That evaluation examined the effectiveness of the Bank instru-

Objectives are to support development of a reciprocally open trading system and to make trade an important part of country development strategies.

ments employed—research, participation in global policy discussions and advocacy, trade capacity building, and mainstreaming of trade—and assessed progress on the two objectives outlined above.

IEG finds the objectives to be relevant, timely, and responsive to the rapidly changing global environment on trade issues. However, it recommends greater attention in the future to the balance between the two objectives. In particular, given the Bank's limited direct role in global negotiations, and the importance of country-specific policy dialogue, the study recommends strengthening the analytical tools, processes, and systematic interactions within Bank operations.

Advocacy to redress issues in the global trading system can be handled by the Trade Department and senior management alone.

Within the Bank, global advocacy can be handled by the Trade Department and senior management alone. But the other impediments to global integration *have to be dealt with in concert with other sector networks within the Bank and with the support of Country Management Units.*

In areas where the Trade Department worked with other networks or provided intellectual leadership—such as sanitary and phytosanitary standards and trade facilitation—the Bank has been successful in ensuring the operational relevance of its activities. In other areas where the Bank could have potentially made an impact—agricultural trade and policies, trade and poverty linkages—inadequate investment by the Bank and relatively little intellectual leadership early on has resulted in less success on the operational side.

To enhance the effectiveness of its trade activities, the Bank will have to face more squarely the multisectoral nature of the current trade agenda.

To enhance the effectiveness of its trade activities, the Bank will have to face more squarely the multisectoral nature of the current trade agenda. It will have to improve links between the various sectors and the Trade Department on trade issues on all fronts (research, trade-related capacity building, knowledge management, and development of tools and templates). In particular, the Trade Department can bring the global perspective to bear on sector issues. Success on this front will be the difference between individually competent analytical pieces of work and a more synergistic approach.

Research

Research on trade issues never declined as dramatically as did economic and sector work (see Chapter 3). This made it easier for DEC to gear up quickly in 2001 when interest in trade surged once again. The Bank's trade research has been marked by close collaboration with academia, notably in the Americas and Western Europe.[5] This cross-fertilization has been important in disseminating the Bank's research, while at the same time influencing it.

The Bank's volume of trade-related research has grown rapidly in recent years. Much has been published in respected journals.[6] Since 2001,when the Bank's program on trade was re-energized, Bank staff and collaborators have produced 125 research papers in the World Bank Policy Research Working Paper series[7] and published more than two dozen books and major reports. Forty-three papers have been published (or are forthcoming) in journals (83, counting all refereed journals).[8]

The Bank's trade research focused on the global economy and growth, regionalism, and development; firm-level analysis of the productivity impact of trade policies and foreign direct investment (FDI); trade in services; and some of the behind-the-border barriers to trade.[9] In addition to the Regional ESW that covers Regional trade integration issues and earlier DEC work on regionalism (both covered in Chapter 3), DEC has continued to carry out major research in this area. For example, Schiff and Winters (2003), an expository volume on regionalism, and *Global Economic Prospects* (GEP) *2005* contributed to better understanding of the benefits and obstacles that regionalism presents for the world trading system (see box 5.1). A significant portion of Bank research was innovative (leading in new fields such as services, agricultural standards, transport costs, and other behind-the-border issues). Particularly successful research (in terms of quality of research and links to operational activities) has been done on agricultural standards.

Bank research on several issues related to the multilateral trading system was timely. In the run-up to the Doha Trade Ministerial, for example, Bank staff contributed significantly to a *World Economy* volume on how to ensure that developing countries were full and active participants (Hoekman 2000) and released the *Global Economic Prospects* report *Making Trade Work for the World's Poor* (2002). *Global Economic Prospects: Realizing the Development Promise of the Doha Agenda* (2004) was published in the run-up to the Cancun Trade Ministerial. In the structured interviews that IEG carried out for this study, WTO members said that these studies contributed positively to their understanding of the issues and the debate (Appendix E5).

A number of pieces of DEC research had important implications for the poor. Work on preferences (Schiff 2002) and research on China and India (referred to in Chapter 3), where many of the world's poor live, was particularly significant. Missing was research on some trade areas with implications for the Bank's poorest clients, such as the impact of external (including commodity) trade-related shocks. For example, despite the long-anticipated phase-out of the multi-fibre arrangement in 2005 and its implications for several of the Bank's clients (such as Bangladesh, Dominican Republic, El Salvador, Kenya, Lesotho, Mauritius, and Nepal), no major cross-country strategic analysis was done. Another gap in research, until recently, has been migration.[10]

Migratory pressures have been building up internationally since the breakdown of communism, but the Bank is only beginning to focus on this issue.[11] The Bank has a natural comparative advantage in studying migration (a global issue that requires data-gathering expertise and facility and a cross-country focus), yet it has not taken the lead. A critical amount of work in this area might have given the Bank the information necessary to participate more actively in the debate that is building in the context of the Doha Round. Such research also might have enabled the Bank to assume leadership similar to the way it has in the debate on regionalism.

Bank trade-related research has often been timely and is of high quality.

In addition, several areas in the trade agenda have been slow to yield important insights. Much of the more detailed work relating to market access in agriculture—and to the effects of a reduction in barriers to trade in agriculture, in general—became available only in late 2004 and has yet to have an observable impact on country programs. As to the functioning of the world trading system, quantitative work on the functioning of the Dispute Settlement Understanding has started only recently.

But research on some areas that affect the Bank's poorest clients was missing, and several areas have been slow to yield insights.

Because research is a long process, the Bank can experience gains from being forward-looking and anticipating topics likely to be on the policy agenda soon. Five topics were covered only marginally in the review period but merited more resources. These are discussed in the following paragraphs.

Export-processing zones. For political economy reasons, reducing protection unilaterally may be difficult. Some countries (China, Madagascar, and Mauritius) have managed to integrate into the world economy by relying on export-processing zones rather than tariff reductions. The Bank has carried out relatively little research in this area (Madani 1999).

Agricultural trade and policies. While advocacy and analytical work for agriculture have long been important Bank activities, the amount of research published in refereed journals has

Five topics were covered only marginally in the review period but merited more resources.

Box 5.1: Do Regional Trading Arrangements Help Liberalize Trade?

Regional preferential trading arrangements (bilateral and plurilateral) have mushroomed in every region of the world. There are currently over 300 RTAs.[a] Several factors underlie the proliferation of RTAs—strategic and geopolitical interests, uncertainties about the future of the multilateral trading system following the failure to launch a round in Seattle and the subsequent difficulties in reaching agreements following the Doha Ministerial meeting, and a desire to leverage the strength of numbers into larger markets and enhance regional cooperation on a range of trade and non-trade issues. The Asia-Pacific Economic Cooperation (APEC) arrangement, the European Union, the Southern Common Market (MERCOSUR), the North American Free Trade Agreement (NAFTA), and numerous other free trade areas and customs unions now exist with the multilateral system and its rules. In the view of some researchers, these arrangements reduce global welfare and undermine the institutional architecture of the multilateral trading system.

There are two schools of thought on whether RTAs should be viewed as "building blocks" or "stumbling blocks" to liberalizing trade.[b] Supporters of RTAs discount the extent to which trade diversion exceeds trade creation under RTAs, and argue that in some circumstances smaller RTAs may be easier for countries to negotiate. Those skeptical of RTAs argue that they are likely to result in a "hub and spoke" type of growth, with the smaller spokes being disadvantaged.

Empirical evidence on the extent to which RTAs help liberalize and expand trade is less common and, similar to the theoretical literature, there is no clear consensus. In a recent review of regional trading arrangements in Africa, which is home to over 30 RTAs (or an average of 4 per country),[c] Yang and Gupta (2005) find that RTAs have been ineffective in expanding trade or investment. Limão (2005) shows empirically that U.S. preferential trading arrangements have harmed multilateral liberalization.

Given the proliferation of RTAs, the issue then is no longer one of whether or not to have RTAs, but of how to use them in ways that are complementary to the multilateral trading system. The issues revolve around the following themes:

- How can RTAs be implemented to maximize benefits (internalizing externalities at the regional level and coordinating on standards) and to minimize negative spillovers (reduction in market access to non-partners)?
- How can RTAs be negotiated to bring about "deep integration" beyond what one might expect is possible at the multilateral level?

a. Global Economic Prospects 2005 (World Bank 2004b) provides an up-to-date and comprehensive overview of current RTAs.
b. The theoretical literature on preferential trade agreements is reviewed in Baldwin and Venables (1996), Bhagwati and Panagariya (1997), and Panagariya (2000). Schiff and Winters (2003) and World Bank (2000, 2004a) review the empirical literature and place it in a development context.
c. World Bank (2004b).

been relatively low: only 4 of 83 articles appeared in specialized and refereed academic journals.[12] Developing countries continue to need specific advice on appropriate policy in the transition to a fully liberalized global agricultural system. Such advice requires additional analysis. While more attention is now being paid to the impact of the external environment through, for example, a series of commodity market studies edited by Aksoy and Beghin (2005), a more systematic approach that integrates research, operational implications, and capacity-building is needed.

Trade-poverty linkages and adjustment costs. Until recently, little research had been done on trade and poverty. Given the importance of the topic—and surrounding controversies—carefully chosen case studies might have helped the Bank's understanding. Because gains from trade liberalization are diffuse and sometimes barely visible in the short run, and losses are all too visible, generating support for reform is difficult. This suggests not only spreading the benefits of reforms to the extent possible to reduce the bias against reform, but, more important, looking into the adjustment costs with a view to minimizing them. So far, research and Bank country programs have largely neglected this area, despite high-level expressions of support and intent by senior managers.[13]

Micro-level adjustment. Another aspect of adjustment that was inadequately researched between 2001 and 2004 is the response of firms to trade liberalization. The emphasis of macro-level aggregates such as exports, imports, and GDP masks firm-level transitions such as the exit and entry of firms, and individual responses such as movements in and out of employment.

Services liberalization. Considering that services research is a relatively new area, the Bank has produced timely results, including articles in journals. Its research has provided useful estimates of the efficiency benefits from well-functioning regulatory environments, demonstrated the necessity of drawing distinctions in policy advice across different types of services, and underlined the importance of a complementary regulatory environment. However, the research results have not yet been effectively translated into policy advice or changes in lending activities. This would require more resources than have been allocated thus far, as well as a clearer strategy to engage operational staff.

The views of Bank staff surveyed for this evaluation overlapped with some of the points made above. In particular, when asked what the single most important area for further attention was, staff identified "adjustment and transitional costs from liberalization" and the "links between trade and poverty at the operational level." In addition, the survey results suggested that staff felt it would be beneficial to have additional research drawing on country experience. This would take advantage of the Bank's extensive knowledge of country experience. A review of the reasons why staff found particular trade reports useful emphasized the "presentation of new evidence" or "the existence of a new perspective."

Conclusions. The Bank's trade research between 2001 and 2004 has been of high quality and has contributed to ongoing debates, notably with respect to the global trade architecture and the multilateral trading system. To strengthen the ongoing work and enhance its contribution to the Bank's mission, the Development Research Group (DECRG) needs to consider a more systematic and continuous assessment of the operational linkages and impact of its research program on trade.

Bank Participation in Global Policy Discussions and Advocacy

For much of the 1980s and 1990s, the Bank's approach to advocacy on trade was muted, taking the external trade environment as given,[14] but the tenor, emphasis, and approach to advocacy intensified after 2000, and particularly in the run-up to the Doha Trade Ministerial meeting in November 2001. The collapse of the WTO talks in Seattle in 1999 and the urgency to retain the credibility of the multilateral trading system as a mechanism to improve the development prospects of the poorer countries galvanized the interest of all major development partners in a revitalized and fair global trading system.

For much of the 1980s and 1990s, the Bank's approach to advocacy was muted.

Advocacy was first established as a formal objective soon after the Trade Department was created in July 2002 (World Bank 2002d, e). The rationale was for the Bank to use its influence with the Organisation for Economic Co-operation and Development (OECD) countries (notably the QUAD),[15] to serve as a counterweight to the richer countries, and to promote a trading system that was more open, rule-based, predictable, and transparent and that addressed the needs of developing countries. In this role, since 2001, the Bank has emphasized more strongly the importance of reducing protectionism in both industrial and (more recently) developing countries.

This shift toward greater advocacy is viewed by surveyed Bank staff and WTO members as appropriate and relevant. In particular, Bank staff surveyed viewed the advocacy work as the single most important contribution of the Trade Department thus far. WTO members interviewed recognized the Bank's advocacy efforts as important to the global dialogue on multilateral trade liberalization.

Advocacy was first established as a formal objective soon after the new Trade Department was created in July 2002.

The Bank's main instruments of advocacy were initially research pieces, editorials by Bank management in influential media (*Financial Times, Washington Post, New York Times, Le Monde*), and speeches by senior management at the WTO, at conferences, and on country visits. These targeted and personal interventions were closely tied to major research outputs such as the *Global Economic Prospects* reports. Since 2004, the annual *Global Monitoring Report* (produced jointly by the IMF and World Bank) has been a major tool to synthesize the Bank's advocacy on trade issues.

Assessing and distinguishing the Bank's achievements in advocacy is difficult.

Between 2000 and 2004, several speeches on trade by the Bank's chief economist and senior Bank management focused on market access in agriculture (Appendix E3). The Bank argued that tariff peaks and OECD agricultural subsidies were high (exceeding per capita aid contributions) and put developing countries at a competitive disadvantage (Rajapatirana 2003 and De Melo 2005 summarize these speeches). The increased emphasis was accompanied by a joint IMF-Bank paper to their respective Boards in 2003.[16] Apart from market access, the most frequently reiterated message by the Bank was the importance of the Doha negotiations for development.

Broadly speaking, the research reports that underpin the advocacy work are well done, reach a broad audience, and are widely picked up by the popular press. But no appraisal of the volume or type of press coverage is available from the Trade Department. Members of the WTO and trade community spoke highly of these reports and indicated that they found them useful (Appendix E5). By contrast, the staff survey indicated that Bank staff found them less useful, indicating that they were sometimes repetitious (Appendix E6).

Given the proliferation of advocacy reports intended for broad audiences, the Bank should reflect on the extent of product differentiation across reports. The trade research and analytical work generated by the Bank (in collaboration with outsiders) warrants either fewer reports, shorter reports, or less frequent reports to avoid repetition.

Assessing and distinguishing the Bank's achievements in advocacy is difficult for several reasons. First, the Bank has a somewhat circumscribed role in multilateral trade negotiations (given its observer status). Second, several other agencies have also been active in this area (for example, Oxfam and the U.K. Department of International Development [DFID]). Oxfam has been extremely active in carrying out advocacy (and some research) and in articulating its findings in an effort to draw attention to how the multilateral trading system can be made fairer. In some cases, their work preceded that of the Bank (as on the issue of cotton).[17] DFID has been one of the most active development partners, producing extensive analytical work related to the Doha Development Round. Together with other development partners, it has been a consistently strong advocate for the Doha Development Agenda.[18] Third, monitoring the impact of advocacy efforts requires not only an assessment of changes in policy, but also of their implementation and impact.

Though one can only guess what would have happened without Bank advocacy, even with the presence of other active partners, the Bank has positioned itself more effectively as an advocate for developing countries, compared with its stance in the 1980s. Given the wide reach of its publications, this has contributed to increasing awareness of the issues. The Bank has been successful in aligning itself with the view that the Doha Development Round must yield greater reciprocity. Surveys carried out for this study with Bank staff and other stakeholders confirmed a generally positive view of the Bank's contributions in the global dialogue.

The Bank has been less successful in changing actual outcomes, though it may still be too early to assess this given that the trade discussions are ongoing and the long-term nature of the change that is required. Participants in the talks (WTO members) felt that the Bank was limited in how much its actions could directly influence outcomes because of the complex political dynamics involved.[19] WTO members also expressed the view that the Bank was constrained in how sharply it could articulate messages, in contrast to nongovernmental (NGOs) and other organizations. The Bank's role could therefore be seen more accurately as indirect—contributing ideas and adding to the pressure to influence changes.

The Bank's initial narrow focus on OECD agricultural subsides may have been at the expense of emphasizing other areas where improvements would also lead to a better functioning of the world trading system (such as nonagricultural market access, reducing protection in developing countries, and reducing barriers to the temporary movement of people). It was also at odds with the Bank's own research, which suggested that the bulk of gains for many developing countries would be derived from addressing "behind-the-border" constraints. However, with agricultural subsidies as an egregious example of the unequal global trading system that is widely perceived as unfair by developing countries, one could argue that there were (and continue to be) relevant political economy arguments for the system to be reformed, and hence for the Bank's intense focus on subsidies.

In any event, the Bank's later messages have struck a more balanced note on the importance of both types of constraints (domestic developing country policies and market access considerations) and highlighted the importance of nuanced messages that take into account the varied outcomes for different groups of countries and commodities.

In this regard, the Bank's advocacy may have generated some unintended consequences. By emphasizing that a less than complete liberalization by the OECD will result in marginal benefits for many developing countries, the Bank may have raised the risk that those countries will be disappointed by what increasingly looks like a modest agricultural liberalization and will refrain from carrying out beneficial unilateral trade liberalization.[20]

Building Trade Capacity

Trade-related capacity building (TCB) means different things to different people, but a relatively recent Organisation for Economic Co-operation and Development–Development Assistance Committee (OECD-DAC)/WTO definition is now commonly accepted (box 5.2).[21]

TCB has become a prominent part of the discussion of integration into the global economy. Three factors explain this increased interest:

The Bank's advocacy work is viewed positively by staff and WTO members.

- First, developing countries were "burned" by their experience with the Uruguay Round. They signed onto commitments that they were unable to meet, partly because of a lack of capacity, and partly because of inadequate programs to help build their capacity.
- Second, and related to this experience, the Doha and Monterey meetings featured far-reaching promises by development partners to provide TCB to developing countries.
- Third, the complexity and intensity of the trade-negotiating process for developing countries at several levels—the Doha Development Agenda, and various bilateral, plurilateral free trade arrangements in almost every Region of the world—have heightened realization that managing integration into the global economy is complex and demanding, and that achieving the benefits is more difficult than anticipated.

The Bank's influence is indirect—contributing ideas and adding to the pressure for change.

Therefore, increasing capacity to manage the process is more critical than ever.[22]

The renewed interest in TCB at the global level has increased pressure for the Bank to identify and delineate its work in this area, even while Bank TCB continues in a dispersed fashion across the institution. Organizationally, TCB is spread over several units, with no single unit having overall responsibility for tracking institution-wide developments in TCB.

In its September 2003 trade progress report to the Executive Board, the Bank identified its objectives in TCB as "to build capacity in client

Box 5.2: What Is Trade-Related Capacity Building?

An activity is classified as trade-related technical assistance/capacity building if it is intended to enhance the ability of the recipient country to accomplish one of the following:

- Formulate and implement a trade development strategy and create an enabling environment for increasing the volume and value added of exports, diversifying export products and markets, and increasing foreign investment to generate jobs and trade.
- Stimulate trade by domestic firms and encourage investment in trade-oriented industries.
- Participate in and benefit from the institutions, negotiations, and processes that shape national trade policy and the rules and practices of international commerce.

In addition, the activity should fulfill the following criteria for eligibility:

- Trade-related technical assistance/capacity building is explicitly promoted in activity documentation.
- The activity contains specific measures to develop trade policy and regulations, enhance the ability of enterprises to participate in international trade, or increase national capacity to participate in the multilateral trading system.

Source: OECD-DAC 2001.

The Bank's trade capacity objectives aim to help client countries participate more effectively in the global trading system.

countries to: (i) formulate and implement sound trade policy to enhance growth and reduce poverty; (ii) manage the adjustment costs of trade reform and external trade shocks; (iii) participate effectively in international negotiations; and (iv) develop appropriate regional trade policies"(World Bank 2003). The report identified as the main levers to achieve TCB objectives ongoing activities in project components, the Integrated Framework for Trade-Related Technical Assistance initiative, World Bank Institute training activities, and analytical work.

Capacity Building Components in Operational Lending

The Bank has augmented resources devoted to trade capacity building, and the Trade Department has extended its learning program to provide training and research support. New lending for TCB more than doubled, from $132 million in 1998–2000 to $267 million in 2001–03, resulting in a portfolio of 50 operations (or components in operations) as of September 30, 2003.[23] TCB has been concentrated in trade and transport facilitation (notably customs), agricultural standards, and trade finance (Appendix E4, table E4.1b). This TCB is primarily intended to strengthen institutions. The Europe and Central Asia Region received the most assistance in TCB by an overwhelming margin—almost half of TCB components are in loans to the Region (Appendix E4, table E4.1a).

While the focus in TCB between fiscal years 2003 and 2004 was correctly targeted thematically toward areas identified in analytical work as critical (such as customs and standards), the TCB components of approved projects, for the most part, do not address the Bank's four strategic objectives, outlined above. Specifically, only 4 of the 15 TCB components addressed any of the 4 objectives outlined above (Appendix E4, table E4.1c). The most glaring gap is capacity building related to helping countries manage external shocks and adjustment costs related to trade liberalization. No project components address this; nor has the Bank done any major research in this area.

The Bank has sporadically helped a few countries participate effectively in international negotiations, but no new TCB loan components focus on negotiations, and other institutions are more important in supporting developing countries in this area. For example, in negotiations regarding training and improving country awareness of the rules of the game, a host of other international organizations are involved (such as the International Trade Centre [ITC], United Nations Conference on Trade and Development [UNCTAD] and the WTO, and, increasingly, development partners such as the European Union [EU], the United Kingdom, and the United States). Bank support to countries acceding to the WTO has been, until recently, largely limited to the Bank's larger clients (China, Russia). Of the 11 least-developed countries in the accession process, 6 are still in the initial stage of negotiations, although some of them have been in the negotiating process for six to nine years.[24] Ethiopia and (more recently) Vietnam are the only ones being assisted by the Bank.

While the Bank's advocacy focus has been on multilateral negotiations, it appears that countries face more pressing demands at the regional level, such as recently completed negotiations in Central America (CAFTA), ongoing negotiations in Africa (EPA), and bilateral free trade arrangements. The extent of Bank support for regional negotiations has varied across regions, but even in regions where it was largely reactive, greater attention is now being paid to how the Bank can best assist regional groupings.

The Integrated Framework for Trade-Related Technical Assistance

The Integrated Framework for Trade-Related Technical Assistance ("the IF") is another instrument in the Bank's TCB portfolio, but has a role and benefits that go beyond TCB.[25] In addition to helping the least-developed countries identify their trade capacity needs, the economic analysis in the Diagnostic Trade Integration Studies (DTIS) is intended to be a useful source for smaller countries that might otherwise not receive that magnitude of resources for diagnosis. As of June 2005, 14 diagnostic studies had been completed, 12 national consultative workshops had taken place, and 4 follow-up donor meetings had been held; 8 diagnostic studies are ongoing.

Two independent evaluations of the IF were undertaken in 2003 and 2004 by Capra (a consulting firm hired by the IF partners) and IEG (as an input into its review of Global Public Programs).[26] The main evaluative findings are summarized in box 5.3. Three key findings are that:

The capacity building components of approved projects generally do not address the Bank's four strategic objectives.

- Despite the 2001 restructuring, weaknesses from the original program remain, including insufficient focus on improved trade outcomes rather than on the process alone, and the shortage of funds (financial and administrative) to meet the identified demands for technical assistance in developing countries.
- There is a divergence in perceptions of the IF within the Bank. The Trade Department provided resources to Regional economists for the management of the DTIS, to increase ownership, to mobilize trade-investment resources, and to offset the initial lack of Regional ownership and the perception of a supply-driven mandate. While Regional management ownership has increased, decentralization of the IF has not fully filtered down to task team leaders in affected sectors at the country level; this has been compounded by the lack of on-the-ground presence.
- The full potential of the IF is not being realized, because the rich analytical work is not being fully translated into operations, highlighting the need to strengthen implementation.

Two independent evaluations of the Integrated Framework initiative suggest that its capacity building impact had been limited.

IEG's review of 26 global public programs provides some useful lessons (IEG 2004a). The most relevant for the IF are the need to link financing to priorities in a systematic fashion, to strengthen and streamline the governance and management of programs, and to develop a results-based management framework.

After a slow start, concrete proposals and approvals for trade capacity projects are finally emerging. As of May 30, 2005, 23 activities ($8.1 million) had been approved. A review of the proposed activities suggests that some overlap

Box 5.3: Independent Evaluations of the Integrated Framework

Relevance: Are the program's objectives right?

- Yes, but outcomes will be limited for some unless external market access and supply-side constraints are addressed.

Efficacy: Has the program met its stated objectives?

- Mainstreaming of trade limited; concrete country-level results highly variable.
- Bridge funding mechanism of $1 million is dwarfed by identified needs in IF matrix and no systematic way of addressing those needs.
- IF raised awareness of trade issues in Bank and participating countries, but country economists stress gap between amounts available for investments and gaps in donor and developing country expectations.
- IF needs to establish a range of concrete country-level outcomes and related performance indicators, with a focus on results and on monitoring outcomes and impacts. IF should monitor changes in donor policies, processes. and practices that inhibit LDC trade performance as identified in the DTIS.

Efficiency: Has the program been cost-effective?

- Still too early to assess if the IF benefits outweigh its high transactions costs.
- Bank Regional staff: Clarifying financing arrangements for identified investment needs critical.
- DEC/PREM staff: individual follow-up examples exist.

Challenges ahead

- Divergence in perceptions of LDCs and participating international agencies on IF role.
- Strong ownership by Bank and partner donor agencies, but developing country ownership limited.

Source: Agarwal and Cutura (2004), Case Study prepared for IEG 2004a; CAPRA-TFOC Consortium 2003.

Concrete trade capacity projects are finally emerging, but they are dwarfed by the identified needs.

with other donor activities persists in some cases, defeating the purpose of donor harmonization.[27] More generally, the pace appears slow relative to the Doha negotiations and the needs identified in the DTIS, and there is no mechanism to ensure that the most critical priorities are funded first.

External Training

WBI has provided external training with the support of other Trade Department staff, primarily the trade researchers in the Development Research Group (DECRG). While the number of staff dedicated to trade in WBI has increased from a single staff member in 2001, the current number of staff (4.5) directly assigned or dedicated to trade training activities remains relatively low.[28] With existing resources, the institute's strategy has been to deliver services (mostly training) and provide research support to selected networks (for example, on Doha issues to the African Economic Research Consortium [AERC] in partnership with country and Regional institutions), rather than to deliver more self-standing products (such as handbooks). Between fiscal years 2002 and 2005, the WBI increased its delivery of learning events from 12 to 61, reaching 3,869 participants (10, 542 participant training days).

WBI has taken a selective approach to capacity building.

While the WBI has been selective in its approach to capacity building, it has used its relatively limited resources effectively and has built capacity in its narrowly focused agenda. Its activities on WTO-related issues that have built capacity on trade issues in China and Vietnam, for example, as well as among African trade researchers, have been timely, have cross-fertilized ideas and experience across countries, and have been identified by the clients as valuable (box 5.4).

Given the importance of TCB in the trade agenda, too few resources have been devoted to training activities. Well-designed training would probably have greater long-run payoff in influence and advocacy than some of the other products reviewed earlier in this chapter, such as GEPs, which have a rather short shelf life.

Tools for trade policy analysis are a product that the Bank could have made available much earlier, had there been emphasis (and resources) to do so. The Bank has finally made the trade database and simulation tool, the World Integrated Trade Solution (WITS), widely available. The current WITS program appears to meet external demands. It provides data and simple simulation programs for trade analysts, thereby helping to develop local trade research capacity in Bank client countries. The number of external users (split evenly between developing and developed countries) has been growing steadily, and they currently account for over three-fourths of all users.

Internally, additional functionality appears to be warranted. A review of trade-related ESW in the past three years and the results of the staff survey suggest that the demand is less for simulation of negotiating scenarios, and more for accessible analysis of the fiscal and welfare implications of changes in tariff regimes, as well as comparative analysis related to international benchmarking and competitiveness assessments. For the future, the Bank will need to ensure that WITS is adequately funded, be more systematic about obtaining timely feedback from both groups of users, and streamline interface and report presentation and online help functions.

Given the stated importance of capacity building in the trade agenda, too few resources have been devoted to training activities.

Conclusions: The above review of Bank TCB activities suggests that the institution is doing an uneven job of meeting its objectives as stated in the September 2003 trade progress report (Appendix E4). The content of the dramatically increased volume of trade-related analytical work that is the basis for country policy dialogue and the focus of TCB components of existing projects (half of TCB

Box 5.4: Effective and Timely Leverage of Knowledge—WTO-Related Trade Capacity Building

Vietnam WTO accession assistance

The trade group has devoted considerable support to Vietnam as it negotiates accession to the WTO. Stakeholder workshops have been conducted to build political commitment among policy makers and parliamentarians, as well as to improve understanding in the private sector and civil society. In addition, the analytical capacity of the Vietnamese was strengthened by linking national researchers at the Institute of Economics with foreign experts and local policy makers to write sector and thematic papers. This has helped them understand when further liberalization might be in their national economic interest and has provided them with stronger arguments to resist pressures from WTO members where these pressures are considered to be inappropriate. The assistance was provided jointly by the Trade Department (WBI) and the Bank country team, which sees WTO accession as a critical entry point for a whole series of second-generation reforms.

AERC/African policy makers

The Trade Department (WBI and DEC) supported the African Economic Research Consortium (AERC) between 2002 and 2004 to enhance understanding of trade liberalization, the constraints imposed by domestic supply conditions and foreign market access, and the ways in which African countries might use the WTO process to further their development objectives.

At the AERC gathering in November 2002 in Kampala, 50 researchers from 25 African countries presented work in progress on country case studies in the manufacturing, agriculture, and services sectors, reviewing each others' work and receiving feedback from WBI, World Bank, WTO, and AERC resource persons.

Several AERC researchers act as trade advisors to their governments and were critical to the preparations of both pre-Doha and pre-Cancun technical and ministerial meetings. Their active role was a major reason why Africa was decidedly better prepared for the launch of the new round than at the time of the Uruguay Round, and their contribution was formally acknowledged by the Africa Group at Doha. WBI support for African trade researchers is continuing, albeit through other channels, since the AERC is placing less emphasis on its trade-related activities.

Source: E-mail communications with Bank staff and partners.

interventions between 2003 and 2004 targeted this objective) suggests that the Bank is at least providing the inputs to meet its objective of helping countries formulate sound trade policy. The Bank is doing less well helping countries adopt appropriate regional policies (third objective) and participate more effectively in negotiations (fourth objective) and has been least effective thus far in helping countries manage external shocks (see box 5.5) and adjustment costs related to trade liberalization (second objective).

Knowledge Management

In the mid-1990s, the software for industrial, trade, and incentives analysis (SINTIA) that country economists used to analyze potential changes in country tariff regimes was decommissioned. Since then, simple tariff analysis tools have been introduced slowly. Not surprisingly, few trade reports contain simulations of fiscal or other implications of reforming the tariff regime. Even where they do, country economists essentially construct their own "model or program," and therefore no standard set of tables appears across reports, and cross-country comparability is limited. The rollout of WITS will help fill this gap.

Two recent handbooks, on the WTO and customs modernization, illustrate the contribution that other products can make to internal and external learning and capacity building. The publication of the trade policy handbook *Development, Trade, and the WTO* in June 2002 (World Bank 2002a) was timely, and the handbook well-conceived. It summarized the economics of sound trade policy and offered guidance on many behind-the-border issues that were being discussed in the seven negotiation bodies under the Trade Negotiation Committee. The crisp and nontechnical handbook is accessible to trade negotiators and offers an opportunity for developing countries to enhance their participation in trade negotiations.[29] The recently released *Customs Modernization Handbook* (World Bank 2005c) is another learning tool with advice, best practice lessons, and templates dealing with managing and monitoring customs reform.

Handbooks and Trade Notes are contributing to internal and external learning and capacity building.

More generally, after a slow start, knowledge management activities are picking up. A series of *Trade Notes* was initiated in 2003 (Appendix E8 lists them). Learning activities targeted at Bank staff have focused on such timely matters as WTO-related issues, the new trade agenda, and standards-related activities. Acknowledging the need for a focal point on knowledge management issues, the PREM Network announced in April 2005 that the Trade Competitiveness Thematic Group, which had been defunct for several years, was to be reconstituted. This has not happened yet, however. But given the cross-sectoral nature of trade and the Bankwide movement to streamline thematic groups, the Bank may also wish to identify linkages with existing thematic groups.

However, a gap still exists between these knowledge management activities and the needs of country economists. Results from the survey of Bank country economists done for the evaluation suggested a desire for more knowledge about transitional costs associated with trade reform, empirical analyses, comparative analysis, and practical research on global value chains. No systematic method of gauging demand exists and, of necessity (and as currently designed), some of these activities, such as the trade brown bag lunches, remain driven by the interests of researchers (both inside and outside the Bank), rather than operational staff.

Mainstreaming Trade into Country Work

"Mainstreaming of trade" is one objective of the Bank's trade strategy, but it is not clearly defined. A precise definition is important, because "mainstreaming" means different things to different people inside and outside the Bank. The use of the phrase in connection with trade appears to date back to a seminar convened under the auspices of the Integrated Framework initiative in January 2001. At that meeting the definition used was as follows: "mainstreaming trade involves the process and methods of identifying and integrating trade

Box 5.5: Minimizing the Effects of Commodity Shocks

Over a period of several years, the Bank has explored ways of helping developing countries minimize the effects of commodity shocks, including a Board paper in 2000, but until 2003, no concrete instruments had been developed. The introduction of a hedging product for IBRD clients that year is an innovation. In the past, the effort was hindered by the complexity of the issue, a lack of consensus on the definition of shocks, and differing views on the optimal triggers and approaches (ex-ante and ex-post).

A 2005 Board Paper, "Managing the Debt Risk of Exogenous Shocks in Low- Income Countries," analyzes the risk of exogenous shocks in low-income countries and evaluates measures (such as financial instruments) to mitigate these risks. While IDA has been able to provide assistance to countries experiencing shocks, there are no automatic instruments to provide a given level of assistance in the face of a given shock.

The paper found that past instruments developed by the international community intended to address terms of trade shocks at the sovereign level have been "hampered by ... speed, conditionality and effectiveness" (p. 15). The Resource Mobilization Department is currently undertaking further research to explore the feasibility of strengthening IDA countries' response to shocks as a follow-up to the Board Paper, taking into consideration the roles of other entities, including the IMF.

The International Task Force (ITF) on Commodity Risk Management in Developing Countries is a public-private partnership established in 1999 to help small-scale farmers better manage their vulnerability to price and weather commodity risks. Within the Bank, the Commodity Risk Management Group is the implementing agency for the ITF. While a few successful pilot projects emerged early on, initial impact was modest, and ITF faced many challenges: scaling up their activities, mainstreaming the concept and garnering support within the Bank, and building capacity in the countries.

There is now evidence of successful scaling up. For example, a weather insurance pilot launched in India in 2003 for 27 farmers has now been replicated, and up to 150,000 farmers have currently bought weather insurance; an impact assessment suggests that the product is timely and meeting demand from farmers.

Source: Interviews with Bank Staff; World Bank 2005a.

priority areas of action into the framework of country development plans and poverty reduction strategies." The Bank has largely followed this definition,[30] which this evaluation views as constituting an overly narrow and operationally incomplete picture of mainstreaming. An important aspect that it does not capture is the degree to which the current trade agenda overlaps with other sectoral agendas.

Accurately defined, mainstreaming trade in Bank operations has several dimensions (diagnostic work, trade in assistance strategies, knowledge management, and incorporation of relevant trade issues in sector activities and strategies). The Bank is doing better along some dimensions than others. The Bank has responded remarkably quickly to keep up with the global agenda and catalyze the rapid increase in trade-related analytical work in both the center and at the country level. Trade Department staff members have been an important part of this response—sharing their expertise through mission participation, contributions to and leadership of reports, and as peer reviewers. Over 90 percent of trade reports done between 2001 and 2004 had Trade Department involvement. At the Regional level, the Bank has increased its engagement with regional organizations and conducted additional (and timely) analysis on regional arrangements (for example, EPAs and common external tariffs in Africa, U.S.-CAFTA arrangement). The Bank has done less well in mainstreaming trade in Country Assistance Strategies and in sector activities and policies.

But gaps persist between these knowledge management activities and the needs of country economists.

Trade in Country Assistance Strategies

A review of all Country Assistance Strategies (CASs)[31] from 2001 to 2004 suggests that the importance of trade varies in Bank assistance to countries, but that the treatment of mainstreaming has improved over time. Trade was initially examined along three dimensions in CASs: (i) identification of issues; (ii) proposed actions to deal with the identified issues; and (iii) trade as part of the objectives (or pillars) of the strategy. About half of country strategies have an extended discussion of trade and about 60 percent of all strategies identify specific actions intended to support trade. However, the quality of the discussion and the extent to which trade's linkages with the macroeconomy and other sectors are analyzed varies significantly.

A more in-depth look confirms that the mainstreaming of trade in assistance strategies is uneven. The existence of trade-related ESW does not appear to make an appreciable difference in whether the CAS has a well-integrated, in-depth discussion of trade issues. In some cases, existing ESW is used effectively to underpin the trade analysis in the CAS, focus on the most critical constraints to expanded trade, and help identify the most critical interventions for the Bank (see box 5.6). In other cases, there is little or no analysis of trade, despite significant strategic issues associated with trade. Table 5.1 summarizes the results of the review, while Appendix E7 summarizes the main actions in more detail.

A comparison with earlier country strategies from 1998 to 2000 shows a mixed pattern in how attention to trade has evolved over time. In half the Regions (Africa, East Asia and the Pacific, Europe and Central Asia), trade is now more likely to be an objective of the strategy. In more recent CASs, trade is more likely to be the focus of a section of the report in four of the six Regions compared with past CASs, but trade-related activities (lending or nonlending) are less likely to be a focus, perhaps reflecting the lag between analytical work and lending.[32]

Integrating Trade and Sector Activities

The Bank has had the most success in linking trade and sector strategies in the areas of sanitary and phytosanitary standards (SPS) and in trade facilitation. Particularly for SPS, the intellectual leadership of the Trade Department, backed by operationally relevant analytical work and close collaboration with key partners in the Agriculture and Rural Development (ARD)Department and operations, has led to actual changes in operational ESW and lending (box 5.7). For trade facilitation, while the intellectual leadership was more limited (and perhaps less essential), the Trade Facilita-

Box 5.6: Trade in Country Assistance Strategies: Mixed and Uneven

A few examples illustrate the diversity of trade-related issues across countries and Regions. In Sub-Saharan Africa, where much remains to be done to reduce constraints and barriers to trade, 12 of the 17 CASs examined mention trade as an objective. But in two reports, no specific measures were proposed. Nor was there any extensive supportive analysis (of the type that would refer to analytical work suggesting why trade is important). Generally, the reports emphasize the need for trade facilitation measures, and three reports cite the Diagnostic Trade Integration Studies carried out under the Integrated Framework as a basis for the Bank's strategy in the country (without further detail).

In Europe and Central Asia, mention of trade as an objective suggests diverse needs across the Region (for example, support for WTO accession, a more export-friendly tariff structure, trade and transport facilitation, and one mention of a Diagnostic Trade Integration Study). In East Asia trade always figures prominently in the Country Assistance Strategy, most often in terms of enhancing competitiveness.

In Latin America and the Caribbean (13 CASs), trade figures prominently and precisely in a little under half (notably Chile, Colombia, and El Salvador) of the CASs. The Middle East and North Africa Region has only three country assistance strategy reports—one on Yemen states (without further details) that the Diagnostic Trade Integration Study had helped identify trade policy and technical assistance needs, and one on Jordan supports export development through enhanced logistics and fertilizer support.

Source: De Melo (2005).

Table 5.1: Trade in CASs by Region (fiscal 2001–04)

Region	Number of documents	Section (a)	Action (b)	Objectives (c)	Only briefly mentioned (d)
CASs	**59**	**29**	**36**	**32**	**9**
Africa	17	13	15	12	
East Asia and Pacific	6	2	5	5	
Europe and Central Asia	17	6	7	7	4
Latin America and the Caribbean	13	6	5	5	3
Middle East and North Africa	3	1	1	2	
South Asia	3	1	3	1	2

Source: Appendix E7.

a. Trade is the focus of a section in the report.

b. Trade-related action (lending or nonlending) is mentioned in the report.

c. Trade is part of the objectives (or pillars) of the strategy.

d. Trade and trade-related issues are only briefly mentioned in the report.

tion initiative and the Customs Handbook have benefited from good collaboration with the Transport Unit, the PREM Public Sector Unit, and the Regions internally, and with the World Customs Organization externally.

While the Bank has done well in cross-fertilizing trade issues in trade facilitation and agricultural standards, there is less coherence with other sectors, notably on agricultural policies with the Rural Development Department, on competitiveness issues with the Private Sector Development Vice-Presidency, on trade and environment issues with the Environmentally and Socially Sustainable Development (ESSD) Network and on poverty issues. There is no formal or informal understanding with the Private Sector Development Vice-Presidency (similar to those for Transport Logistics or with ARD), which is crucial given the synergies (and in some cases overlap) on competitiveness and supply-side issues that both groups cover.

Conclusions on Mainstreaming

The absence of a clear operational definition of "trade mainstreaming" is a disadvantage in several ways. First, given the Bank's extensive relationship with developing countries on trade issues through its lending operations and policy advice, its intellectual leadership is important in clarifying this concept. Second, in the absence of this leadership, guidance and templates on how to incorporate trade at the operational level are also missing. They would help create a more systematic way for country and sector economists to ascertain the extent to which trade should fit into the Bank's strategy of assistance. Third, given the neglect that trade faced in the early part of the decade, mainstreaming trade requires a more active approach.

The integration of trade into sector activities is mixed.

In contrast, other thematic areas that have faced the task of mainstreaming (and other agencies that have faced the task of mainstreaming trade) have used more clearly defined and activist strategies to bridge the gap between the corporate mandate and agenda and the operational actions (table 5.2). They have also monitored regularly the progress in mainstreaming in their respective areas.

Experience from both the Gender and Environment Units in the Bank, each of which had to deal with mainstreaming their respective areas into sector operations, suggests that while senior management leadership and

Box 5.7: Intellectual Leadership Plus Collaboration Yield Operational Relevance in Sanitary and Phytosanitary Standards

For SPS, a well-integrated program of analytical work and policy analysis has generated more detailed understanding of the economic, institutional, and policy aspects of standards and trade, including the strategic and policy options available to governments and the private sector in a range of developing countries.

This has been complemented operationally by an initiative to mainstream SPS through (i) participatory national strategies for strengthening capacities to manage sanitary, phytosanitary, and other standards for export and domestic markets; (ii) preparation of project subcomponents related specifically to capacity building for sanitary, phytosanitary, and other standards that will be integrated into Bank investment loans; (iii) design and implementation of pilot projects that effectively link smallholder farmers and small enterprises with larger agribusinesses or food distributors through coordinated supply chain pilots; and (iv) sharing implementation lessons. Stand-alone projects are unlikely; instead, small to medium-size ($0.5 to $15 million) components of agricultural services, export promotion, and competitiveness projects will likely be the norm.

The program has been accompanied by a rich learning program (including distance learning). Future learning events will be more operationally focused, involving Bank (and other development agency) field staff together with country (official and private) counterparts through facilitated e-learning courses and dialogue. Internally, the program has been marked by close collaboration between the operational Regions, the Agriculture and Rural Development Department, and the Trade Department. Externally, it involves active collaboration with various external agencies (public/private; bilateral/multilateral) that have greater technical expertise and/or implementation experience than the Bank in this field. The Bank is also trying to build bridges among practitioners working on SPS standards, on the one hand, and social and environmental standards, on the other, as such standards are increasingly bundled in agro-food trade and distribution channels, and developing country suppliers need to address the challenges and opportunities in these areas concurrently. The Bank's emerging comparative advantage in this field relates to economic analysis and in positioning SPS analytical and planning matters in the mainstream of (trade and agricultural) policy and planning.

Source: Interviews of Bank staff working on standards issues; World Bank Trade Web site: http://web.worldbank.org/WBSITE/EXTERNAL/TOPICS/TRADE.

Table 5.2: Trade Mainstreaming Lags behind Other Thematic Areas and Organizations

	World Bank			UK DFID
Action	**Trade**	**Environment**	**Gender**	**Trade**
Participatory institutional sector strategy prepared		X	X	X
Conceptual framework for integration of issue into operational strategy		X	X	
Development of diagnostic tools (ESW)	X	X	X	X
Identifiable staff tasked with helping to mainstream issue at operational level	Partial	X	X	X
Formal links with other related sectors	Partial (transport. ARD)	X	X	Partial
Upstream involvement of sector staff in CAS		X	X	X
Systematic monitoring of mainstreaming against benchmarks		X	X	X
Systematic identification of skills mix, gaps, and strategy for medium-term needs		X	X	

Sources: Interviews with network staff in Gender and ESSD and DFID staff in February–April 2005. DFID Trade Strategy paper (April 2005).

support is important and necessary, it is far from sufficient. To make an appreciable difference, the establishment of a widely disseminated conceptual framework, network intellectual and advisory support to Regional staff, dissemination of best practice examples, and proactive and upstream identification of the support needed are critical. While not guaranteeing immediate success, these actions lay its foundation. Together with monitoring against established benchmarks, they enable adjustments as needed.

Chapter 6: Evaluation Highlights

- Bank strategies on trade have been largely relevant.
- But strategies took too narrow a view on critical factors for trade to contribute to growth.
- The institution was also initially slow to react to the changing global environment and to incorporate those issues in operations.
- Research and (increasingly) advocacy have played important roles, externally.
- But the greatest challenge remains at the country level, where greater coordination across sectors is required, as well as greater attention to poverty and distributional implications.

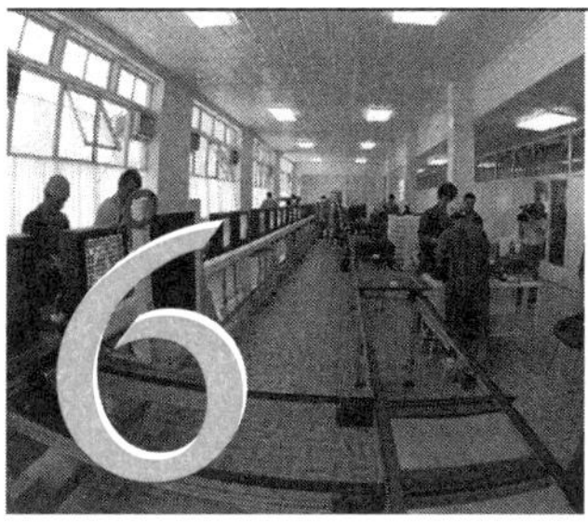

Findings and Recommendations

Since the 1980s the Bank has committed about $38 billion to developing countries in all Regions through a diverse group of stand-alone trade adjustment and investment loans, as well as trade components of loans. It has also conducted wide-ranging trade-related analysis and supported trade-related capacity building.

Bank assistance on trade issues encompasses three phases of intervention, as noted in Chapter 1—two intensive phases with a lull in-between. The earlier intensive phase focused to a greater degree on the traditional trade agenda related to opening up trade regimes in developing countries. It was characterized by significant trade adjustment lending.

Following a slowdown in trade activities during the second half of the 1990s, the WTO Trade Ministerial in Doha catalyzed a resurgence of Bank work on trade after 2001. This recent intensive phase has focused on the global trading system and "behind-the-border" barriers to trade. This phase has not focused so much on lending as on analytical research, trade-related capacity building, and advocacy on behalf of the developing countries.

Findings

Was the Bank's Assistance Relevant?

1987–2001 period

The objectives of the Bank's trade assistance, notably in lending, between 1987 and 2001 were to improve resource allocation, expand and diversify exports, enhance client integration into the global economy, and contribute to overall economic growth. These objectives were relevant and appropriate.

In spite of the absence of formal strategies governing trade for part of the review period, the implicit strategies that existed provided an adequate framework at the general level, were broadly consistent with the literature, and succeeded in providing a clear sense of the Bank's views and approach. The focus on removing other domestic market distortions to complement trade reform was also appropriate.

The strategy was too narrow, however, in terms of its focus on what matters for trade and growth. Specifically, it underestimated the complexity and sequencing of other complementary policies, the role of the external environment, the importance of institutions, and the interaction between trade and distributional outcomes. Consequently, the Bank was too optimistic about the benefits from trade.

Domestic distortions. The focus on marketing and pricing distortions in domestic markets to support the traditional trade agenda was appropriate given the poor performance arising out of the latter stages of import substitution, distortions in the client countries, and the bias against the rural sector and exporting inherent in the initial trade regimes.

Complementary policies. While the Bank correctly identified the importance of complementary supply-side policies, it underestimated the complexity and difficulties of implementing those reforms. Conditions related to these complementary policies have been repeated over time in lending operations, reflecting partial implementation from the time they were first recommended. Compliance with policies intended to improve the regulatory framework and the competitive environment lagged behind compliance with trade policies. These policies, which now commonly fall under the rubric of the investment climate, influence overall outcomes from trade policies.

External environment. Through its balance-of-payments support, the Bank provided general support during exogenous shocks for several countries, and trade elements were often present in the context of those loans. Through its ESW and research, the Bank provided advice on agricultural policy reform. Yet overall, the Bank was sometimes slow to react. For example, despite several attempts, until recently exogenous shocks and external factors were also not systematically addressed or acknowledged in project design and ESW, despite being an important factor in poor project performance.[1] However, until recently, no overarching strategic advice or instruments existed to help developing countries to manage commodity shocks, which are particularly important given the continued agricultural dependence of many client countries.

A missed opportunity was an issue that cut across several developing countries—the phasing out of the multi-fibre arrangement (later renamed Agreement on Textiles and Clothing). This was anticipated for several years. Yet despite the importance of garments and textiles for many Bank clients, no cross-country analysis was carried out and individual country analysis (such as for Nepal) was late. In this context, the Bank's country and Regional focus may not have lent itself efficiently enough to issues that cut across countries.

Trade and poverty linkages. Social and economic vulnerability was not addressed sufficiently. Economic and sector work, as well as project design, were weak in systematically incorporating or monitoring social outcomes such as poverty and employment, even where economic analysis existed. While earlier on, the issue appeared to be one of low prioritization, that no longer appears to be the case. Surveys of Bank staff and managers indicated considerable interest in the links between trade and poverty. The difficulty in incorporating poverty considerations appears to be a combination of having the right expertise at the operational level (staff skilled in designing these types of interventions); the complexity of the issue, which requires a multidisciplinary team cutting across the Bank's sector/network boundaries; and, in some cases, lack of data to underpin the required analysis.

2001–04 period

The objectives of the Bank's activities in trade since 2001 were to make the world trading system more reciprocally open and to make trade an important part of country development strategies. These objectives were appropriate and relevant given the importance of the WTO in the multilateral trading system, the difficulties with the Seattle trade meeting in 1999, the linkages between trade and other aspects of development, and the potential benefits to its clients of improved trade performance.

The Bank's strategy, however, did not articulate clearly enough the separation of the Bank's research and its advocacy, its limitations with respect to influencing change, or identify risks associated with the strategy.[2] The Bank could have presented a more nuanced message from the start that distinguished between groups of developing countries and also clarified the relative importance of the multilateral system for different developing countries. For example, the emphasis on the multilateral trading system may have been misplaced in the case of individual countries where the more pressing demand was in the context of regional trading arrangements (especially Free Trade Association Agreements) and the need for those countries to make decisions in the negotiating context. Insufficient attention was given to the non-agricultural market access aspects of the global negotiations.

The Bank's support for TCB lacks a holistic strategy. The Bank has attempted to respond to developing country demand for TCB by working with external partners (U.N. agencies, bilateral and multilateral donors) through the Integrated Framework for Trade-Related Technical Assistance (IF) initiative. While the revamped IF has dealt partly with the risks associated with donor commitment and funding for analysis, it has made less progress in streamlining processes and accelerating implementation, and continues to be marked by the absence of a results-based management system (IEG 2004a; Capra-TFOC 2003). Weaknesses in the existing set-up for the IF pose risks for timely and relevant delivery of TCB to meet LDC needs and represent a potential reputational risk for the Bank (and other agencies involved in the initiative).

Was the Bank's Assistance Effective?

1987–2001 period

The Bank was effective in helping countries liberalize their trade regimes. Average tariffs fell, coverage of nontariff barriers diminished, foreign exchange shortages became nonexistent, and the exchange rate was reinstated as a viable instrument for export development. Overall, the Bank has helped its clients reduce the bias against exports considerably.

Exports grew in most countries and the associated industrial policy reforms (such as those in competition policy) contributed toward a more open playing field. Countries that received Bank loans were able to free up their imports. Countries undertaking trade reform with Bank support experienced greater economic growth than those that did not, but this outcome may also reflect the larger set of economic reforms they undertook concurrently.

Despite these gains, Bank assistance has in some cases fallen short in important aspects. Many of the Bank's clients, notably in Africa, have not been successful at diversifying their exports, and they continue to be vulnerable to commodity price shocks. Because of the lack of diversity in their exports, some countries have not successfully integrated into the global economy and have actually lost market share. The Bank's interventions in aspects of trade logistics (ports, customs, and trade finance) and export incentives have had a mixed but improving record. The investment response was slow in a number of countries—reflecting, perhaps, credibility of policies and government crowding out.

The evaluation found that some countries experienced both faster export growth and declining per capita consumption. Three factors appear to underlie why the link between export performance and poverty reduction has been weaker than theory would predict. First, export growth has a better chance of reducing poverty if it is broad-based. In countries where exports baskets continue to be narrowly based, the benefits of good export performance may not reach the poor for geographic reasons or because transfer/distributional mechanisms are inadequate. Second, for some of the Bank's clients, exports have grown in goods for which there is a declining world demand, capping the extent to which they can derive benefits. Third, in many countries there has not been a strategic approach to incorporating trade in a national development strategy, except at a superficial level.

2001–04 period

While the objectives of the Bank's strategy were relevant, the institution could have defined more clearly how it would monitor and operationalize the strategy. Partly because of donor and other external interest and pressures associated with the WTO negotiating timetable, the Bank has put more emphasis on this aspect of the strategy (through Board progress reports, partnerships, outside media) than on operationalizing trade at the country level.

The Bank's research and advocacy on the multilateral trading system has, in the eyes of international trade officials and non-Trade Department Bank staff surveyed for this study, contributed to increased awareness of the costs associated with tariff peaks and agricultural protection in OECD countries.

Bank research has contributed significantly to the thinking on trade in several different areas. External surveys and interviews indicate that its research on services liberalization, the global trade architecture, and agricultural standards are viewed as innovative and of high quality.

Greater research and operational attention is needed, however, in the following areas: agricultural trade and policies, links between trade and poverty and adjustment costs associated with trade, and migration.

The Bank has been slow to translate its extensive work on the development aspects of WTO issues into practical policy advice for staff. Services liberalization is a particular gap in this regard. Despite high-quality work at the center, there appears to be no clear strategy on how to share this knowledge and apply it to operational work, particularly in the financial and private sector units.[3] This is particularly critical given the complexity of the services negotiations and the sectors that they span. In another example, no strategic approach has been planned for the 26 countries (all Bank clients) currently in the process of accession to the WTO. The poorest and those least likely to have the capacity to articulate their needs have received less support (such as Cape Verde and Sao Tome and Principe) and have been in the accession process for several years.

The greatest operational successes have occurred where the Trade Department has provided intellectual leadership and put together a team involving the networks and operational staff, such as in standards and trade facilitation. Conversely, priority areas such as agricultural trade, services liberalization, and the distributional outcomes associated with trade have suffered from the lack of intra- and intersectoral partnerships. The incorporation of trade into country development and Bank assistance strategies has been uneven and little guidance has been given to country teams on incorporating trade considerations in their work.

Recommendations

Key challenges lie ahead in trade for the Bank's clients, as trade issues increasingly cut across multiple sectors and involve complex negotiations at the bilateral, Regional, and multilateral levels. But there are also opportunities as a result of heightened interest in Africa by development partners, greater attention to an equitable global trade system, the building of coalitions that may help various groupings of developing countries negotiate more strategically and effectively in the global arena, and continued interest in aid and trade-related capacity building to support developing countries in their trade and growth agendas.

In general, there is greater consensus on what constitutes an appropriate trade strategy,[4] its limits in the context of the multilateral trading system, and the importance of complementary policies. "New industrial strategy" is being looked at again within the Bank to see how best the state can strategically support development by offsetting "market failures in information and communication" (see Leipziger 2005).

The current trade agenda is significantly more globalized than previously and very much tied in with overall economic growth. To pay greater attention to export-led growth in the future, continued efforts to reduce anti-export biases in trade policy are needed, with priority given to removing constraints to specific promising exports. Second, as is already emerging, greater attention needs to be paid to the investment climate, infrastructure, and trade facilitation more broadly. Third, selective promotion of export development, such as support for training, improved information about market opportunities, linkages, technology development, and so on would be useful.

The time is right to consider the direction of the Bank's future work in trade. The Doha trade negotiations that catalyzed and invigorated trade work at the Bank are likely to conclude in the next few years. Moreover, the establishment of the Trade Department includes a sunset clause that requires revisiting its mandate in 2005. It is appropriate for management to look ahead and focus on future priorities. This study makes three recommendations.

Recommendation 1: Address Poverty-Distributional Outcomes and External Shocks in a Balanced Approach

This evaluation found that despite the increasing volume of research on poverty issues in the Trade Department and of poverty and social impact analysis more generally, trade-related projects do not consistently or systematically address poverty and distributional outcomes. While much import liberalization has already occurred, further liberalization appears possible for some developing countries, notably within agriculture. With that in mind, three actions are critical. First, IEG recommends that at the country level, all new projects with trade policy components include a discussion of this issue that, at a minimum, draws on the cross-sectoral expertise from economic policy, poverty, gender, PSD, and (as appropriate) agricultural and rural development units, as well as existing research in the country. Identification of possible transitional costs, an assessment of the existing institutional framework for cushioning shocks and actions to mitigate or minimize shocks would be important considerations in the discussion.[5] Placing trade in a broader discussion of the determinants of poverty will help ensure that this is not a mechanical exercise, but rooted in its expected importance.

Second, at the institution-wide level, and following the Bank's statement at the Cancun Ministerial in 2003, IEG recommends that a concrete program of adjustment assistance be developed more rapidly to respond to trade-related shocks that developing countries may face.[6] To the extent that such a program is no longer deemed relevant, it would be helpful for management to clarify this.

Third, IEG recommends a more systematic program of research on micro-level adjustment to trade policies, looking at firms, individuals, and households.

Recommendation 2: Revisit the Balance between Global and Country Agendas and Strengthen Operational Links on Trade Issues

IEG recommends that management revisit the balance between its activities at the global level on the one hand, and on the Regional and country agenda on the other. Given the multisector nature of trade issues, a participatory process that involves operational sector colleagues, other networks, and the Trade Department is likely to yield the greatest benefits. Operational linkages need to be strengthened between different units of the Bank, and greater emphasis placed on country and field operations.

Three actions are necessary. First, greater strategic and intellectual guidance is needed from the Trade Department with respect to the conceptual framework within which country teams should consider trade issues. The design of a guidance note and upstream support on a pilot basis to country teams planning Country Assistance Strategies would be practical first steps and would help determine those cases in which trade is logically a priority element in the country dialogue.

Second, in three thematic areas of focus, a more formal set of arrangements between operations, networks, and the Trade Department is needed to maximize synergies—agricultural trade and policies, services liberalization, and distributional outcomes associated with trade policies.

Third, as has been done between the Transport and Agriculture units on the one hand, and the Trade Department on the other, IEG recommends that working arrangements with the Private Sector Department Vice-Presidency be established to highlight the interface between the two areas and to bring the global dimension to bear more precisely. This cross-fertilization of trade and the need for better integration of trade and the Finance, Private Sector, and Infrastructure (FPSI) work program is especially evident in the work on trade in services. Greater interaction between the Trade Department staff specialized in trade in services and the sub-sectoral expertise in transport, power, finance, telecoms and so on located in FPSI is needed.

Recommendation 3: Strengthen Knowledge Management Efforts

Two actions are important.

First, a concerted effort to bring all country economists up to date with the main features and application of the WITS software would enhance their awareness of the global trade issues and implications for the countries they work on and enable them to supervise research assistants/consultants and seek further training, if and when needed.

Second, knowledge management efforts could reflect greater cross-fertilization with other networks and better integrate trade work done in the center and country-level work on agriculture, economic policy, labor markets, and private sector development. As part of these efforts, the possibility of joint thematic groups with other networks should be explored.

More generally, IEG recommends a more effective use of knowledge management tools tailored to key target groups—across different sectors. A mechanism to obtain regular systematic feedback from operational staff on the most immediate and relevant trade-related topics would be helpful, as the survey identified gaps, despite the canvassing conducted by Regional trade coordinators during the year. Finally, greater sharing of country experience in particular areas, much as was done with the work in agricultural standards, is needed. This will require greater support from the center to ensure quality-at-entry for project design as well as economic and sector work.

APPENDIXES

APPENDIX A1: TIMELINE OF MAJOR DEVELOPMENTS IN INTERNATIONAL TRADE, 1987–2005

Table A1.1: Annotated Timeline of Major Developments in International Trade in the World Bank

Year	Analytic activities	Strategy/institutional response	World Bank events
1987	WDR 1987 on *Industrialization and Foreign Trade.* World Bank publishes *The Uruguay Round - A Handbook for the Multilateral Trade Negotiations* (Finger and Olechowski 1987). It serves as a handbook, giving background information and guidance for developing countries participating in the Uruguay Round of the GATT negotiations. World Bank and UNDP begin Trade Expansion Program to provide integrated technical assistance to countries embarking on trade reform programs by fielding specialized teams to diagnose obstacles to integration and suggest options for reform.	At the start of the timeline, the Bank has been lending directly for trade since the mid-1970s and number of trade-related projects is expanding.	On May 8, Mr. Conable announces that implementation of an institutional reorganization will begin, and be completed by September. Affects way trade is organized in Bank. Regional Technical Departments created; include trade experts with a Regional mandate. Trade units in Policy Research and Country Economics Departments moved to International Economics Department (IEC). Anne Krueger leaves the Bank as Chief Economist and VP Development Economics; replaced by Stanley Fischer.
1988		Development Committee paper on trade. World Bank and IMF Boards reach agreement ("Concordat") on cooperation and collaboration.	
1989		Review of lessons from trade policy reform in developing countries.	President Conable addresses the Reuters Information Services in London. He calls the worldwide severity and pervasiveness of poverty a "moral outrage," and identifies the key elements of "sustainable development:" solution to the debt problem; policy reform efforts in developing countries; secure long-term investment; **unrestricted international trade;** sound environmental policies.

(Table continues on the following page.)

Table A1.1: Annotated Timeline of Major Developments in International Trade in the World Bank (continued)

Year	Analytic activities	Strategy/institutional response	World Bank events
1990	Papageorgiou, Michaely, and Choksi (1991). Major cross-country study on lessons from trade liberalization.		
1991	Thomas and Nash (1991); lessons from trade liberalization.		
1992		O.D. 8.6 issued on adjustment lending with a section on trade.	World Bank reorganization is announced. All research is consolidated under the Chief Economist and Vice President for Development Economics. Regional Technical Departments are made smaller and partially consolidated (ECA/MNA; SAS/EAP); the sector operations divisions are strengthened.
1993			President Preston congratulates participants on the completion of the Uruguay Round of the GATT trade negotiations.
1994			Trade policy analysis unit in IEC split; commodities analysis moved to DECPG.
1995			Mr. James D. Wolfensohn becomes World Bank President in May.
1996	Martin and Winters (1996)—Uruguay Round assessment.		Major reorganization; Managing Directors Gautam S. Kaji, Caio Koch-Weser, and Sven Sandstrom announce the launch of the "networks" initiative, beginning with the Human Development Network. Abolition of Regional technical departments that housed dedicated trade experts.
1997	Having provided technical support for reforms in 17 countries, World Bank/UNDP Trade Expansion Program concludes as planned with a global conference and the preparation for publication of the *Trade Policy Reform: Lessons of Experience* was started.	World Bank and the World Trade Organization (WTO) sign a formal agreement of cooperation to coordinate efforts to further integrate developing countries into the global economy.	Trade unit in IEC moved into DECRG.
1998	Published *Trade Policy Reform: Lessons of Experience* (Nash and Takacs, 1998).	Integrated trade research/capacity-building program launched between DECRG and EDI.	
1999	Doha Round conference in Geneva (DRG/WBI); Stiglitz paper on need for balanced outcome.	Partnership established between DECRG/EDI and DFID: Trade Policy Development Project.	Presidential Speech at Seattle: "Global Trade and the 'Development Round': Seizing the Day." In his his speech, Wolfensohn urges wealthy nations to eliminate trade barriers for the sake of the three billion people who live on less than $2 a day. Manufactured goods exported from developing countries to the industrialized world face barriers four times higher than those from industrialized countries. At the same time, barriers blocking manufactured goods flowing between developing countries are even higher.

Year	Analytic activities	Strategy/institutional response	World Bank events
2000	Hoekman and Martin (2000): Doha agenda research.		James D. Wolfensohn begins his second term in May as President of the World Bank. President Wolfensohn began a tour of Southeast Asia. He addressed the Tenth Ministerial Meeting of UNCTAD in Bangkok, saying that globalization must have a "human face," and should promote social equity. Trade liberalization was an important tool for reducing poverty and he called on the international community to give free market access for all the exports of the countries eligible for debt relief under the Heavily Indebted Poor Countries (HIPC) Initiative. The World Bank's Trade and Transport Facilitation in Southeast Europe Program announced the signing of a memorandum of understanding between six Balkan countries. The program was created to reduce the costs of trade and transport, and to reduce smuggling and corruption at border crossings in southeast Europe. The Development Committee's Spring meetings in Washington are marred by protests of thousands demanding an end to globalization. 6,000 – 10,000 demonstrators gathered in Washington to shut down the meetings by tying themselves together using lengths of pipe and chain. The meetings were conducted in spite of the protests.
2001		Launch of periodic Board Progress Reports on Trade. Nick Stern makes trade a core element of investment climate policy agenda.	Presidential Speech: "Making Globalization & Trade work for the Developing World." In a speech to the U.N.'s Economic and Social Council, President James D Wolfensohn called on G7 leaders to take steps to open their markets to developing country products. No centralized Trade Department exists in the World Bank. Trade researchers in DECRG and commodity analysis in DECPG, 2 trade economists in Economic Policy unit of PREM.
2002	Hoekman, Mattoo, and English (2002): Handbook on Development/WTO. Globalization, Growth, and Poverty Report. GEP takes hard-hitting look at market access issues.	Trade-related lending is at low point. Progress Report "Proposed Priorities for Trade Work at the Bank, 2002-2005." The World Bank and the World Trade Organization establish a new fund, (Standards and Trade Development Facility), as part of their efforts to link aid to trade opportunities in the fight	In a speech at the Woodrow Wilson International Center for Scholars in Washington, President Wolfensohn called on wealthy donor nations to double foreign aid over five years and tear down trade barriers that harm the world's poorest workers and rob them of markets for their products. Presidential Speech: "The Developing World needs the Opportunity to Trade out of Poverty."

(Table continues on the following page.)

Table A1.1: Annotated Timeline of Major Developments in International Trade in the World Bank (continued)

Year	Analytic activities	Strategy/institutional response	World Bank events
2002 (cont.)	LAC Trade Flagship.	against poverty by helping them shape and implement international standards on food safety, and plant and animal health. The goal is to provide grants and financial support for technical assistance projects in developing countries through enhanced collaboration between the international organizations involved. The Food and Agriculture Organization (FAO), the World Health Organization (WHO) and the World Organization for Animal Health (OIE) are expected to join the Bank and the WTO in the facility. Also expected to participate are the Codex Alimentarius (the food safety standards-setting organization run jointly by the FAO and WHO), and the Secretariat of the International Plant Protection Convention at the FAO. World Bank issues a press release announcing creation of International Trade Department. Uri Dadush appointed first director of the International Trade Department.	In his address to the 2002 World Bank/IMF Annual Meetings, Wolfensohn called on rich countries to improve donor coordination, untie aid, and agree a "fixed timetable" for the elimination of agricultural subsidies. "We know that there is so much that can be done by rich countries without waiting for Doha. I urge you to act sooner."
2003	MNA Trade Flagship *Cotton and Developing Countries: A Case Study of Policy Incoherence* identified policy intervention in the cotton sectors of the U.S. as detrimental to developing countries.	World Bank's publishes *Lessons from NAFTA for Latin America and the Caribbean Countries: A Summary of Research Findings.* Progress Report: "Leveraging Trade for Development: The World "Bank's Agenda." Trade Sector manager hired.	Chief Economist Stern delivered a statement regretting the failure of the World Trade Organization meetings, and urging participants to take action on reductions in domestic support, export subsidies, and market openings for agricultural products. Joint WTO-IMF-World Bank statement to the WTO General Council meeting on coherence.
2004	EAP Trade Flagship. LAC NAFTA report.	Progress Report: "Leveraging Trade for Development: The World Bank's Research Agenda."	IEG conducts independent evaluation of IF as part of its Global Public Goods Evaluation.
2005	SAR Trade Flagship. The World Bank issued a report on the economic benefits of the Central American Free Trade Agreement, signed between Costa Rica, Dominican Republic, El Salvador, Guatemala, Honduras, Nicaragua and the United States.	Aid for Trade Paper presented to World Bank Board and Development Committee in September.	

Table A.2: Timeline of Global Trade Events

Year(s)	International	Industrialized world	Developing world
1986–93	GATT Trade ministers launch the Uruguay Round in Punta Del Este, Uruguay, embarking on the most ambitious and far-reaching trade round so far. The round extended the range of trade negotiations, leading to major reductions in agricultural subsidies, an agreement to allow full access for textile and clothing from developing, and an extension of intellectual property rights.		
1991			Brazil, Argentina, Uruguay, and Paraguay sign Mercosur trade pact.
1994	North America Free Trade Association (NAFTA) goes into effect between Canada, U.S., and Mexico. Trade ministers meet for the final time under GATT auspices at Marrakesh, Morocco to establish the World Trade organization (WTO) and sign other agreements.		In West Africa, the CFA franc is devalued for the first time since its creation, changing a critical parameter for Bank policy in that region.
1995	The World Trade Organization is created in Geneva.		"Single Undertaking" implies large number of new disciplines for many countries.
1996	Singapore WTO Ministerial Conference introduces investment, competition, procurement, and trade facilitation to the multilateral arena.		
1997	High-level WTO meeting creates the Integrated Framework for Trade-related Technical Assistance to LDCs (IF) in October.		Devaluation of Thai currency sets off regional economic crisis.
1998	Geneva WTO Ministerial.		Asian currencies and stock markets continue to plunge, creating an economic crisis for the continent.
1999	Mike Moore, former Prime Minster of New Zealand, is appointed WTO Director General for a three-year term to replace Renato Ruggiero following a contentious battle. At least 30,000 protestors disrupt WTO summit in Seattle, U.S. Seattle Trade Ministerial ends in debacle as protestors take over the meeting and developing counties complain about lack of voice.		
2000	Independent evaluation of IF conducted.	1st Joint Communiqué by IF Heads of Agency	
2001	Doha Trade Ministerial held in November in Doha, Qatar and the Doha Development Agenda is born.	The term "trade mainstreaming enters the lexicon.	LDC Ministerial held in Zanzibar.

(*Table continues on the following page.*)

Table A.2: Timeline of Global Trade Events (continued)

Year(s)	International	Industrialized world	Developing world
2001 (cont.)	Sells itself as more "development friendly" than previous rounds. China formally joins the WTO. Taiwan is admitted immediately afterward. IF revamped and three pilot studies initiated (Cambodia, Madagascar, Mauritania).	United States establishes the African Growth and Opportunity Act (AGOA) preference scheme. EU adopts Everything But Arms (EBA) preference scheme. DAC Guidelines on Strengthening Trade Capacity for Development published.	
2002	Former Thai deputy prime minister, Dr. Supachai Panitchpakdi begins a three-year term as Director General of the WTO. First WTO head to come from a developing country.	Oxfam launches "Make Trade Fair" campaign. U.S. Farm Bill passed. 2nd Joint Communiqué.	
2003	World Trade Organization talks in Cancun, Mexico collapse after a group of developing nations reject farm subsidies proposed by wealthier nations. An international high-level Round-Table on the coffee crisis, organized by the International Coffee Organization (ICO) and the World Bank, called for rich countries to share the burden of the coffee crisis that affected the living standards of 125 million people, mainly in small-holdings in developing countries. The Round-Table urged the U.S. Government to rejoin the ICO and demanded that rich countries reduce their internal agricultural subsidies and tariffs in order to allow potential diversification in those coffee-producing countries willing to move to other crops. Independent evaluation of IF undertaken by CAPRA International (consulting firm hired by participating partners).	First OECD-DAC Meeting of trade development communities in Paris. Second Joint WTO/OECD report on Trade-related Technical Assistance and Capacity Building. Third joint IF Heads of Agency Communiqué issued to reaffirm the organizations' commitment to effective integration of least developed countries into the multilateral trading system and to articulate plans for improving progress under the Integrated Framework. In a letter to heads of governments of all member countries, World Bank President James D. Wolfensohn and International Monetary Fund Managing Director Horst Köhler called for renewing progress on world trade talks. Wolfensohn and Kohler emphasize the centrality of multilateral trade liberalization to growth and prosperity over the past fifty years and stressed that expanding trade by collectively reducing barriers is the single most powerful tool that countries, working together, can deploy to reduce poverty and raise living standards.	Emergence of the G-20. G-90 meeting held in Mauritius. Christian Aid review of trade in PRSPs.
2004	WTO rules that U.S. subsidies to cotton farmers are unfair and rules against EU sugar subsidies. Framework Agreement reached in Geneva in August to move forward on Doha agenda; three "Singapore issues" taken off the table.		

Year(s)	International	Industrialized world	Developing world
2004 (cont.)	IEG conducts independent evaluation of IF as part of its Global Public Goods Evaluation.		
2005	Elimination of Multi-fibre Arrangement. Pascal Lamy appointed new Director General of WTO. Aid for Trade Paper presented to World Bank Board and Development Committee in September.	Africa Commission and UN MDG Trade taskforce call for stronger linkages between trade reform and development assistance. G-8 endorses aid for trade concept.	

Source: IEG staff compilation from various sources.

APPENDIX A2: CONCEPTUAL FRAMEWORK FOR THE EVALUATION

Capturing the overall development effectiveness of the Bank's trade work is difficult for three reasons:

- First, several country conditions influence the effectiveness of trade reforms and assistance: the country's macroeconomic environment, its endowments, non-trade factors in the investment climate (notably institutions), governance and political economy, and institutional capacity. While the Bank may support countries in some of these areas, it is important to attempt to disentangle (a) the Bank's actual contribution and (b) the relative importance of these other determinants.
- Second, a host of international external factors also influence government attitude toward trade reform and its ability to implement reforms; especially relevant are commodity price shocks, market access, and the country's participation in regional, bilateral, or multilateral trading arrangements.
- Third, other actors such as the private sector, bilateral and multilateral development agencies, and nongovernmental organizations may influence the pace and nature of reforms. These external variables and the extent to which Bank support and assistance takes them into account are important determinants of the results achieved.

The conceptual framework underpinning the evaluation's analysis is illustrated in figure A2.1. It builds on a logical framework of the links between Bank actions and outcomes and impacts. The main apparent desired *outcome* of the Bank's support for trade is improved trade performance: higher export volumes, faster export growth rates, a more diversified basket of exports, cheaper and more readily available imported inputs, and greater integration in the global economy. The assumption (often explicitly stated) is that expanded trade will contribute to the Bank's overarching goal of poverty reduction in two ways—by contributing to overall economic growth and by creating jobs—with an overall beneficial *impact*.

The Bank's approach to helping countries achieve better trade performance has been to use its budget, staff, and partnerships through lending, economic and sector work, policy advice, and technical assistance to clients, as well as research and advocacy *(inputs)*. The outcomes associated with these inputs depend to some extent on the policies and strategies followed by governments; they are expected to improve the competitive environment for exporters, reduce rent-seeking opportunities, improve access to imported inputs, and strengthen the institutional capacity of officials and institutions dealing with trade-related issues. Through this support, the Bank influences trade-related *outputs*—for example, commitment by governments and the actual trade reforms they introduce and improved customs clearance times for exporters. These in turn are expected to contribute to improved trade performance *outcomes*.

Figure A2.1. Conceptual Framework for the Evaluation

Inputs	Trade adjustment and investment lending Economic and sector work (ESW) and policy advice Technical assistance—for example, for trade negotiations Research and advocacy Country Assistance Strategies
Objectives	**Competitiveness** Transparent incentives Neutral to importers/exporters Access to inputs at world prices Allocative efficiency gains **Institutional Capacity** Policy makers Exporting firms Trade promotion institutions (customs, standards)
Outputs	Tariffs: Lower levels, narrower ranges, less dispersion Shorter customs clearance times Increased trade financing
Outcomes	**Improved Trade Performance** Increase in exports and faster growth rates Greater export diversification Increased market shares Higher firm-level productivity Reduced rent-seeking and greater import competition
Impact	Economic growth Poverty reduction

APPENDIX B1: TRADE AND DEVELOPMENT—THE STATE OF THE DEBATE

The effect of trade and related policies on country economic performance has been debated for more than a century. The literature generated by that debate, especially since the 1960s, concludes that although trade offers long-term benefits for developing countries, trade liberalization alone is not sufficient for economic growth. Rather, it has become clear that maximizing trade and welfare outcomes depends on the underlying macroeconomic environment, industrial policies for export development, the design and sequencing of trade policies, external constraints and opportunities, and complementary policies. These factors in the outcome of trade liberalization and a summary of current debates are the subject of this appendix. The objective is to provide the context for the Bank's approach to trade. The first half of the appendix draws on Oyejide (2004).

Trade Policy Reform and Economic Growth: Implications for Bank Advice

Belief that international trade is critical for economic growth underpinned the Bank's policy advice to its client countries from the early 1980s—there were few alternatives, as import substitution had run its course. The first multicountry studies of developing countries' trade regimes (Little, Scott, and Scitovsky 1970 and Balassa and Associates 1971 and an influential study done by the NBER and summarized in Bhagwati 1978 and Krueger 1978) had systematically detailed the inefficiencies of the import-substituting development strategies that prevailed throughout the developing world. The studies were influential in promoting export orientation as a path to more rapid economic growth.[1]

Despite differences of opinion among econometricians on the causal relationship between trade reform and economic growth, the long-term benefits of increased trade are unchallenged. Few countries have grown rapidly and reduced poverty by following a long-term autarkic approach. As noted in Panagariya (2004), neither Rodrik (1999) nor Stiglitz (2002), critics of the Bank's approach to trade liberalization, dispute the benefits countries can gain by opening up their economies. Researchers on both sides of the issue also increasingly agree on the importance of country specificity and of institutions in disentangling the various policies that affect trade and growth.

Macroeconomic Environment and Trade Policy Reform

Three macroeconomic factors contribute to maximizing the success of trade reform: macroeconomic stability, the real exchange rate, and the timing of foreign exchange market liberalization and trade reform.

Macroeconomic stability

There is a strong consensus in the literature regarding the necessity of macroeconomic stability for trade liberalization to have significant effects on resource allocation within an economy. In Papageorgiou and others (1991), smaller budget deficits kept inflation low and thus supported a real depreciation of the domestic currency during trade policy reform. The study showed that poor macroeconomic policies were more commonly associated with reversals in trade liberalization than any other factor. Nominal currency devaluation must often be combined with anti-inflationary monetary and fiscal policies, as well as appropriate aid management policies, to ensure that it is converted to real depreciation and not subsequently reversed.

The literature is less clear on whether trade policy reform should be implemented after macroeconomic stability has been achieved or whether liberalization and macroeconomic adjustment should proceed simultaneously (Dean, Desai, and Riedel 1994). Some analysts maintain that stabilization should precede liberalization (Rodrik 1992, p. 88); some go so far as to say that stabilization may be all that matters; while others insist that an outward-orientation already implies commitment to maintaining macroeconomic stability (Bhagwati and Srinivasan 2001, pp. 3, 11).[2]

The real exchange rate

There is also a strong consensus on the relevance of the real exchange rate for export promotion. Williamson (1997, p. 17) asserts that "perhaps the most important single instrument in implementing outward orientation is exchange rate policy." Considerable empirical evidence exists on the relationship between export performance and the real exchange rate. Studies such as those of Diaz-Alejandro (1984), Paredes (1988), and Caballero and Corbo (1989) show that real exchange rate misalignment can be detrimental to export growth, and that real exchange rate variability and uncertainty are associated with negative effects on export performance in some Latin American countries. On the positive side, the literature also suggests that the exceptional export growth performance of East Asian countries and Chile is closely related to the ability of these countries to avoid real exchange rate overvaluation while minimizing exchange rate volatility.

Timing of trade policy and exchange rate reform

Debate continues on the role of exchange rate policy in trade liberalization and whether exchange rate changes need to precede or accompany trade reform. As pointed out by Krueger (1978) and Pritchett (1996), in countries where foreign exchange shortages due to overvalued exchange rates and extensive exchange controls are binding constraints on trade, the removal of import restrictions would be ineffective without reform of the foreign exchange market. In particular, trade liberalization without devaluation may be rendered incompatible by the resulting adverse balance-of-payments effect. To resolve this incompatibility, a "trade-liberalizing devaluation" (Collier 1991) may be necessary; this would be designed to permit a relaxation of trade and payments restrictions without creating an adverse balance-of-payments effect. The possibility that trade liberalization without devaluation may create a short-run external balance problem suggests that the two policy initiatives are strongly complementary (Corden 1989; O'Connell 1997).

These considerations may explain the results of several studies of trade liberalization in developing countries during the 1980s and early 1990s. For instance, Papageorgiou and others (1991) report that most of the successful trade liberalization programs began with a depreciation of the real exchange rate. The results reported in Elbadawi and Soto (1997) for a sample of African and other developing countries "corroborate the view that without real depreciation, trade liberalization would be difficult to sustain." The policy implications from these results is that, for countries with overvalued currencies, the first step in the adjustment process should be to bring about a sustained real devaluation, which would enable the real exchange rate to be then held stable before implementing any trade liberalization.

Policies for Export Development

Two other types of policy measures are important for export development: compensatory measures designed to offset any inherent anti-export bias in a trade regime[3] and additional incentives meant to address specific problems of exports.

To develop exports, governments can compensate for the adverse effects of policies that penalize the export sector by designing measures that restore incentive neutrality between production for export and import substitution. The required neutrality of incentives can be achieved by allowing export producers to purchase their inputs and sell their outputs at competitive prices; that is, by granting exporters and their main suppliers duty-free access to inputs, and granting exporters the right to retain all their export proceeds. Several mechanisms exist for granting duty-free access to exporters for imported inputs. These include duty drawback or rebate systems, and bonded manufacturing warehousing arrangements. In addition, geographically separated entities (export processing zones) may be set aside from which all import trade barriers are excluded.

Export development can also be promoted by applying additional incentives to tackle specific export problems. Falvey and Gemmell (1990) categorized those used in Asian countries into three groups: input-related incentives, output-related incentives, and incentives associated with externalities. Prominent in the first group are subsidies on public utility services, special depreciation allowances on capital inputs, and preferential credit arrangements. The second group includes tax exemptions, export credits, export subsidies, provision of infrastructure, and assistance with overseas export marketing. Government services in aid of export quality promotion are among the incentives in the third group.

The effectiveness of these incentives—and other industrial policy measures—continues to be debated (Pack 2000). But the literature notes some successes. In particular, it is generally agreed that export processing zones have been effective in Madagascar, Mauritius, and Mexico. In addition, Agosin (2002) suggests that temporary subsidies were a powerful tool for stimulating the growth of non-traditional exports in Chile.

Developing countries currently face greater constraints in using selective and industrial policies compared to the period when the East Asian "tigers" did. This is due to the changing economic environment and changes in the international "rules of the game."

As noted by Lall (2004, p. 28), technical changes and the globalization of production complicate the use of industrial policies, compared to the past. He noted that rapid technical change "reduces the scope for, and raises the risks of some forms of industrial policy." Isolation from fast-moving technologies may hold back the development of competitive capabilities and make targeting more difficult. Globalization also makes some past industrial policies less useful or more risky and costly. For example, excluding foreign direct investment (FDI) is now less feasible as a means of boosting domestic technologies as few countries have the ability to match international innovation on their own. Similarly, few developing countries have domestic enterprises with the ability to mount export drives to match the integrated production networks of multinational companies. Finally, the ability to impose conditions on multinationals is also more limited as more countries compete for FDI.

Several of the export promotion measures described above have had their use constrained or prohibited by recent WTO agreements. For instance, the Agreement on Subsidies and Countervailing Measures (SCM) prohibits export subsidies by countries with per capita incomes above $1,000. Similarly, the Agreement on Trade Related Investment Measures (TRIMs) mandates the removal of local content and trade balancing requirements from the export promotion and industrial policy arsenal of WTO members. These measures were used with some success in East Asia.[4]

Chang (2004) contends that while the changing international economic environment and new rules have imposed considerable extra constraints on the use of industrial policies, these constraints are not overwhelming. In particular, the least-developed countries can use exemptions and longer transition periods. He notes that the demands for a more development-friendly trade round may also offer additional flexibility for industrial policies in the future.

Design, Sequence, and Duration of Trade Policy Reform

Design issues related to trade policy reforms include: the components of the trade reform package, the sequence in which the various elements should be reformed, and how long it should take to complete trade reform.[5]

Design questions arise from the need to ensure that the elements of the reform package have effects that are mutually reinforcing. Questions about sequence arise for two reasons. First, trade policy reforms in developing countries can be complicated and difficult to manage; hence, they often strain implementation capacity that may be eased by sequencing the various components. Second, sequencing is desirable to the extent that it permits the policy reform program to consider the varying adjustment needs of the different sectors of the economy as well as the interactions between different elements of the package (Winters 2000).

The literature is clear that import policy reform should begin with the elimination of quantitative restrictions. Where these are transformed first into tariffs the economy gains through the removal of distortions associated with rent-seeking and monopoly power, increased transparency of the trade regime, and increased tariff revenue (Dean, Desai, and Riedel 1994).

A similar sequence applies on the export side. The removal of export licensing and prohibitions typically occurs first, simultaneously with elimination of restrictions on imported inputs used in the production of exports. Next, export taxes (usually on agricultural exports) are removed and other export incentives (including direct and indirect subsidies) introduced. In practice, easing exporters' access to imported inputs at world prices has had a more significant impact on export growth than more general export incentives (Thomas and Nash 1991).

Whether trade policy reform should be strong and sudden or moderate and gradual remains in dispute. For instance, Bhagwati and Srinivasan (2001, p. 2) assert that "nothing requires that, faced with high trade barriers, a country's tariff reforms must be on a shock therapy path." The deliberate, systematic, and sequential implementation of trade policy reform also resonates with Collier, Greenaway, and Gunning (1997, p. 307) who note: "in the presence of multiple policy instruments and conflicting interest groups competing for attention, policy reforms are more likely to be incremental than comprehensive." In any case, there are circumstances in which adjustment costs associated with policy reforms may be lower if adjustment can be spread over time (Winters 2000), provided the delay does not become an excuse for aborting an otherwise necessary reform. On the other side, sometimes a "big bang" approach is viewed as necessary to take advantage of an opportunity for reform and to signal credibility and commitment of new leadership.

Empirical evidence on the speed of reform is not conclusive. Papageorgiou and others (1991) suggest that strong programs that start boldly tend to have a better chance of success and sustainability than weaker, more prolonged ones; they claim that a reform program that endures six years is very likely to last indefinitely. However, Lal (1995) suggests that the gradualist approach to trade reform, initiated by India and China in the early 1990s, may turn out to be both successful and sustainable.

External Constraints and Opportunities

Early World Bank support for trade policy reform in developing countries was predicated on the expectation that most gains from such reforms would accrue from each country's own liberalization efforts. Hence, the resulting reform programs emphasized unilateral rather than multilateral trade liberalization. Yet, much of the trade policy reform undertaken by the industrial countries up to the mid-1990s took place under the auspices of GATT.

The importance of multilateral negotiations for promoting trade liberalization in developing countries eventually was recognized and has been associated with a number of advantages, including that it enables countries to obtain external market access "concessions" through an exchange process, binding their reforms to an international framework as a means of resisting internal anti-reform interests, preventing reversals, and endowing their reforms with greater security, transparency, and credibility.

From the early 1990s, why and how external market constraints may cause problems for developing countries that adopt outward-oriented trade strategies has been increasingly recognized (Cline 1989 and Ghosh 1992). Industrial countries are the primary export markets of newly industrializing developing countries and market access barriers in those industrialized countries limit export opportunities of developing countries. One of the first manifestations of this concern was "export pessimism"—the belief that developing countries' exports could not successfully penetrate the economies of the developed countries (Hughes 1992). This was because industrial country imbalances at that time, combined with unfavorable trends in international markets, would sharply limit the extent to which world markets could continue to absorb exports from developing countries. Ghosh (1992) argued that unless the industrial economies enjoyed faster growth, there would be little room for developing countries to adopt and successfully implement outward-oriented trade policy reform.

Some researchers agree that trade policy reforms in developing countries are likely to be more successful if they are supported by improved economic performance and more accommodating policy changes by the developed countries (World Bank 2002b). In particular, improved market access for poor countries in the developed countries may be necessary (Ianchovichina, Mattoo, and Olarreaga 2001).

Developed countries have made some efforts to provide developing countries with special market access. For example, the high-income countries have offered the generalized system of preferences as a means of mitigating the effects of high tariffs on developing countries' exports. These schemes have helped some developing countries to take advantage of export opportunities in preference-giving countries. But the schemes have not fully eliminated the trade barriers faced by low-income countries for several reasons. First, the schemes are unilateral and can be eliminated or modified at will by the preference-granting countries. Second, they have limited product coverage, and the preference mainly applies to products that already face relatively low tariffs. Third, the preferences are easily eroded by non-tariff measures such as safeguards, anti-dumping, rules of origin, and "graduation" mechanisms.

A more effective remedy suggested by some researchers is to extend duty-free and quota-free market access to all exports of the least-developed countries. This could achieve two important objectives: help mitigate the deficiencies of existing preferential market access schemes and significantly increase the export growth of this set of countries.[6] But while agreeing that improved and predictable market access for African products could be helpful, at least to some extent, Helleiner (2002b) suggests that before market access, the poorest countries must first be assisted to address their export supply capacity constraints through increased investment in infrastructure and skills.

Research suggests that developing countries should focus on both increasing their access to industrial country markets and reducing their own protection levels to reap the gains from liberalization in the context of multilateral trade negotiations (Anderson et al. 2002).[7]

Complementary and Mitigating Measures

Trade policy reforms generally are expected to work with lags that may vary by country, sector, and the periods over which the reforms are implemented. In principle, therefore, trade policy reforms tend to yield their full efficiency and welfare gains in the long term. But trade policy reforms also have costs that often are incurred well before the related stream of benefits can be realized. In addition, there is an inherent distributional problem: the "burden" of the reforms may not fall on the same agents who reap the benefits or the cost may not be shared in the same proportion as the benefits across different groups. Trade policy reform works by reallocating resources from less efficient to more efficient uses. This reallocation is not without costs. In particular, as workers are displaced from inefficient enterprises, some amount of transitional unemployment and output loss is likely.

Trade policy reform may be associated with a second type of problem. When import barriers are reduced, imports may increase sharply and rapidly, thus generating a balance-of-payments deterioration. For these and similar reasons, policymakers are often concerned that trade policy reform may have negative effects on the balance-of-payments, output, employment, as well as income distribution.

These concerns are unjustified in certain cases. Papageorgiou and others (1991) suggests that for many countries studied, the costs of trade policy reforms were very small, even in the short term. In most of these countries, the balance-of-payments position improved as a result of policy since the improvement in export performance was both quick enough and large enough to more than offset the surge in imports. Other studies (such as Oyejide, Ndulu, and Gunning

1999) show that short-term costs constitute realistic concerns for countries contemplating or implementing trade policy reforms. Furthermore, while cautioning against broad generalizations about the depth and duration of possible transition losses associated with trade policy reform, Winters (2000) suggests a few pointers. First, the more protected the sector being liberalized the greater the transitional costs are likely to be, although this sector may also offer the largest long-run returns to reform. Second, if the labor market is exposed to very large shocks emanating from policy reforms that render it dysfunctional, transitional unemployment may be larger in volume and longer in duration. Third, rapid or concentrated reforms are more likely to generate transitional losses through unemployment than more diffuse reforms.

Complementary, compensatory, and mitigatory measures are typically designed to address the costs associated with trade policy reform. In particular, complementary measures may be used to reduce the adjustment cost of reform and provide households the assistance that they may need to avoid poverty by enabling them to attain a greater degree of economic viability (Winters 2000). Thus, complementary policies may need to be put in place before or at the same time as a trade policy reform is implemented.

Compensatory and mitigatory policies include measures designed to protect in some way those who suffer losses as a result of trade policy reform. For these policies, targeting is critical because of the need to focus especially on those who lose rather than offer general support that could be costly and wasteful. For example, when trade policy reform leads to employment losses it should be possible to identify those affected and arrange redundancy payments and re-training programs. Sometimes the pattern of loss has a regional dimension and hence, mitigative measures may have to reflect this. In general, therefore, compensatory and mitigatory policies involve the creation of "safety nets" for those who suffer from the transitional costs of trade policy reform.

With respect to the sequencing of mitigatory measures, to the extent that they must be appropriately targeted, it is reasonable to assume that they should be put in place after trade policy reform has been implemented and the transitional costs begin to show.

By comparison, opinion is divided regarding whether complementary policies should precede or be implemented simultaneously with trade policy reform. It has been suggested (for instance by Winters 2000) that if a trade policy reform program is credible and it includes significant transition periods, it could be an important stimulus for the complementary measures that are required. Hence, it may not be necessary for complementary measures to precede trade policy reform. However, this point of view may underestimate the extent of institution building and capacity creation required before a low-income country can effectively realize the full potential of a major trade policy reform.

The sequencing of complementary measures may not, in fact, be fully amenable to theoretical or even empirical generalizations. It may be necessary to evaluate the structure and performance of relevant market institutions as well as the economy's supply response capacity constraints before designing a major trade policy reform program.

Trade and Growth

The role of trade and hence trade-related policies on country performance has been a subject of controversy for well over a century. The debate about whether trade was a handmaiden or an engine of growth was theory-based before becoming more empirical from the late 1960s onwards, when developing countries were first subjected to intensive scrutiny.

This rest of this Appendix traces the main "turning points" in the debate over trade and growth to help place the evaluation in context.[8] The focus is on three main areas: the role of international trade in economic growth, the approaches to trade liberalization, and the links between trade, distribution, and poverty.

The Role of Trade in Economic Growth

The belief that international trade is critical to economic growth underpinned the World Bank's policy advice to its client countries from the early 1980s. The Bank and its clients had few alternatives as import substitution of non-durable consumer goods had run its course. Little, Scott, and Scitovsky (1970) Balassa and Associates (1971) were the first multi-country studies of trade regimes in developing countries, the former commissioned by the OECD Development Centre, and the latter by the World Bank. These were followed by an influential study carried out by the NBER and summarized in Bhagwati (1978) and Krueger (1978).

The multi-country studies, following a common methodology, were the first to detail systematically the inefficiencies of the then-prevalent import-substituting development strategies followed throughout the developing world. The studies were influential in promoting export orientation as a path to more rapid economic growth. The experience of the East Asian "tigers" that moved the furthest away from the purely import substitution model was simplified and generalized to support the export-led growth model.[9]

As pointed out by Little in his analytical appraisal of changes in the field of development economics, this vision of the role of trade in a country's development strategy was a minority view in the profession. It was only with the advent of the two oil shocks and debt crisis that the failure of what Sachs and Warner (1995) called the "state-led" development strategy became apparent and more widely accepted in development thinking. World Bank researchers had contributed to the literature; but this thinking was not put into practice until lending conditions were used in structural adjustment lending, and was subsequently crystallized in the 1987 World Development Report (WDR), which focused on trade policies.

Despite the potential benefits from trade, policies related to trade liberalization remain controversial in some circles for at least three reasons. First, critics assert that it led to instances of too rapid liberalization, resulting in severe transitional costs of adjustment reflected in increased poverty, de-industrialization, and job loss. They also argue that the impact of trade reform on exports has been limited.[10] While the long-term gains from trade appear to be well established, the benefits may be less visible in the short run for at least three reasons: (i) inappropriate macroeconomic policies, such as incomplete stabilization resulting in contractionary fiscal or monetary policies that squeeze out credit from the private sector and reduce the entry of new firms or result in appreciation of the real exchange rate, thereby reducing competitiveness; (ii) missing complementary (so-called "behind the border") policies and institutions to support faster export growth such as customs, rule of law, quality and standards, as well as trade logistics;[11] and (iii) insufficient or inadequate skills and capital to take advantage of emerging opportunities that arise from the liberalization. The dissatisfaction with the outcomes associated with more open economies culminated in large protests at the World Trade Organization's 1999 meetings in Seattle.

The second reason trade is controversial is that, in contrast to the "first best" world that underpins standard trade theory, the "real" world has several deviations that are likely to influence the outcome of unilateral trade liberalization. The existence of protectionism in industrial and other developing countries, the rise of regionalism and unanticipated political events are just three factors that can result in unanticipated outcomes. Therefore, some critics of trade have denounced the Bank for not taking these factors into account.

The third reason is related to the politics of any reform, but especially trade. Changes in relative prices under trade are important and hence, anticipated distributional shifts lead to strong opposition and controversies that, at times, end in policy reversals.

Beyond these points on imperfect trade liberalizations, there are questions about the link between trade reform and economic growth. The econometric evidence on the links between trade reform, economic growth, and trade performance remains mixed.[12] It has proven difficult to use the cross-sectional approach to establish causality and identify the role of other intervening factors such as geography and institutional factors. In particular, the verdict is still out on the relative importance of each factor.

Researchers continue to extend existing methodologies to explore the links between trade reform and growth. Specifically, they have focused on refining the measurement of "openness" and on incorporating additional economic variables that influence whether and the extent to which trade liberalization results in accelerated economic growth. In particular, by identifying the years when non-reversed trade liberalization programs were launched and using panel regression techniques, Wacziarg and Welch (2003) find that on average, growth, investment, and openness increase after trade liberalization. Others have focused on the role of additional country-specific factors, such as the role of institutions, in determining the success of trade reform (Rodrik, Subramanian, and Trebbi 2004; Freund 2003).

The new growth theory predicts that openness to trade (and investment) increases access to new technology, enhances efficiency by making market structures more competitive, allowing the exploitation of economies of scale and by spurring innovation. In a study of 93 countries, Edwards (1998) finds that total factor productivity growth is faster in more open economies. Subsequent work in this area has supported this finding.[13] De Melo (2005) documents how the Bank's research in this area has contributed to establishing the microeconomic channels at the firm and sector level through which trade openness contributes to economic growth. Building on firm and census surveys in manufacturing, Bank research contributed to establishing the beneficial impact of "import discipline" on pricing and productivity gains. More recently, De Melo notes that Bank industry studies have complemented firm-level studies by establishing the links among a variety of factors (R&D embodied in trade, foreign direct investment, and product variety) and productivity growth.

Despite differences of opinion among econometricians on the links between trade reform and economic growth, areas of common ground exist. While the econometric evidence on the causality between trade openness and economic growth is equivocal, few countries have grown rapidly and reduced poverty following a long-term autarkic approach. As noted in Panagariya (2004), neither Rodrik (1999) nor Stiglitz (2002) ultimately disputes the benefits from countries opening up their economies. Researchers on both sides of the issue also increasingly agree on the importance of country specificity and of individual country case studies in disentangling the various policies that affect trade and growth. Thus, if trade is necessary for sustained economic growth, countries that have followed largely different approaches to liberalization can have equally good performance (see for example the country examples in the Rodrik [2003] survey). Finally, while international trade is necessary for sustained economic growth, countries take different paths to liberalizing trade with no assurance that doing so will by itself necessarily lead to accelerated growth.

The Approaches to Trade Liberalization

The relative importance of the three primary routes to trade liberalization—multilateral, preferential regional trading arrangements, and unilateral—have varied and evolved. The institutional framework for global multilateral trade liberalization is the World Trade Organization (WTO), and before 1996, the General Agreement on Tariffs and Trade (GATT). The WTO enforces a rules-based system that governs trade relations among its members. The organization affects the trade policies of its members through a number of channels: periodic Trade Policy Reviews, multilateral trade negotiations, the dispute settlement mechanism, as well as the accession process into the organization. Bhagwati (1982), World Bank (World Bank 2002b), and others have argued that participation (and hence liberalization) through the multilateral route ultimately benefits the developing countries as it provides them with a stronger voice than they would have in bilateral negotiations. While the Uruguay Round (launched in 1986 and completed in 1993 under the GATT) was not the first round of liberalization undertaken under the multilateral framework;[14] it was the first in which developing countries participated in large numbers.

Mixed views persist regarding the achievements of the Uruguay Round that preceded the current Doha Development Agenda. On the positive side, large tariff cuts were accomplished compared to previous rounds, "voluntary" export constraints were abolished, agriculture was brought under GATT discipline, a dispute settlement mechanism was codified through the establishment of the WTO, and an agreement was reached on phasing out non-tariff barriers under the Multi-Fibre Arrangement (MFA).

Despite estimated aggregate gains, the impact on individual countries and regions was uneven. Even the elimination of the MFA, while advantageous for exporters in theory, was subsequently found to potentially adversely affect developing country exporters. More generally, developing countries signed the Single Undertaking, committing them to agreements in the Uruguay Round that they later found difficult to implement due to capacity constraints. In addition, many (including World Bank researchers) found the costs associated with implementing some of these new agreements were inconsequential.[15] Trade-related capacity building that was promised under the Uruguay Round was slow to arrive, leading to a Uruguay Round "hangover"[16] for developing countries and setting the stage for their greater caution in subsequent trade negotiations.

The most recent round of trade negotiations, the Doha Development Agenda (DDA), was initiated in November 2001. More than any previous round, the DDA aims to make multilateral trade liberalization more development-friendly. Estimates of the gains from the DDA range widely and depend greatly on the extent to which both developing and industrial countries open up their markets. As industrial countries have not agreed to significant agriculture liberalization, the actual gains from the DDA can be quite low.[17]

Since Doha, the DDA negotiations have limped along. Industrial countries thus far have not been able to offer the type of concessions that researchers deem necessary to make the Round beneficial to developing countries. Developing countries have been much more assertive than in previous rounds and (to some extent based on the experience with the Uruguay Round) are more skeptical of the touted benefits. Following a disappointing interim meeting in Cancun in September 2003, a framework on the modalities for negotiations was agreed in August 2004. Nonetheless, substantial risks persist in reaching agreement on the DDA given the stances of the negotiating parties.[18, 19]

In the meantime, regional preferential trading arrangements[20] have sprung up in every region of the world. Over 300 such RTAs currently exist.[21] Several factors underlie the proliferation of RTAs—strategic and geopolitical interests, uncertainties about the future of the multilateral trading system following the failure to launch a round in Seattle and subsequent difficulties in reaching agreements following the Doha meetings, and a desire to use the strength of numbers to develop larger markets and increase regional cooperation on a range of trade and non-trade issues. The Asia-Pacific Economic Cooperation (APEC) arrangement, the European Union, MERCOSUR, the North American Free Trade Agreement (NAFTA), and numerous other free trade areas and customs unions now co-exist (uncomfortably) with the multilateral system and its rules.

Two camps of thought exist on whether RTAs should be viewed as "building blocks" or "stumbling blocks" to liberalizing trade.[22] Supporters of RTAs discount the extent to which trade diversion exceeds trade creation under RTAs and argue that in some circumstances smaller RTAs may be easier for countries to negotiate. Skeptics argue that RTAs are likely to result in a "hub and spoke" type of growth with the smaller spokes being disadvantaged. In the view of some researchers, these arrangements reduce global welfare and undermine the institutional architecture of the multilateral trading system.

Empirical evidence on the extent to which RTAs help liberalize and expand trade is less common and, similar to the theoretical literature, there is no clear consensus. In a recent review of regional trading arrangements in Africa which has more than 30 RTAs (or an average of four per country),[23] Yang and Gupta (2005) find that RTAs have been ineffective in expanding trade or investment. Limão (2005) shows empirically that U.S. preferential trading arrangements have harmed multilateral liberalization.

The primary route to trade liberalization for most Bank clients during the 1980s was unilateral trade liberalization. Much of this liberalization was carried out with the support of the Bank and the International Monetary Fund (IMF).

Not much research has been done on how much protection has been reduced through the different channels. Analyses done by the Bank in 1997 and again in 2004 suggest that a large share of trade liberalization carried out by Bank clients occurred through the dialogue with the Bank and associated lending.[24] In a recent paper, Rose (2004) questions the extent to which the multilateral system has actually influenced levels of protection. By refining the econometric approach used in the gravity model to take into account different groups of countries and the asymmetric liberalization pattern, Subramanian and Wei (2003) find a positive and strong, albeit rather uneven, impact of the WTO on trade liberalization. In particular, their results suggest that the WTO has not contributed to greater openness in developing countries. But it may be more important to separate the rules-making aspect of the WTO from its ability to liberalize trade.

Trade, Income Distribution, and Poverty

With the establishment of the Millennium Development Goals (MDGs), reducing poverty and facets of poverty such as vulnerability and deprivation have been strengthened as development priorities. The extent to which economic growth reduces poverty depends on, among other factors, the pattern of growth, the extent to which it is broad-based, and the degree to which it is labor-absorbing. The discussion of the links between trade, distribution, and poverty is thus part of the larger discussion on the circumstances under which economic growth is "pro-poor."

A major contribution to the analytical underpinnings of the links between trade liberalization and poverty is provided by McCulloch, Winters, and Cicera (2002). They identify the three main channels through which macro-level trade liberalization influences poverty at the household and individual level as enterprises, markets, and the state. Their analysis then examines how changes in border prices, tariffs, and other trade reforms work through each of these channels, recognizing that market imperfections, non-market factors, institutions, and gender can all influence the linkages between trade and poverty.

Empirical evidence on unambiguous links between trade and poverty is limited. Ben-David and Winters (2000) note that trade reform can result in losers in the short-run but argue that improving supporting policies such as safety nets and job retraining are ultimately more beneficial in reducing the hardships of the poor rather than abandoning the reforms. Hertel and Reimer (2004) provide an up-to-date summary of the results of recent studies. As they note, research in this area is evolving rapidly. In another contribution to the literature, UNCTAD (2004) finds that trade liberalization and expansion in the least developed countries during the 1990s did not lead to poverty reduction. It attributes this result in part to the pattern of economic growth as well as civil conflicts in some of these countries.

As women are disproportionately represented among the poor, international trade can improve employment opportunities for women. In a survey of the empirical literature on the impact of international trade on gender equality, Swamy (2004) finds that increasing trade is generally associated with narrowed gender wage gaps. However, for a country to maximize the gains from trade, she illustrates that education, skills acquisition, and a nondiscriminatory labor market are also needed. In Sub-Saharan Africa, a particular consideration is enhancing female farmers' control over resources so they can fully reap the benefits from trade expansion.

Overall, the literature emphasizes macroeconomic approaches and is narrowly focused on trade policy. This approach is insufficient at a number of levels—not the least of which is the magnitude of the impact when trade policy is the solitary focus. The fact is that direct effects may be quite small; therefore, researchers need to look at other factors that can affect the ability of individuals to take advantage of the opportunities offered by more open trade regimes such as their access to markets. The other important factor is that trade policy is never conducted in isolation from other policies. These other factors may actually have greater impact on the poor and thus, the role of trade policies needs to be put in relative context. Finally, the consensus also appears to be moving towards the need for more emphasis on tools that help measure the micro effects on firms and households of macro policies including trade (Hertel and Reimer 2004). In particular, they note the importance of better understanding how factor markets, notably labor, work given that it is the most important asset of the poor.

APPENDIX B2: LESSONS FROM PREVIOUS IEG EVALUATIONS

Agriculture

IEG (1996a) evaluated agricultural sector adjustment loans (AGSECALs) including its trade policy components. According to this study, throughout the 1970s, agricultural development programs mistakenly relied on public enterprises, over-valued exchange rates, high tariffs, and quantitative restrictions. In the 1980s, the Bank's agricultural sector adjustment operations supported the public production model and sought to increase its efficiency. However, the output impact of most completed AGSECALs had been rather small, as they did not tackle the basic policy constraints. Although IEG project evaluations rated 66 percent of the 35 completed AGSECALs as satisfactory, their objectives were deemed irrelevant by this study since most of them were designed within the policy framework of the 1980s. IEG (1996a) noted that only since the late 1980s was there a clear rejection of the state-led model with AGSECALs starting to aim at liberalization, competitive marketing, and reduced state intervention in international trade.

Industrial Activities

An IEG study of Bank funding for industrial activities in Korea, India, and Indonesia, calls for more decisive support to state-led activities (IEG 1991b). The study reports that up to the end of fiscal 1990, lending to all industrial activities constituted 16.9 percent of the Bank's total cumulative lending. From those loans, 63 percent was channeled through financial intermediaries, and 37 percent went to industrial projects. After backing import substitution strategies in the 1950s and 1960s, Bank support for industrialization increasingly moved toward outward-oriented industrialization. IEG considered that in the case of Korea, a restrictive framework underlying the analysis of industrialization has led the Bank to downplay the micro-level process of capability acquisition that underpins its industrial success. IEG notes that the Bank reports merely pointed at orthodox explanatory factors such as human capital and export orientation without mentioning selective government intervention in capability development, technological search and effort, or interaction with other firms and institutions. According to this study, Bank project work shows a much clearer appreciation of capability building, selectivity, and institutions.

Similarly in the case of Indonesia, IEG suggests that the Bank's analyses did not develop sufficient understanding of Indonesian industry at the subsectoral level. As in the case of Korea, the Bank's orthodox stance coexisted with a pragmatic approach that the IEG report judged as better geared to the needs of particular sectors during the liberalization process. Considering inefficient state intervention in the case of India, the study commended Bank's insistence on deregulation and outward-looking policies, though arguing that more effective industrial strategies could have been formulated for this country. IEG concluded that the emphasis of the Bank on non-selective interventions seemed to undermine a potentially valid case for selective promotion to help countries tackle the next stage of the learning process.

An assessment of industrial restructuring also recommended support for active state intervention in this process (IEG 1995). After arguing that trade liberalization and real exchange rate devaluation were common characteristics of successful industrial restructuring, this evaluation advised the Bank to extend its role into support for technology development; improved information about market opportunities, particularly for exports;

and labor training, redeployment, and other actions to mitigate the costs of restructuring.

Trade Liberalization

Since the early 1990s, several IEG studies have evaluated Bank-supported trade liberalization. In 1992, IEG evaluated trade reforms backed by adjustment programs in nine countries (IEG 1992a). Conditions usually attached to these loans included measures to promote a more open economy, improve macroeconomic management, and remove price distortions and impediments to efficient resource allocation. The Bank had also worked to facilitate consensus building and to encourage borrower ownership through dialogue, training, and coordination. The report noticed that all countries reduced quantitative restrictions, but only some of them reduced tariffs significantly. In two countries, early trade reforms were reversed due to economic instability. Though reforms required changes in the market policy frameworks that encourage competition, the Bank supported such changes in only four countries, and in only one case were reforms sufficiently comprehensive according to IEG.

After noting that higher export growth is fostered by easier access to imports of raw materials and capital goods as a result of trade reform, IEG (1992a) suggested that sound general economic policies, greater transparency in the regulatory framework, greater private sector access to credit, and improved productivity contributed to a higher supply response. In addition, the report noted that the most successful adjusters pursued a more active exchange rate policy than the less successful.

IEG drew several lessons from the nine sampled liberalization episodes in this review. In general, it suggested that conditionality should emphasize a few key variables that are easy to monitor. The evaluation also argued that trade reform should be undertaken in three stages: (i) tariffication; (ii) equalization of tariffs without reducing tariff revenues; and (iii) reduction of tariffs. This sequence was generally followed in all nine countries, although three are yet to move to the third stage. Complementary actions should include a previous analysis of debt dynamics; the attainment of internal balance before the reduction of tariffs; and the maintenance of real interest rates on savings above international levels to keep external balance. Considering the need to maintain fiscal and internal balance during reforms, IEG suggested coordination between tax reforms and tariff reductions. Governments should also foster internal competition to prevent domestic regulatory policies from eventually being used as anti-trade devices. Comparing the experiences of Ghana and Indonesia, the report deemed investments in human capital crucial for project sustainability. It also argued for the need to consider country-specific characteristics such as a low tax base (e.g., Pakistan) or volatility of terms of trade (e.g., Jamaica). Borrower ownership was considered necessary to increase the likelihood of countries actually meeting loan conditions and for enhanced credibility of the reforms.

IEG (1992a) urged Bank ESW to identify population groups negatively affected by trade reforms, and to use well-targeted relief measures for losers. According to IEG (1992b) the rural population had benefited more when reforms led to increases in tradable crops or agricultural incomes and less when the gains were concentrated on exportable crops, since the poor usually participate less in exportable crop production than in the rest of the agricultural sector. Although the poor may benefit indirectly from growth in agricultural exports, income inequality in rural areas rises in such cases. The report found that Structural Adjustment Loans (SALs) have usually included special programs to mitigate the social costs of adjustment mainly in the form of programs for the newly unemployed and the chronically poor (e.g., public work programs, nutrition support schemes for children and pregnant women, and targeted food subsidies). However, IEG highlighted poor design of special programs, inadequate attention to the development of appropriate institutions, and lack of proper and timely financing.

Social Impact of Adjustment

IEG has paid special attention to the effects of trade and adjustment reforms in Sub-Saharan Africa. A first evaluation on this issue (IEG 1993) found that many assessments of African adjustment operations did not deal with the basic question of sequencing. The study demands more attention in this regard, citing for example the need for export promotion to proceed over import liberalization, though with adequate coordination to avoid an anti-export bias of protectionist policies. A later update on this report (IEG 1997) noticed that out of 30 countries with trade-related conditionality in SALs between 1980 and 1996, compliance was good in 19 and weak or poor in 11 (though this was a better performance than other elements of adjustment lending). More seriously, conditions dealing with the social impact of adjustment were only present for half of the reforming countries. Similarly, IEG (1999) reports that nearly half of the Bank poverty assessments do not adequately evaluate individual elements of the poverty reduction strategy, failing to address the links between poverty and macroeconomic policies such as trade and exchange rate policy.

IEG (1996a) argued that since AGSECALs switched focus toward trade liberalization, their impact had been significantly positive for a large number of countries. However, the study still perceived some deficiencies in the Bank's approach to agricultural policy reform. More than 85 percent of AGSECALs ignored food security; Bank directives did not require performance indicators; more than 75 percent of AGSECALs did not address the issue of trade in agricultural equipment and inputs; and little attention was devoted to institutional and policy improvements to domestic markets. Furthermore, the Bank usually overestimated borrower performance; lent only to borrowers with external financing or fiscal problems; was not being effective in supporting institutional reforms; and usually did not establish a proper connection between the amount of financing of AGSECALs and their outcomes. Finally, this evaluation noted that Operational Directive 8.60 on adjustment lending did not cover the peculiarities of agricultural pricing, marketing, regulations, and trade liberalization.

An IEG evaluation of adjustment lending (IEG 1992b) also analyzed trade reforms implemented under these operations. Considerable progress is recognized in reforming the trade regimes affecting industrial sectors, mainly in removing export barriers. The report asserts that measures to replace or eliminate non-tariff barriers to imports were also widespread.

Trade Infrastructure

IEG (1996b) assessed Bank lending for port development, analyzing 35 out of 57 related projects between 1980 and 1992. Most projects aimed at developing and rehabilitating general cargo and container ports. Out of 35, 27 had substantially achieved their objectives at the time the Bank completed its loan disbursements, and most ports had performed adequately without suffering any significant congestion. However, only five had a substantial impact on institutional development, and sustainability of benefits was likely in only 19. Moreover, few projects recorded their progress toward their stated efficiency goals, and project objectives were usually considered attained when intermediate goals were achieved. Average economic rate of return was 17 percent, although appraisal returns were estimated at 28 percent. On average, implementation took 50 percent longer than projected and used larger amounts of Bank staff than the average project. Many of the projects reviewed in this evaluation initially facilitated adaptations to technological changes, but had continuing problems related to labor illiteracy, falling revenues, and increased competition from other ports and transportation. The evaluation recommended that opening to private capital should be the next step.

Source: Salinas, G. (2003), "Internal Evaluations of World Bank Supported Trade Activities," Background Paper prepared for the Trade Assistance Evaluation.

APPENDIX C1: DEFINING TRADE IN THE BANK PORTFOLIO

Trade Project Database Technical Notes

General Description: The database was built using two main approaches: (i) Trade-related keywords (for example, export, imports, trade, WTO, customs, and the like) were searched for in project document descriptions on ImageBank. This approach was necessary as the Business Warehouse descriptions associated with trade were not always accurate. The initial search was refined by a manual examination of project objectives. (ii) For projects approved after fiscal year 2002 when the Business Warehouse introduced a more refined and accurate definition of trade projects, the Business Warehouse categories of export development and competitiveness, regional integration, trade facilitation and market access, and other trade and integration were used to identify trade-related projects.

Time Period: The database contains information for the period covering fiscal 1981–2004. The Trade Assistance Evaluation, however, focuses on the fiscal 1987–2004 period.

Classification: Trade-related projects are classified under the following categories:

(a) *Trade Liberalization:* Includes projects with policy changes related to the exchange rate, tariffs, import surcharges, non-tariff barriers, export barriers, trade-related subsidies, foreign exchange markets, liberalization of an export-related economic sector, and privatization or de-monopolization of trade activities. Most of these policies imply liberalization of trade activities, but in some cases they include heterodox policies (frequently regarding trade-related subsidies). Trade policy studies are also included in this category.

(b) *Trade Facilitation, Institutional:* Includes Bank operations aimed at developing trade-related institutions such as customs, trade promotion institutions, trade financing institutions, drawback systems, institutions in charge of setting trade policies, technical assistance to exporters, antidumping and standards systems, institutions dealing with regional and multilateral agreements, and trade-related environmental regulators (including those for forestry exports).

(c) *Trade Facilitation, Infrastructure:* This category includes projects supporting the development of trade-related facilities, such as export processing or free trade zones, storage facilities for trade products, sector-specific infrastructure for exports/imports, or railways and roads that are explicitly intended to facilitate external trade according to the project objectives and description in ImageBank. Operations supporting port development that are explicitly tied to trade logistics objectives are included.

(d) *Trade Financing, Public:* This includes Bank financing of state exporters and public imports. Imports under structural adjustment projects are intentionally excluded, but public imports for economic recovery or rehabilitation projects are only partially included. In particular, rehabilitation projects included are those that also contain additional trade-related actions beyond mere critical imports.

(e) *Trade Financing, Private:* Includes IBRD/IDA finance for private exporters and of imports for the private sector. This category excludes those operations that provide general financing to the private sector, without earmarking funds for exporters. Neither does it include those projects that finance imports through the foreign exchange market.

(f) *Technical Assistance for WTO Accession and/or Negotiations:* This category includes projects that support countries in their negotiations and accession to the World Trade Organization.

(g) *Mitigation Policies:* This includes operations with trade-related components that are complemented with some measures and policies to alleviate its potential negative effects over some sector of the population.

Data collection was updated in April 2005 and revised summary tables were prepared in May 2005.

APPENDIX C2: PORTFOLIO DATA FOR TRADE-RELATED PROJECTS

Table C2.1: World Bank Lending for Trade-Related Projects (number of projects)

	I	II	III	IV	V	VI	VII	VIII
		Trade facilitation		Trade financing				
Approval fiscal year	Trade liberalization	Institutional	Physical infrastructure[a]	Public	Private	TA for WTO accession/ negotiations	TR-related Bank projects[b]	Total evaluated Bank projects[c]
1987–94	135	122	44	24	39	1	247	1,841
1995–99	70	76	43	3	18	1	146	948
2000–04	25	65	35	3	11	2	116	191
1987–2004	**230**	**263**	**122**	**30**	**68**	**4**	**509**	**2,981**

Source: Trade Assistance Evaluation Database.

a. Includes only lending components for physical trade facilities in projects that have also other trade-related actions.

b. This covers the same set of projects as in column IX, table C2.2. Columns I-VI do not sum to VII because the categorization of projects by trade-related theme is not mutually exclusive.

c. Total may not add up due to rounding.

Table C2.2: World Bank Trade-Related Commitments and Cofinancing (US$ million)

	IX	X	XI	XII	XIII	XIV	
Approval fiscal year	TR-related Bank lending[a]	TR-related cofinancing	TR-related total project financing[b]	Cost of trade actions[c]	TR-cost / TR-related financing (XII/XI)	Total Bank lending of evaluated projects[e]	Est. Bank share of TR-cost/total Bank lending (XII*XIII/XIV)[d, e]
1987–94	30,433	10,507	40,940	21,738	53%	142,335	8.1%
1995–99	14,834	7,643	22,477	10,172	45%	72,529	6.3%
2000–04	6,877	3,822	10,700	6,309	59%	21,688	17.2%
1987–2004	**52,144**	**21,972**	**74,117**	**38,219**	**52%**	**236,578**	**8.3%**

Source: Trade Assistance Evaluation Database.

a. Total lending in projects that contain trade-related components.

b. World Bank lending plus cofinancing, including government's contributions to Investment and technical assistance project costs.

c. Sum of XV to XX (table C2.3). This column differs from XI (table C2.2) as it only captures the share of multi-sector lending operations related to trade actions.

d. This ratio was not calculated using the exact amount of Bank funds that supported trade actions, but an estimation based on the share of project costs devoted to trade accounts.

e. Total may not add up due to rounding.

Table C2.3: World Bank Trade-Related Projects (cost of trade actions in US$ million)

	XV	XVI	XVII	XVIII	IXX	XX	XXI
		Trade facilitation		Trade financing			
Approval fiscal year	Trade liberalization	Institutional	Physical infrastructure[a]	Public	Private	TA for WTO accession/ negotiations	Total cost of trade actions[b]
1987–94	6,453	1,880	2,140	4,996	6,607	14	22,091
1995–99	1,562	1,159	4,511	212	2,726	1	10,172
2000–04	196	1,153	4,418	140	395	6	6,309
1987–2004	**8,212**	**4,192**	**11,069**	**5,349**	**9,728**	**21**	**38,571**

Source: Trade Assistance Evaluation Database.

a. Includes only lending components for physical trade facilities in projects that have also other trade-related actions.

b. Sum of XV to XX (Table C2.3). This column differs from XI (table C2.2) as it only captures the share of multi-sector lending operations related to trade actions.

Figure C2.1: Ratings of Projects with Trade Components > 80 percent, 1987–2004

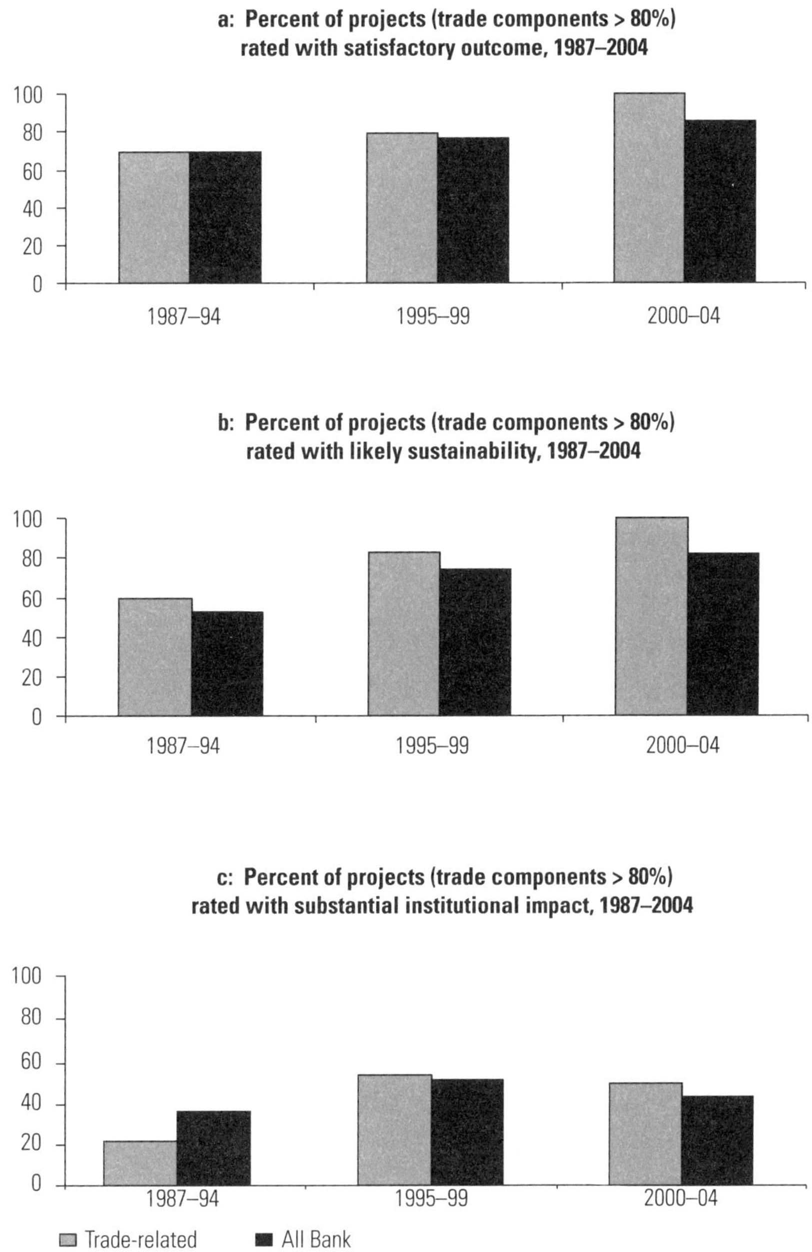

Source: Trade Assistance Evaluation Database.

Table C2.4: IEG Ratings of Projects with Trade Components > 80 percent[a] (number of projects)

	Approval fiscal year			
	1987–94	1995–99	2000–04	1987–2004
Number of IEG evaluated projects with trade components > 80%	75	24	2	101
IEG ratings of trade-related projects (%)				
Satisfactory outcome[b]	69	79	100	72
Likely sustainability[c]	60	83	100	66
Substantial institutional development impact[d]	22	54	50	30
Satisfactory Bank performance	62	83	100	70
Satisfactory borrower performance	64	75	100	68
Number of TAE evaluated projects with trade components > 80%	42	8	0	50
TAE implicit ratings of trade components (%)[e]				
Satisfactory outcome	74	88	NA	76
Likely sustainability	58	88	NA	63
Substantial institutional development impact	15	43	NA	20
Satisfactory Bank performance	65	100	NA	73
Satisfactory borrower performance	83	71	NA	80
TAE satisfactory outcome by area (implicit, %)				
Trade liberalization	93	50	NA	88
Institutional	26	50	NA	30
Physical infrastructure	100	100	NA	100
Public financing	64	100	NA	69
Private financing	59	67	NA	60
TA for WTO accession/negotiations	NA	NA	NA	NA
Mitigating measures	100	0	NA	100
Memo:				
1987–2004				
Satisfactory outcome	70	77	85	73
Likely sustainability	53	74	82	61
Substantial institutional development impact	37	52	44	42
Satisfactory Bank performance	71	79	88	76
Satisfactory borrower performance	66	74	79	70

Source: Trade Assistance Evaluation Project Database.

a. TAE evaluations based on 494 projects. Percentages are calculated based on the total number of evaluated projects for each category, which may be lower than the total evaluated projects shown.

b. Satisfactory refers to Highly Satisfactory, Satisfactory, and Marginally/Moderately Satisfactory.

c. Likely refers to Likely and Highly Likely.

d. Substantial refers to Substantial and High.

e. Implicit ratings from IEG project documents, estimated under the TAE. TAE ratings could not be extracted for all evaluated projects.

Figure C2.2: Ratings of Projects with 80 percent > Trade Components > 50 percent, 1987–04

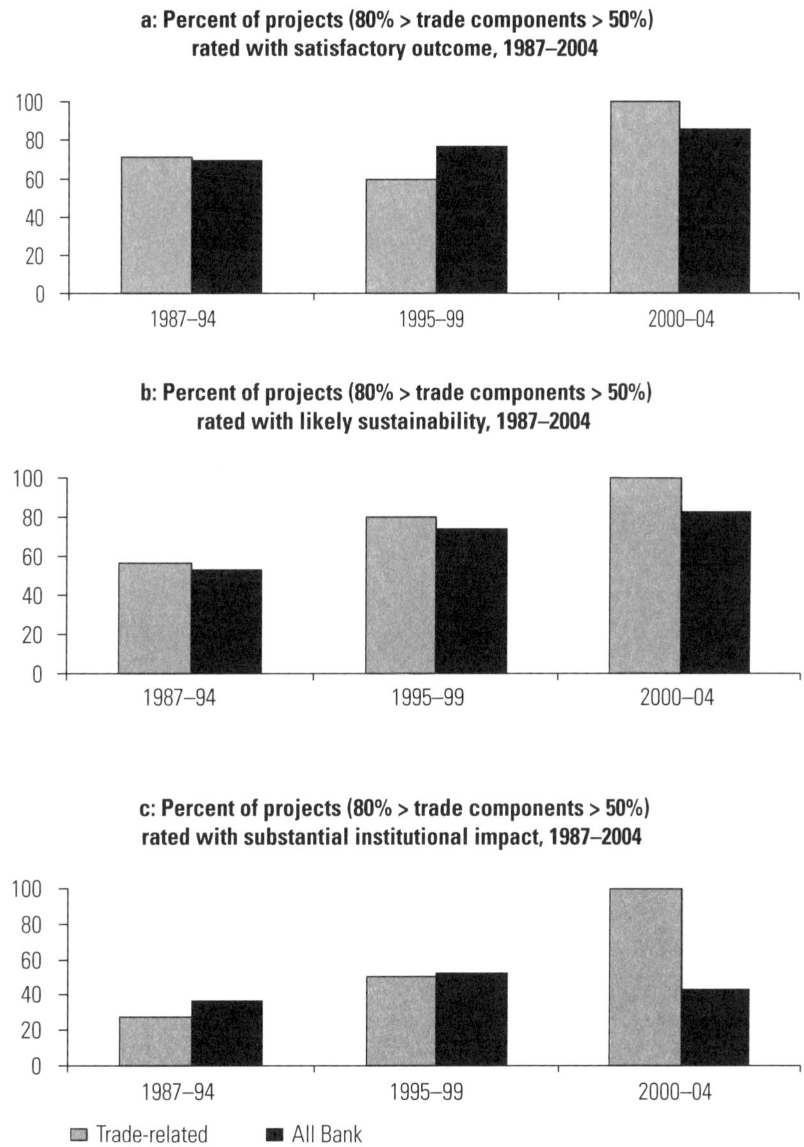

Source: Trade Assistance Evaluation Project Database.

Table C2.5: IEG Ratings of Projects with 80 percent >Trade Components > 50 percent[a] (number of projects)

	Approval fiscal year			
	1987–94	1995–99	2000–04	1987–2004
Number of IEG evaluated projects with 80 % > trade components > 50%	24	5	2	31
IEG ratings of trade-related projects (%)				
Satisfactory outcome[b]	71	60	100	71
Likely sustainability[c]	57	80	100	63
Substantial institutional development impact[d]	27	50	100	36
Satisfactory Bank performance	63	80	100	73
Satisfactory borrower performance	0	67	100	50
Number of TAE evaluated projects with 80% > trade components > 50%	21	4	0	25
TAE implicit ratings of trade components (%)[e]				
Satisfactory outcome	76	100	NA	80
Likely sustainability	60	100	NA	65
Substantial institutional development impact	17	100	NA	21
Satisfactory Bank performance	63	100	NA	67
Satisfactory borrower performance	88	100	NA	78
TAE satisfactory outcome by area (implicit, %)				
Trade liberalization	77	100	NA	82
Institutional	54	100	NA	60
Physical infrastructure	75	67	NA	71
Public financing	100	0	NA	100
Private financing	40	0	NA	40
TA for WTO accession/negotiations	0	0	NA	0
Mitigating measures	0	0	NA	0
Memo:				
1987–2004				
Satisfactory outcome	70	77	85	73
Likely sustainability	53	74	82	61
Substantial institutional development impact	37	52	44	42
Satisfactory Bank performance	71	79	88	76
Satisfactory borrower performance	66	74	79	70

Source: Trade Assistance Evaluation Project Database.

a. TAE evaluations based on 494 projects. Percentages are calculated based on the total number of evaluated projects for each category, which may be lower than the total evaluated projects shown.

b. Satisfactory refers to Highly Satisfactory, Satisfactory, and Marginally/Moderately Satisfactory.

c. Likely refers to Likely and Highly Likely.

d. Substantial refers to Substantial and High.

e. Implicit ratings from IEG project documents, estimated under the TAE. TAE ratings could not be extracted for all evaluated projects.

Table C2.6: IEG Ratings of Trade-Related Projects[a] (total project cost in US$ million)

	Approval fiscal year			
	1987–94	1995–99	2000–04	1987–2004
Cost of IEG evaluated trade-related projects	40,011	15,748	2,936	58,696
IEG ratings of trade-related projects (%)				
Satisfactory outcome[b]	74	61	94	71
Likely sustainability[c]	62	69	93	65
Substantial institutional development impact[d]	41	39	32	40
Satisfactory Bank performance	67	76	98	73
Satisfactory borrower performance	66	55	94	64
Cost of TAE evaluated trade-related projects	29,952	10,206	60	40,218
TAE implicit ratings of trade components (%)[e]				
Satisfactory outcome	78	96	100	83
Likely sustainability	57	62	100	58
Substantial institutional development impact	38	54	0	41
Satisfactory Bank performance	73	92	0	76
Satisfactory borrower performance	79	87	100	81
TAE satisfactory outcome by area (implicit, %)				
Trade liberalization	86	95	100	89
Institutional	66	97	0	75
Physical infrastructure	79	43	0	63
Public financing	77	100	0	79
Private dinancing	60	82	0	61
TA for WTO accession/negotiations	0	0	0	0
Mitigating measures	100	55	0	86
Memo:				
1987–2004				
Satisfactory outcome	77	75	96	78
Likely sustainability	64	77	92	70
Substantial institutional development impact	43	48	55	46
Satisfactory Bank performance	75	84	97	81
Satisfactory borrower performance	72	73	96	75

Source: Trade Assistance Evaluation Project Database.

a. TAE evaluations based on 494 projects. Percentages are calculated based on the total number of evaluated projects for each category which may be lower that the total evaluated projects shown.

b. Satisfactory refers to Highly Satisfactory, Satisfactory, and Marginally/Moderately Satisfactory.

c. Likely refers to Likely and Highly Likely.

d. Substantial refers to Substantial and High.

e. Implicit ratings from IEG project documents, estimated under the TAE. TAE ratings could not be extracted for all evaluated projects.

Table C2.7: IEG Ratings of Projects with Trade Components > 80 percent[a] (project cost in US$ million)

	Approval fiscal year			
	1987–94	1995–99	2000–04	1987–2004
Cost of IEG evaluated projects with trade components > 80%				
IEG ratings of trade-related projects (%)				
Satisfactory outcome[b]	66	86	100	70
Likely sustainability[c]	61	85	100	66
Substantial institutional development impact[d]	25	79	17	35
Satisfactory Bank performance	64	87	100	71
Satisfactory borrower performance	65	84	100	71
Cost of TAE evaluated projects with trade components > 80%	9,027	547	0	9,574
TAE implicit ratings of trade components (%)[e]				
Satisfactory outcome	70	95	NA	71
Likely sustainability	56	95	NA	58
Substantial institutional development impact	15	50	NA	16
Satisfactory Bank performance	72	100	NA	74
Satisfactory borrower performance	80	88	NA	80
TAE satisfactory outcome by area (implicit, %)				
Trade liberalization	86	57	NA	84
Institutional	61	100	NA	63
Physical infrastructure	100	100	NA	100
Public financing	76	100	NA	78
Private financing	54	82	NA	55
TA for WTO accession/negotiations	0	0	NA	0
Mitigating measures	100	0	NA	100
Memo:				
1987–2004				
Satisfactory outcome	77	75	96	78
Likely sustainability	64	77	92	70
Substantial institutional development impact	43	48	55	46
Satisfactory Bank performance	75	84	97	81
Satisfactory borrower performance	72	73	96	75

Source: Trade Assistance Evaluation Project Database.

a. TAE evaluations based on 494 projects. Percentages are calculated based on the total number of evaluated projects for each category which may be lower that the total evaluated projects shown.

b. Satisfactory refers to Highly Satisfactory, Satisfactory, and Marginally/Moderately Satisfactory.

c. Likely refers to Likely and Highly Likely.

d. Substantial refers to Substantial and High.

e. Implicit ratings from IEG project documents, estimated under the TAE. TAE ratings could not be extracted for all evaluated projects.

Table C2.8: IEG Ratings of Projects with 80 percent > Trade Components > 50 percent[a] (project cost in US$ million)

	Approval fiscal year			
	1987–94	1995–99	2000–04	1987–2004
Cost of IEG evaluated projects with 80% > trade components > 50%	3,953	1,096	105	5,154
IEG ratings of trade-related projects (%)				
Satisfactory outcome[b]	71	36	100	64
Likely sustainability[c]	69	90	100	74
Substantial institutional development impact[d]	67	31	100	61
Satisfactory Bank performance	35	90	100	68
Satisfactory borrower performance	60	27	100	44
Cost of TAE evaluated projects with 80% > trade components > 50%	**4,017**	**1,074**	**0**	**5,091**
TAE implicit ratings of trade components (%)[e]				
Satisfactory outcome	73	100	n.a.	79
Likely sustainability	59	100	n.a.	66
Substantial institutional development impact	29	100	n.a.	31
Satisfactory Bank performance	70	100	n.a.	78
Satisfactory borrower performance	82	100	n.a.	66
TAE satisfactory outcome by area (implicit , %)				
Trade liberalization	76	100	n.a.	82
Institutional	46	100	n.a.	52
Physical infrastructure	80	53	n.a.	71
Public financing	100	0	n.a.	100
Private financing	57	0	n.a.	57
TA for WTO accession/negotiations	0	0	n.a.	0
Mitigating measures	0	0	n.a.	0
Memo:				
IEG ratings for all Bank projects (%)				
Satisfactory outcome	70	77	85	73
Likely sustainability	53	74	82	61
Substantial institutional development impact	37	52	44	42
Satisfactory Bank performance	71	79	88	76
Satisfactory borrower performance	66	74	79	70

Source: Trade Assistance Evaluation Project Database.

a. TAE evaluations based on 494 projects. Percentages are calculated based on the total number of evaluated projects for each category which may be lower that the total evaluated projects shown.

b. Satisfactory refers to Highly Satisfactory, Satisfactory, and Marginally/Moderately Satisfactory.

c. Likely refers to Likely and Highly Likely.

d. Substantial refers to Substantial and High.

e. Implicit ratings from IEG project documents, estimated under the TAE. TAE ratings could not be extracted for all evaluated projects.

Table C2.9a: Trade-Related Projects by Region (number of projects)

Region	Fiscal year of approval			
	1987–94	1995–99	2000–04	1987–2004
Africa	96	55	51	202
East Asia and Pacific	20	13	7	40
Europe and Central Asia	34	50	28	112
Latin America and the Caribbean	60	13	13	86
Middle East and North Africa	22	12	8	42
South Asia	15	3	9	27
Total	247	146	116	509

Source: Trade Assistance Evaluation Project Database.

Table C2.9b: Average Number of Trade-Related Projects per Bank Client with Trade Loan by Region (number of projects)

Region	Fiscal year of approval			
	1987–94	1995–99	2000–04	1987–2004
Africa	2	1	1	5
East Asia and Pacific	2	1	1	3
Europe and Central Asia	1	2	1	4
Latin America and the Caribbean	3	1	1	4
Middle East and North Africa	3	2	1	5
South Asia	2	0	1	3
Total	2	1	1	4

Source: Trade Assistance Evaluation Project Database.

Table C2.10: Trade-Related Projects by Region (project cost in US$ million)[a]

Region	Fiscal year of approval			
	1987–94	1995–99	2000–04	1987–2004
Africa	9,437	6,738	4,939	21,114
East Asia and Pacific	4,969	4,424	1,121	10,514
Europe and Central Asia	9,156	6,261	1,473	16,890
Latin America and the Caribbean	9,242	3,260	1,076	13,578
Middle East and North Africa	3,689	1,518	838	6,045
South Asia	4,447	277	1,252	5,976
Total[b]	40,940	22,477	10,700	74,117

Source: Trade Assistance Evaluation Project Database.

a. Represents total project costs of which trade-related portions is a component.

b. Total may not add up due to rounding.

APPENDIX C3: CHANGES IN THE FOCUS OF TRADE CONDITIONALITY

Between 1987 and 1990, the main focus of Bank trade policy advice was on import-related policies, which comprised almost half of all lending conditions (or 6.4 conditions on average per loan).[1] Within the imports category, conditions related to quantitative restrictions were most frequent, followed by those associated with tariff reform. The next most important conditions were industrial policies (in Africa, East Asia, and Middle East and North Africa) and those related to exports (Latin America). South Asia was an exception to the pattern, its loans focused heavily on industrial policy, with as many conditions in that area as all the other areas combined (figure C3.1).

Over the next decade, as adjustment lending peaked and countries became more open, the emphasis shifted toward industrial policies, though reforming import policies remained important, notably in Latin America and South Asia. In almost all regions, the emphasis on industrial policies was greater between 1991 and 1999 compared to the earlier period; the exception was South Asia. Conditionality in this period reflected the importance the Bank placed on increasing enterprise efficiency resulting in continuing and expanding privatization as a priority. Actions related to privatization (general privatization strategies, initiating privatization of state-owned exporters) and investment promotion (legislation related to investment codes, streamlining business regulations and incentive, strengthening investment promotion institutions, liberalizing foreign investment) accounted for over half of all conditions related to industrial policy. The exception to the pattern was South Asia where a gradual approach meant still significant outstanding reforms remained on the import side.

In the five most recent years, trade-related conditions have been quite diverse across regions. Industrial policy has been prominent in three regions (East Asia and Middle East and North Africa), while conditions related to export incentives have been more prominent in Africa, but overall no clear pattern emerges. This could be in part due to the relatively small size of the sample during this period (20 lending operations), which renders regional breakdowns less informative.

Conditions related to the exchange rate and foreign exchange rate management were the least frequent as a share of all conditions (7 percent) throughout the period. The numbers were likely to have been biased downwards, however, by two factors. First, for a major group of Bank's clients—12 French-speaking West African countries—the tying of their currency (the CFA franc) to the French franc meant they had no flexibility to adjust the exchange rate even when doing so was warranted by economic factors. Second, the steps involved in reforming exchange rate regimes were often less complex and thus fewer conditions would be associated with them. In recent years, exchange rate–related conditionality has been absent, reflecting the overwhelming move towards market-determined exchange rate regimes.

Figure C3.1: Focus of Trade Conditions in Adjustment Loans Over Time, 1987–2004

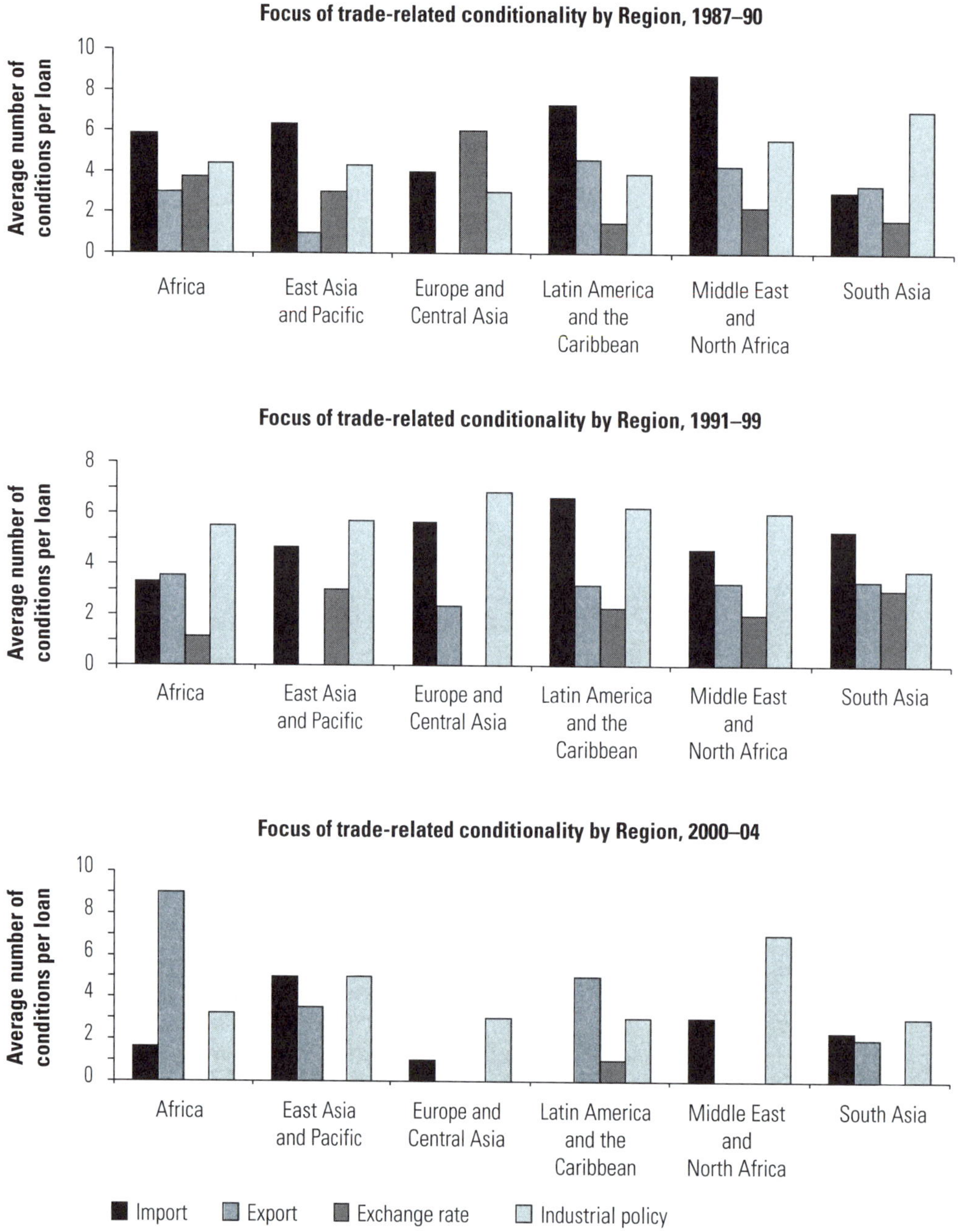

Source: Tsikata (2005).

APPENDIX C4: IMPLEMENTATION OF CONDITIONS

Table C4.1: Implementation of Conditions

Region/country	Overall policy implementation rating	Time period covered	Number of operations evaluated
Africa			
Burkina Faso	Good	2000–00	1
Burundi	Poor	1992–95	1
Cape Verde	Good	2002–?	1
Central Africa	Good	1988–90	1
Ethiopia	Good	2002–?	1
Madagascar	Good	1987–94	2
Malawi	Moderate	1988–01	4
Mali	Good	1991–01	2
Mauritania	Good	2000–01	1
Mauritius	Moderate	1987–89	1
Mozambique	Good	1988–99	3
Niger	Moderate	1999–03	2
Nigeria	Moderate–	1987–92	2
Senegal	Poor	1995–?	3
Tanzania	Moderate	1987–00	4
Zambia	Good	1991–?	6
Zimbabwe	Moderate+	1992–98	2
East Asia and Pacific			
Cambodia	Moderate	2000–?	1
Indonesia	Good	1999–99	1
Papua New Guinea	Poor	1996–97	1
Philippines	Good	1987–95	2
Vietnam	Good	1995–?	2
Europe and Central Asia			
Bulgaria	Good	1992–?	3
Georgia	Moderate	1998–99	1
Kazakhstan	Good	1994–97	1
Macedonia	Good	1997–99	1
Romania	Moderate	1992–98	2
Yugoslavia, Former	Good	1990–92	1

(*Table continues on the following page.*)

Table C4.1: Implementation of Conditions (continued)

Region/country	Overall policy implementation rating	Time period covered	Number of operations evaluated
Latin America and the Caribbean			
El Salvador	Moderate+	1991–95	2
Guatemala	Good	1993–96	1
Jamaica	Moderate	1987–96	3
Mexico	Good	1987–94	6
Nicaragua	Good	1992–97	2
Panama	Good	1987–99	3
Trinidad and Tobago	Good	1990–93	1
Venezuela	Poor	1989–93	1
Middle East and North Africa			
Egypt	Moderate	1991–94	1
Jordan	Good	1990–93	1
Morocco	Moderate	1998–92	2
Tunisia	Moderate– (moderate going with most recent)	1987–?	4
South Asia			
Bangladesh	Moderate– (moderate going with most recent)	1987–95	2
India	Moderate	1992–93	1
Pakistan	Good	2001–04	2
Sri Lanka	Moderate	1990–95	1

Source: IEG staff assessment.

Note: May not add up to the total number of loans as some loans have not been evaluated, or were evaluated but rated non–evaluable, either because project documents did not contain enough information or because the loan had no legally binding conditionality.

APPENDIX D1: CORE AND NON-CORE TRADE PROJECTS

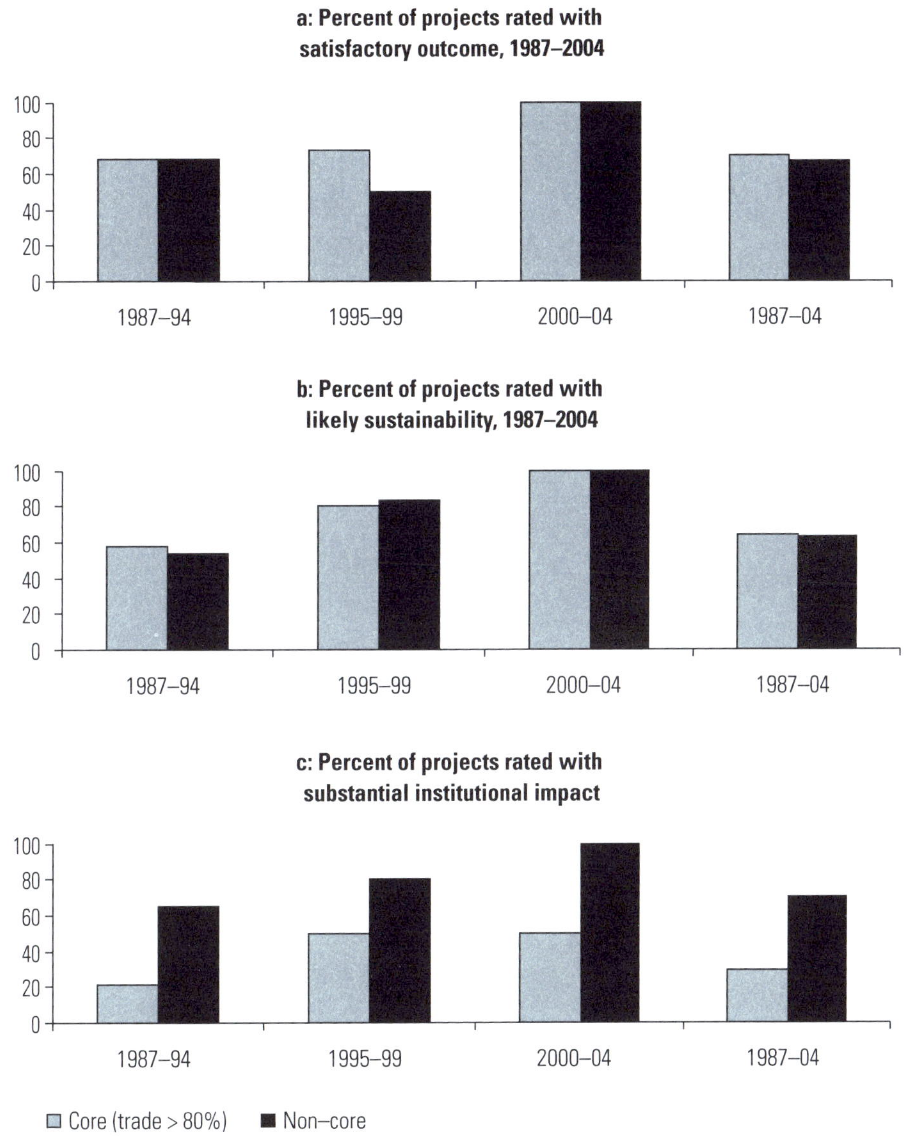

Source: Trade Assistance Evaluation Project Database.

Note: Core = > 80% trade; non-core = < 80%.

APPENDIX D2: IEG PORTFOLIO RATINGS

Table D2.1: IEG Ratings of Projects with Trade Component > 50 percent[a] (number of projects)

	Approval fiscal year			
	1987–94	1995–99	2000–04	1987–2004
Number of IEG evaluated projects with trade component > 50%	**99**	**29**	**4**	**132**
IEG ratings of trade-related projects (%)				
Satisfactory outcome[b]	70	76	100	72
Likely sustainability[c]	59	82	100	65
Substantial institutional development impact[d]	23	54	75	31
Satisfactory Bank performance	62	83	100	70
Satisfactory borrower performance	67	69	100	69
Number of TAE evaluated projects with trade component > 50%	**64**	**12**	**0**	**76**
TAE implicit ratings of trade components (%)[e]				
Satisfactory outcome	75	92	NA	78
Likely sustainability	59	91	NA	64
Substantial institutional development impact	17	50	NA	21
Satisfactory Bank performance	65	100	NA	72
Satisfactory borrower performance	84	75	NA	83
TAE satisfactory outcome by area (implicit, %)				
Trade liberalization	85	83	NA	85
Institutional	58	100	NA	65
Physical infrastructure	88	80	NA	85
Public financing	71	100	NA	74
Private financing	55	67	NA	56
TA for WTO accession/ negotiations	0	0	NA	0
Mitigating measures	100	0	NA	100
Memo: 1987–2004				
Satisfactory outcome	70	77	85	73
Likely sustainability	53	74	82	61
Substantial institutional development impact	37	52	44	42
Satisfactory Bank performance	71	79	88	76
Satisfactory borrower performance	66	74	79	70

Source: Data on all World Bank projects.

a. TAE evaluations based on a subset of 494 projects. Percentages are calculated based on the total number of evaluated projects for each category, which may be lower than the total evaluated projects shown.

b. Satisfactory refers to Highly Satisfactory, Satisfactory, and Marginally/Moderately Satisfactory.

c. Likely refers to Likely and Highly Likely.

d. Substantial refers to Substantial and High.

e. Implicit ratings from IEG project documents, estimated under the TAE. TAE ratings could not be extracted for all evaluated projects.

APPENDIX D3: TRADE-RELATED INVESTMENT PROJECTS

Table D3.1: Approved Amounts for Customs Components of Technical Assistance Projects, Fiscal Years 1982–2004 (US$ million)

Region	1982–86	1987–91	1992–96	1997–2002	2003–04	1982–2004
Africa	0.2	8.6	5.3	11.7		25.8
East Asia and Pacific			20.3	1.1		21.4
Europe and Central Asia		0.3	48.2	164.5	11.0	224.0
Latin America and the Caribbean	2.6	1.2		22.0	0.8	26.6
Middle East and North Africa			3.8	9.0	29.2	42.0
South Asia				10.5	31.0	41.5
Total	2.8	10.1	77.6	218.8	72.0	381.3

Sources: 1982–2002: Customs Modernization Handbook; 2003–2004: IEG staff compilations from Trade Assistance Evaluation Database (project documents).

Table D3.2a: Summary of Objectives, Fiscal Years 1982–2004 (number of projects)

Objective	1982–93	1994–2002	2003–04	1982–2004
Revenue enhancement	1	9	2	12
Trade facilitation	3	17	5	25
Security	0	0	0	0
Strengthening customs agency	8	19	3	30
Integrity	1	3	1	5
Improving compliance	1	11	2	14
Improving trader services	0	13	0	13
Participation of stakeholders	0	0	0	0

Sources: 1982–2002: Customs Modernization Handbook; 2003–2004: IEG staff compilations from Trade Assistance Evaluation Database (project documents).

Table D3.2b: Summary of Objectives, Fiscal Years 1982–2004 (number of projects, annual averages)

Objective	1982–93	1994–2002	2003–04	1982–2004
Revenue enhancement	0.1	1.0	1.0	0.5
Trade facilitation	0.3	1.9	2.5	1.1
Security	0.0	0.0	0.0	0.0
Strengthening customs agency	0.7	2.1	1.5	1.3
Integrity	0.1	0.3	0.5	0.2
Improving compliance	0.1	1.2	1.0	0.6
Improving trader services	0.0	1.4	0.0	0.6
Participation of stakeholders	0.0	0.0	0.0	0.0

Sources: 1982–2002: Customs Modernization Handbook; 2003–2004: IEG staff compilations from Trade Assistance Evaluation Database (project documents).

Table D3.3a: Performance Indicators, Fiscal Years 1982–2004 (number of projects)

Indicator	1982–93	1994–2002	2003–04	1982–2004
Efficiency-Intended Results				
Revenue collected per customs staff	0	8	2	10
Total customs agency costs compared to revenue collected	0	7	2	9
Salaries compared to revenue collected	0	7	2	9
Trade volume per number of staff	0	8	2	10
Annual number of declarations per customs staff	1	9	1	11
Effectiveness-Intended Results				
Release time (import clearance time)	1	12	3	16
Physical inspection and introduction of risk management	0	14	2	16
Trade community information	0	4	2	6
Irregularities per number of examinations	0	8	2	10
Surveyed occurrence of corruption/integrity	0	2	2	4
More effective physical inspections	0	4	1	5
Rejection of incomplete or inaccurate declarations	0	1	0	1
Timely and accurate production of trade statistics	0	2	0	2

Sources: 1982–2002: Customs Modernization Handbook; 2003–2004: IEG staff compilations from Trade Assistance Evaluation Database (project documents).

Table D3.3b: Performance Indicators, Fiscal Years 1982–2004 (number of projects, annual averages)

Indicator	1982–93	1994–2002	2003–04	1982–2004
Efficiency-Intended Results				
Revenue collected per customs staff	0.0	0.9	1.0	0.4
Total customs agency costs compared to revenue collected	0.0	0.8	1.0	0.4
Salaries compared to revenue collected	0.0	0.8	1.0	0.4
Trade volume per number of staff	0.0	0.9	1.0	0.4
Annual number of declarations per customs staff	0.1	1.0	0.5	0.5
Effectiveness-Intended Results				0.0
Release time (import clearance time)	0.1	1.3	1.5	0.7
Physical inspection and introduction of risk management	0.0	1.6	1.0	0.7
Trade community information	0.0	0.4	1.0	0.3
Irregularities per number of examinations	0.0	0.9	1.0	0.4
Surveyed occurrence of corruption/integrity	0.0	0.2	1.0	0.2
More effective physical inspections	0.0	0.4	0.5	0.2
Rejection of incomplete or inaccurate declarations	0.0	0.1	0.0	0.0
Timely and accurate production of trade statistics	0.0	0.2	0.0	0.1

Sources: 1982–2002: Customs Modernization Handbook; 2003–2004: IEG staff compilations from Trade Assistance Evaluation Database (project documents).

Table D3.4: Approved Amounts for Export Processing Zone (EPZ) Components of Trade-Related Projects, 1987–2004 (US$ million)

Region	1987–90	1991–94	1995–99	2000–04
Africa		19.5 (1)	46.1 (4)	16.0 (2)
East Asia and Pacific	NC (1)			
Latin America and the Caribbean	30.0 (2)	0.3 (2)		
Middle East and North Africa			NC (1)	
Total	NC (3)	19.8 (3)	NC (5)	16.0 (2)

Source: IEG Staff compilations from Trade Assistance Evaluation Database (project documents).

Note: Number of Projects in Brackets; NC – Non-calculable.

Table D3.5: Summary of EPZ Component Objectives, 1987–2004

Objective	Number of projects	Percentage share (out of 13 projects)
Establish the physical infrastructure needed to operate free trade zone	5	38.5
Establish/strengthen institutions that manage free trade zones and promote trade and investment through operational support, technical assistance, and consulting services	4	30.8
Finance training activities for sectors directly involved in investment and free zone-related businesses	4	30.8
Remove administrative bottlenecks to facilitate trade	4	30.8
Enhance country's foreign exchange earnings, attract foreign investment (through reducing FDI barriers) and improve the performance of private enterprises	4	30.8
Create employment in the formal sector	3	23.1
Achieve more effective export free trade regime, mainly through privatization of free trade zones	3	23.1
Become globally competitive export and processing center and achieve broad-based, export-oriented, and sustained growth	3	23.1
Pass new legislation, which enables private operation of free trade zones	1	7.7

Source: IEG staff compilations from Trade Assistance Evaluation Database (project documents).

Table D3.6: IEG Ratings of EPZ-Related Projects

	Number of projects	Percent of total
Closed projects	10	76.9
Moderately satisfactory or better rating	8	61.5
Moderately unsatisfactory or lower rating	2	15.4
Unrated	3	23.1
Total	13	100.0

Source: IEG staff compilations from Trade Assistance Evaluation Database (project documents).

Table D3.7: Reasons for Poor Performance

Category	Number of projects
Lack of clearly defined management of EPZ	2
Delayed privatization of EPZ	2
Lack of an appropriate fee structure for EPZ (lack of economic viability)	1
Lack of responsibility for the operation and maintenance of the off-site infrastructure	1
Environmental concerns	1
Absence of sound sector policies (underdeveloped financial system; reliance on a poorly-capitalized banking system, etc.)	1
Lack of effective project management	1

Source: IEG staff compilations from Trade Assistance Evaluation Database (project documents).

Table D3.8: List of Projects with EPZ Components

Country	Project name	Fiscal year of approval	Total project amount (US$ m)	EPZ component (US$ m)	IEG rating
Cape Verde	Capacity Building Project for Private Sector Promotion	1996	11.4	2.8	S
Dominican Republic	Industrial Free Zone Development Project	1989	30.0	30.0	MS
El Salvador	Second Structural Adjustment Loan Project	1994	50.0	NC	HS
Gambia, The	The Gateway Project	2002	16.0	16.0	—
Ghana	First Trade and Investment Promotion Gateway Project	1999	50.5	43.2	—
Indonesia	Second Export Development Project	1988	165.0	NC	S
Jamaica	Private Investment and Export Development Project	1994	35.0	0.3	MU
Jordan	Third Economic Reform & Development Loan Project	1999	120.0	NC	MS
Kenya	Export Development Project	1991	149.0	19.5	MS
Madagascar	Rural Transport Project	2003	80.0	NC	—
Senegal	Private Sector Adjustment and Competitiveness Credit	1995	40.0	NC	S
Uruguay	Second Structural Adjustment Loan Project	1989	140.0	NC	S
Zimbabwe	Enterprise Development Project	1996	70.0	0.1	U

Source: IEG staff compilations from Trade Assistance Evaluation Database (project documents).
Note: NC – Non-calculable.

Table D3.9: Main Accomplishments of EPZ Projects

Country	Results
Cape Verde	• The project was to finance the construction of physical facilities (factory shell) for the establishment of foreign enterprises. Three factory buildings were completed and successfully leased to three export enterprises. The project was able to attract foreign investment and increase foreign exchange earnings. • The project effectively contributed to employment creation in the private sector: the project financed in-factory training of 1,180 workers from nine EPZ companies.
Dominican Republic	• Project financing assisted the development of 13 Free Zones.
Gambia, The	• Through open dialogue with the Government, appropriate policies were established to help ensure the success of the project, e.g. The Gambia Investment Promotion Act 2001, The Gambia Free Zone Act 2001, and The Gambia Divestiture Act 2001. In addition, the Agency in charge of promoting investment and Free Zone-related businesses was established in 2001.
Indonesia	• The Kawasan Berikat Nusantara (KBN) has now three EPZs: Marruda, Cakung, and Tanjung Priok. A one-stop service is provided on these EPZs for approvals and processing of all permits and licenses, such as building construction permits, industrial licenses, limited trade permits, expatriate work permit and all other activities related to services required by investors. • Cakung EPZ was fully utilized by 1990 with 128 investors participating.
Jamaica	• New Free Trade Zone (FTZ) legislation was passed, which enabled private operation of FTZs as well as the establishment of Single Factory Free Zones (SFFZ). • A new private FTZ in the informatics sector was established.
Jordan	• Aqaba was designated as a Special Economic Zone (SEZ) in February 2001. • The SEZ is expected to bring in $6 billion in direct and indirect investments and create 70,000 jobs over the next two decades. • EPZs in Jordan have expanded rapidly, and there are currently 11 zones, employing some 100,000 workers according to ILO data.
Kenya	• EPZ is nearly complete, but only one firm is operational.
Senegal	• The project was implemented largely as scheduled and most of the credit conditions met, including those concerning the EPZs.

Source: IEG staff compilations from Trade Assistance Evaluation Database (project documents).

Table D3.10: Approved Amounts for Matching Grants Component of Trade-Related Projects, 1986–2004 (US$ million)

Region	1986–90	1991–94	1995–99	2000–04
Africa	5.7 (1)	NC (2)	30.7 (4)	
East Asia and Pacific	5.7 (1)			
Europe and Central Asia			3.5 (1)	
Latin America and the Caribbean		4.9 (2)	29.5 (2)	
Middle East and North Africa			19.7 (1)	
South Asia	40.0 (2)	NC (1)	16.4 (1)	
Total	51.4 (4)	NC (5)	99.8 (9)	

Source: ImageBank (World Bank).

Note: Number of Projects in Brackets; NC – Non-calculable.

Table D3.11: Summary of Matching Grants Component Objectives, 1986–2004

Objective	Number of projects	Percent share (out of 18 projects)
Help firms to overcome information and expertise gaps in entering export markets and accelerate country's integration into the world economy	9	50.0
Finance part of the costs of consultant fees and foreign travel associated with the preparation and implementation of export development plan/program	7	38.9
Diversification of the export mix by strengthening marketing, export promotion, technical, and research services through joint public and private efforts	7	38.9
Increase international competitiveness of small and medium scale enterprises	7	38.9
Improve the performance of export-related public agencies (institutional strengthening)	4	22.2
Increase non-traditional (and high value added) exports	3	16.7
Promote diffusion of good technology practices through a Technology Diffusion Scheme which will share the cost in improving the private sector's access to productivity, quality, and design services, and to information on new technologies	1	5.6
Simplify and reduce export procedures	1	5.6
Develop the capacity of the local consulting industry	1	5.6

Source: IEG staff compilations from Trade Assistance Evaluation Database (project documents).

Table D3.12: IEG Ratings of Matching Grants-Related Projects

	Number of projects	Percent of total
Closed projects	13	72.2
Moderately satisfactory or better rating	9	50.0
Moderately unsatisfactory or lower rating	4	22.2
Unrated	5	27.8
Total	18	100.0

Source: IEG staff compilations from Trade Assistance Evaluation Database (project documents).

Table D3.13: Reasons for Poor Performance

	Number of projects
Weak administrative capacity, complex and time-consuming application process, and lengthy processing and procurement procedures	5
Delayed implementation of the matching grants scheme	4
Government's failure to provide timely counterpart funds to reimburse the assisted enterprises	1
The absence of a separate special account to facilitate disbursements under the matching grant schemes	1
Economic crisis/recession in the main export markets and resulting decisions by numerous firms to cancel program participation	1
Difficult internal macro-economic conditions that create uncertainties and discourage private investment	1
Internal political crises and associated with that frequent transfer of the project management	1
Failure to properly supervise the assisted firms and cancel the matching grants of those that were not using them effectively	1
Putting the emphasis on meeting quantitative targets (number of firms and amount of grants approved) at the expense of quality considerations	1

Source: IEG staff compilations from Trade Assistance Evaluation Database (project documents).

Table D3.14: List of Projects with Matching Grants Components

Country	Project name	Fiscal year of approval	Total project amount (US$ m)	Matching grants component (US$ m)	IEG rating
Argentina	Agricultural Services and Institutional Development Project	1991	33.5	2.0	S
Argentina	Enterprise Export Development Project	1996	38.5	27.0	S
Armenia	Enterprise Development Project	1997	16.8	3.5	MU
Bangladesh	Second Industrial Sector Adjustment Credit Project	1993	100.0	NC	S
Bangladesh	Export Diversification Project	1999	32.0	16.4	—
Côte d'Ivoire	Private Sector Development Capacity Building Project	1998	12.0	5.7	—
El Salvador	Competitiveness Enhancement Technical Assistance Project	1996	16.0	2.5	—
India	Industrial Export Project - Engineering Products	1986	250.0	20.0	S
India	Export Development Project	1989	295.0	20.0	U
Indonesia	Export Development Project	1986	64.5	5.7	S
Kenya	Export Development Project	1991	149.0	NC	MS
Mauritius	Technical Assistance Project to Enhance Competitiveness	1994	7.7	3.2	HS
South Africa	Industrial Competitiveness and Job Creation Project	1997	46	20.6	—
Trinidad and Tobago	Business Expansion and Industrial Restructuring Project	1992	27.0	2.9	U
Tunisia	Export Development Project	1999	35.0	19.7	—
Uganda[a]	Private Sector Competitiveness Project	1996	12.3	3.0	S
Zambia	Enterprise Development Project	1997	45.0	0.7	S
Zimbabwe	Enterprise Development Project	1996	70.0	6.4	U

Source: IEG staff compilations from Trade Assistance Evaluation Database (project documents).

Note: NC – Non-calculable; a. – Not in the Trade Projects Database.

Table D3.15: Main Accomplishments

Country	Fiscal year of approval	Results
Argentina	1991	• 150 non-traditional export promotion projects were supported through matching grants which were complemented by over 100 training seminars and courses for producers that contributed to an estimated $220 million in export contracts for 336 firms. • The project contributed to creation of an improved business environment in the agricultural sector, and supported Government's restructuring of the public sector to improve efficiency and to concentrate on services complementary to private activity. • Sustainability is likely for most activities.
Argentina	1996	• The objective of helping to increase the competitiveness of a group of SMEs was substantially achieved. Compared to a control group of similar enterprises not assisted by the program, the assisted enterprises consistently showed that they were more likely to adopt export-oriented measures and had better export performance. • The second objective of improving the performance of export-related public agencies was only partially achieved: while the institutional infrastructure for quality control and for commercial services was strengthened, no progress was made in the areas of export procedures and export promotion policy.
Armenia	1997	• Enterprise Support Fund (ESF) was established. • ESF provided grants to 38 projects, from which 10 projects were financed by the repaid amounts.
Bangladesh	1993	• Policy guidelines for matching grants have been approved by the government.
Bangladesh	1999	• Close to 1,100 projects were implemented for a total amount of $21.9 million. More than 700 firms benefited from the program. Over the period 1999-2003, the number of new countries to which assisted firms were exporting had increased by 36 percent compared to a 14 percent increase for the non-assisted group. The number of types of products exported had risen by 21 percent against an 8 percent decline for the non-assisted firms. However, the average growth rate of Matching Grant Facility (MGF) assisted firms (15 percent) and non-assisted firms (17 percent) was not significantly different. • The evaluations confirmed that the matching grants have had a profound effect on participating firms' performance and potential for growth. One important effect has been the introduction of business and market planning, which very few of the participating firms had experience of prior to preparing the plans for their grant applications. The existence of the MGF has meant that many firms, for the first time, got involved in active overseas marketing, and in using outside expertise for technical and management training, for technical, product and market development, and for International Standards Organisation (ISO) certification. The MGF method ensures that these outsourced services are economically tailored to the needs of the individual firms.
Côte d'Ivoire	1998	• Matching grants totaling some $2.2 million with investments totaling $4.2 million were approved by the Export Promotion Association (APEX-CI), which is high considering the developments during project implementation. The $2.2 million financed some 445 grants to 149 firms and 27 associations. • 115 firms (77 percent) and 20 associations (74 percent) used the support for marketing activities. • Main beneficiaries were firms producing chemical pharmaceutical products (14 percent), agro-industry (12 percent) and services (24 percent); the largest number of associations dealt with tourism related activities (16 percent).
El Salvador	1996	• Between June and December 2002, FOEX (a matching-grant program) approved approximately $300,000 in matching grants. • By June 30, 2004 FOEX had commitments for $863,954 and had reimbursed $505,613.

(*Table continues on the following page.*)

Table D3.15: Main Accomplishments (continued)

Country	Fiscal year of approval	Results
El Salvador (cont.)		• Reports by the Ministry of Economy on a sample of 49 firms, which received FOEX funds, show that they experienced an increase in the value of their exports (fob) from $9.8 million in 2001 to $16.7 million in 2003– a 70 percent increase in exports.
India	1986	• Establishment of the Productivity Fund (PF) and Export Marketing Fund (EMF) to promote export awareness and orientation and help firms in the development of viable export marketing strategies. • These two funds disbursed about $15.6 million consisting of 359 grants to 292 firms (63 firms obtained more than one grant), with an average grant size of about $50,000. • By any performance measure, both the PF and EMF had a highly positive impact. In all sub-sector categories, compound annual growth rates of exports for firms receiving assistance from either of the two funds exceeded the growth rate for the overall sub-sector. Of the 180 firms receiving assistance from the Export Development Fund (EDF), 52 percent were first time exporters. Furthermore, there are indicators that assisted firms improved their internal competitiveness and organizational efficiency.
India	1989	• Establishment of the EDF. The fund provided firms with grant support on a matching basis for a range of preinvestment promotion and marketing activities; one-window clearance through an established steering committee for the various Government approvals required for export marketing and product adaptation activities; and term finance and incremental working capital finance to implement an export development plan.
Kenya	1991	• Up to July 1993, 175 grant-aided projects have been approved, compared to a target for the period of 105. The additional export revenues already achieved by clients stand at $21.7 million, representing a ratio of export revenues to grants of 15:1, substantially over the original target ratio, specified during design, of 2:1 within two years of disbursement. • The Government of Kenya updates indicate that as of 1994, 269 grant-aided projects have been approved and that the revenue ratio is 42:1 from 210 projects whose claims have been processed as of March 1994. The Trade Development Institute (TDI) deserves recognition for the way they have implemented this scheme.
Mauritius	1994	• The Technology Diffusion Scheme (TDS) has realized its overall objective of helping Mauritian firms access specialized technical and marketing know-how. The TDS supported 190 firms which implemented 266 different projects. • The export performance of TDS participant firms surpassed industry averages and the national export growth rate. Exports by TDS participant firms rose by 53 percent compared to overall export increase of 21 percent in 1996 and 3 percent in 1997. • There was also a marked increase in the range of products that are exported.
South Africa	1997	• A total of 1,247 Competitiveness Fund (CF) grants were approved, of which 984 CF grants were paid out fully, and 82 were paid out partially. • Achievements in terms of firms served compare favorably with other programs in the region. In total, 261 Business Development Services (BDS) providers participated in the program and 13 percent of these service providers benefited from the program more than once. In addition, 12 percent of BDS providers involved with the CF program were international firms. • The services provided included production systems development (23.2 percent), in-house activity (11.6 percent), financial/project management (11.6 percent), marketing and intelligence (9.5 percent), human resources and training (5.3 percent), website development (5.3 percent), information technology (IT) system development (5.3 percent), specialist consulting (2.1 percent), and (26.1 percent) for other activities.

Country	Fiscal year of approval	Results
Trinidad and Tobago	1992	• Establishment of the Export Technical Assistance Facility. • The matching grant component assisted 43 recipients to explore and access export markets.
Tunisia	1999	• Export Market Access Fund (EMAF) program has transformed traditional public-sector led export promotion. For the first time the private sector is paying for export services and a core of local consultants has been developed around the EMAF program, which can make these market initiatives sustainable. • The EMAF management team was applauded for its efficiency and responsiveness in proactively assisting clients. Through various seminars and twining arrangement with foreign and local experts, the management team facilitated knowledge transfer about foreign markets and requirements, as well as know-how for potential exporters about the process of exporting • Participants pointed out that they have witnessed a sharp improvement (through EMAF) of export service delivery compared to previous methods.
Zimbabwe	1996	• Under the ZimTrade Matching Grant Scheme, 13 grants were approved and about $1 million had been committed to exporters, SMEs and associations. Approximately 15 percent of the total commitments was disbursed.

Source: IEG staff compilations from Trade Assistance Evaluation Database and project documents.

APPENDIX D4: PROBIT ESTIMATION OF THE DETERMINANTS OF PROJECT OUTCOMES

Table D4.1: Probit Estimation of the Determinants of Project Outcomes

	Dependent variable = IEG outcome ratings		
Since 1995 dummy	0.12	0.11	0.09
	(2.14)**	(2.09)**	(1.94)*
Share of trade actions	0.00	0.00	0.00
	(1.70)*	(1.62)	(1.04)
Value of trade part of the loan	–0.00	–0.00	–0.00
	(1.77)*	(1.83)*	(1.28)
Structural-type dummy	0.21	0.21	1.00
	(3.59)***	(3.52)***	(.)
Income groups	0.26	0.26	
	(3.34)***	(3.43)***	
Africa dummy	–0.19	–0.18	–0.14
	(1.47)	(1.47)	(1.34)
East Asia and Pacific dummy	–0.04	–0.06	0.08
	(0.24)	(0.31)	(0.69)
Europe and Central Asia dummy	–0.47	–0.47	–0.24
	(2.89)***	(2.90)***	(1.88)*
Latin America and the Caribbean dummy	–0.32	–0.31	–0.03
	(1.92)*	(1.89)*	(0.31)
Middle East and North Africa dummy	–0.19	–0.19	0.07
	(1.00)	(1.01)	(0.58)
Conflict 1980s	0.08		
	(1.11)		
Conflict 1990s		0.04	0.01
		(0.74)	(0.27)
Conditionality			–0.92
			(30.41)***
Observations	324	324	324

Source: IEG staff estimation.

Note: Robust z statistics in parentheses. * Significant at 10%; ** significant at 5%; *** significant at 1%.

APPENDIX D5: AGGREGATE ECONOMIC ANALYSIS

Table D5.1: Aggregate Economic Analysis: Overview of Data and Country Classification

Variable		t	All	AFR	EAP	ECA	LAC	MNA	SAR
			Region						
Real exchange rates	REER	0	97.5	94.5	96.9	99.6	101.7	97.3	94.5
		1	86.5	74.1	88.0	120.5	101.5	83.1	74.4
		2	85.6	72.9	86.8	121.2	101.8	83.8	68.3
		3	89.4	73.0	86.5	114.0	113.0	84.5	70.8
Inflation	INF	0	103.5	19.7	7.2	56.3	278.2	5.5	6.9
		1	56.5	25.1	8.7	63.2	128.1	12.1	10.4
		2	48.3	13.7	7.1	80.8	117.7	4.2	9.4
		3	17.0	16.9	7.6	84.7	19.5	4.3	9.2
Fiscal balance/GDP	FBAL	0	–4.3	–5.4	–2.7	–3.1	–2.6	–7.2	–7.9
		1	–3.8	–6.0	–1.8	–3.9	–1.3	–4.6	–6.7
		2	–2.6	–4.0	–1.6	–5.0	–1.0	0.0	–5.4
		3	–2.6	–4.0	0.0	–7.0	–1.2	–2.2	–5.6
Tax revenue/GDP	TXRV	0	13.7	13.1	15.1	11.6	14.2	18.5	10.1
		1	14.3	15.1	15.1	11.8	13.6	20.6	8.4
		2	15.5	16.5	14.9	13.8	14.7	22.9	10.2
		3	16.2	17.0	15.0	16.1	16.0	22.8	10.1
Investment to GDP growth	INVG	0	6.0	10.3	8.7	–7.6	2.2	–0.5	2.0
		1	10.3	10.7	9.5	6.9	10.1	21.5	4.6
		2	9.6	11.7	5.5	5.3	8.7	13.5	7.7
		3	6.1	3.7	8.0	15.5	8.6	–0.3	2.4
Per capita GDP growth	GDPKG	0	0.6	–0.8	4.7	3.6	0.0	–0.3	3.4
		1	1.5	0.6	5.5	1.1	1.6	–3.0	2.7
		2	2.2	1.3	6.1	1.0	1.5	3.1	3.4
		3	2.0	0.7	6.1	4.8	1.9	1.5	2.2
Exports to GDP growth	EXG	0	8.1	4.0	4.9	27.6	11.1	23.1	7.7
		1	8.3	9.5	12.7	8.8	4.4	8.4	12.2
		2	7.4	4.8	6.0	10.8	9.2	6.9	15.0
		3	7.3	8.8	8.6	15.9	5.3	3.5	5.6
Imports to GDP growth	IMG	0	–0.9	–4.1	0.3	8.6	0.9	10.4	–3.3
		1	4.7	2.6	7.0	14.7	6.7	–2.0	4.0
		2	3.7	0.5	6.1	1.1	6.3	1.5	7.1
		3	4.7	1.5	8.1	23.6	7.8	–2.5	0.3
Trade to GDP	OPEN	0	53.0	53.0	51.7	34.8	54.9	90.1	27.2
		1	58.8	63.1	55.1	31.8	54.6	117.0	31.6
		2	62.2	65.4	60.2	35.5	59.6	107.8	39.0
		3	64.4	66.2	69.9	49.4	60.4	107.4	39.6
Current account balance to GDP	CABL	0	–3.6	–4.9	–2.9	0.4	–2.5	–2.2	–4.3
		1	–2.7	–4.2	–2.4	–0.2	–0.9	–2.5	–3.7
		2	–2.7	–3.3	–1.5	–0.7	–1.7	–8.8	–2.8
		3	–3.7	–5.3	–1.5	–1.4	–3.2	–2.7	–1.7

Income		Population Size		Borrower?		Reform pace		Intensity		Initial export structure		
Middle	Low	Large	Small	Yes	No	Fast	Gradual	High	Low	Fuel	Manuf	Other
99.2	95.0	98.4	96.8	97.3	98.1	95.9	98.7	95.5	98.1	97.4	97.2	96.0
95.1	74.7	93.7	81.7	85.4	90.3	86.3	86.7	77.2	89.54	90.9	87.6	78.6
93.7	74.6	94.8	79.5	83.7	92.4	86.6	84.9	71.8	90.12	91.3	77.3	77.7
100.2	74.7	100.0	82.3	86.8	98.6	91.1	88.1	71.7	95.12	98.8	78.0	81.1
165.6	18.6	223.9	23.3	98.4	121.4	161.5	57.2	17.7	131.3	50.3	8.9	20.9
80.0	24.3	104.3	24.6	26.1	162.9	30.8	77.1	26.9	66.09	38.6	11.5	25.3
73.9	13.2	92.1	19.1	19.1	150.6	19.6	71.2	16.6	58.53	28.9	12.6	17.0
17.4	16.3	16.3	17.4	16.8	17.4	16.3	17.5	15.4	17.44	21.6	9.3	16.4
–3.6	–5.2	–4.7	–4.0	–4.5	–3.5	–4.4	–4.2	–5.3	–3.96	–2.3	–8.0	–3.5
–2.3	–5.8	–4.0	–3.6	–4.0	–3.0	–4.6	–3.0	–4.1	–3.64	–2.3	–6.0	–4.3
–1.5	–4.2	–2.8	–2.5	–2.6	–2.5	–3.1	–2.2	–3.4	–2.34	–2.1	–2.7	–2.6
–1.4	–4.2	–1.8	–3.1	–2.7	–2.3	–2.9	–2.3	–4.7	–1.92	0.1	–3.5	–2.7
15.4	11.5	14.4	13.3	13.3	15.4	14.3	13.3	12.4	14.15	16.3	15.3	13.6
15.2	13.2	14.7	14.1	14.2	15.0	14.6	14.1	11.2	15.36	15.1	12.3	14.2
16.1	14.6	14.8	15.9	15.2	16.4	16.0	15.1	12.7	16.37	13.0	15.7	15.7
17.0	15.1	14.6	17.2	16.2	16.3	16.7	15.8	14.5	16.74	12.7	18.2	16.2
1.4	12.2	1.6	8.9	9.0	–4.5	7.1	5.1	5.7	6.055	24.0	21.7	18.3
9.7	11.2	7.3	12.3	11.4	6.7	10.0	10.6	12.2	9.725	23.5	22.2	20.0
7.4	12.8	6.1	11.9	7.7	16.4	10.8	8.7	12.3	8.739	25.0	26.1	21.3
7.9	2.7	8.8	4.2	6.4	5.1	6.7	5.5	7.2	5.786	24.6	25.3	21.9
1.0	–0.1	1.9	–0.3	0.3	1.6	0.2	0.9	–1.3	1.177	–0.5	1.1	0.6
2.0	0.9	2.6	0.8	1.4	2.0	1.9	1.3	1.0	1.711	1.4	0.7	0.7
2.6	1.7	3.1	1.7	2.0	3.1	1.8	2.6	2.1	2.265	3.8	3.3	1.7
2.8	1.0	2.9	1.5	1.9	2.4	1.7	2.3	1.7	2.143	1.1	2.1	1.9
10.7	4.6	9.3	7.3	8.4	7.2	8.0	8.2	6.0	8.787	6.4	9.4	4.5
5.8	11.8	9.5	7.6	8.4	8.1	8.6	8.2	5.4	9.306	12.2	8.3	7.2
8.3	6.1	7.6	7.2	8.2	4.3	7.3	7.4	4.8	8.177	8.7	11.2	6.0
6.3	8.7	8.7	6.4	7.8	5.7	7.0	7.5	5.4	7.92	5.8	6.1	7.6
0.8	–3.2	–2.3	0.1	–0.4	–2.7	–1.3	–0.6	–5.2	0.54	–0.3	2.4	2.6
5.0	4.3	7.0	3.2	4.9	4.1	5.9	3.7	1.7	5.658	8.0	10.2	5.4
5.8	0.9	4.6	3.1	3.3	5.0	2.9	4.3	1.5	4.403	14.9	9.8	6.1
7.2	1.3	9.1	1.8	5.0	3.7	5.9	3.7	3.9	4.991	8.3	6.1	8.0
56.7	47.8	39.8	61.7	51.1	59.6	52.3	53.5	52.0	53.25	44.7	64.5	52.6
59.3	58.1	44.5	68.3	58.1	61.3	57.1	60.1	56.8	59.43	46.5	69.3	58.6
62.9	61.4	47.3	72.2	62.7	60.6	61.0	63.2	60.5	62.81	46.9	77.7	63.1
65.5	63.1	51.3	73.2	65.6	60.4	62.8	65.7	62.2	65.18	46.6	78.7	65.5
–2.5	–5.0	–2.4	–4.4	–4.1	–1.8	–2.8	–4.2	–4.7	–3.22	–0.2	–4.6	–4.3
–1.1	–4.9	–2.3	–3.0	–4.0	1.8	–2.1	–3.2	–3.9	–2.31	–0.9	–2.8	–3.9
–2.0	–3.6	–1.1	–3.8	–3.8	1.0	–1.8	–3.4	–4.6	–2.09	–1.7	–4.2	–3.0
–2.6	–5.1	–2.7	–4.3	–4.7	–0.2	–2.5	–4.6	–7.1	–2.57	–2.6	–1.8	–4.7

(Table continues on the following page.)

Table D5.1: Aggregate Economic Analysis: Overview of Data and Country Classification (continued)

Variable		t	Region						
			All	AFR	EAP	ECA	LAC	MNA	SAR
Terms of trade	TOT	0	99.0	97.8	97.6	100.8	101.5	101.3	94.7
		1	97.9	93.9	95.6	102.4	103.9	102.6	92.2
		2	95.9	93.7	95.6	108.7	100.6	91.2	86.1
		3	94.5	90.2	95.8	102.4	101.1	90.9	85.7
Total external debt to GDP	DEBT	0	79.2	88.0	76.0	46.2	79.4	86.8	37.9
		1	83.7	106.8	57.9	34.8	69.6	143.5	44.0
		2	73.0	97.2	48.9	41.3	57.3	102.4	44.7
		3	66.6	97.5	36.6	43.5	45.4	86.5	41.8
Reserves in months of imports	FXRS	0	2.6	1.7	3.1	2.5	3.3	2.1	3.2
		1	3.3	2.6	2.9	3.2	4.1	2.6	4.2
		2	3.2	2.4	3.3	3.0	3.9	2.9	4.1
		3	3.6	2.9	3.6	3.8	4.2	3.6	4.5

Source: Jinjarak, Salinas and Tsikata (2005).

Note: AFR = Africa; EAP = East Asia and Pacific; ECA = Europe and Central Asia; LAC = Latin America and the Caribbean; MNA = Middle East and North Africa; SAR = South Asia.

t = 0 : 0–2 years before trade reform; t = 1 : 0–2 years after trade reform; t = 2 : 3–5 years after trade reform; t = 3 : 6–8 years after trade reform.

Income		Population Size		Borrower?		Reform pace		Intensity		Initial export structure		
Middle	Low	Large	Small	Yes	No	Fast	Gradual	High	Low	Fuel	Manuf	Other
100.5	97.0	96.4	100.8	98.2	101.9	99.7	98.5	99.0	99.06	98.5	98.1	98.7
101.7	92.7	94.0	100.5	96.4	103.4	98.5	97.4	97.7	97.97	92.0	103.4	97.8
99.5	91.1	94.0	97.3	95.1	98.8	96.8	95.3	97.7	95.39	83.7	95.5	96.2
99.8	87.3	92.8	95.7	93.7	97.4	93.8	95.1	95.4	94.26	79.2	97.3	93.8
68.8	93.4	66.8	87.5	90.4	40.1	75.4	82.3	96.9	73.48	38.6	74.7	90.5
68.1	105.1	66.0	95.5	96.1	40.4	76.3	89.7	99.8	78.52	44.4	85.1	100.5
58.2	93.1	57.3	83.4	83.2	37.2	71.8	73.9	96.5	65.35	41.5	77.4	82.3
48.4	91.5	51.1	77.0	75.1	37.1	64.9	68.0	92.1	58.37	38.8	65.4	76.4
2.9	2.1	2.6	2.6	2.4	3.1	2.6	2.5	2.0	2.723	2.8	2.1	2.5
3.5	3.0	3.0	3.5	2.9	4.5	3.6	3.1	3.0	3.351	3.0	2.5	3.2
3.5	2.7	3.5	2.9	2.8	4.3	3.3	3.1	2.8	3.26	2.9	3.0	2.9
3.9	3.1	3.8	3.5	3.3	4.7	3.9	3.3	3.5	3.619	3.2	3.7	3.3

Table D5.2: Country Groupings

Region		Income		Size by population	
AFR	Cameroon	Low	Cameroon	Small	Cameroon
AFR	Central AFR Rep.	Low	Central AFR Rep.	Small	Central AFR Rep.
AFR	Côte d'Ivoire	Low	Côte d'Ivoire	Small	Chile
AFR	Ghana	Low	Ghana	Small	Costa Rica
AFR	Kenya	Low	India	Small	Côte d'Ivoire
AFR	Lesotho	Low	Kenya	Small	Dominican Rep.
AFR	Madagascar	Low	Lesotho	Small	Ecuador
AFR	Malawi	Low	Madagascar	Small	Ghana
AFR	Mali	Low	Malawi	Small	Honduras
AFR	Mauritius	Low	Mali	Small	Jamaica
AFR	Morocco	Low	Nepal	Small	Jordan
AFR	Niger	Low	Niger	Small	Lesotho
AFR	Nigeria	Low	Nigeria	Small	Madagascar
AFR	Senegal	Low	Pakistan	Small	Malawi
AFR	South Africa	Low	Senegal	Small	Mali
AFR	Tanzania	Low	Tanzania	Small	Mauritius
AFR	Zambia	Low	Vietnam	Small	Nepal
AFR	Zimbabwe	Low	Zambia	Small	Niger
EAP	China	Low	Zimbabwe	Small	Panama
EAP	Indonesia	Middle	Argentina	Small	Paraguay
EAP	Korea, Rep. of	Middle	Brazil	Small	Senegal
EAP	Philippines	Middle	Chile	Small	Trinidad andTobago
EAP	Thailand	Middle	China	Small	Tunisia
EAP	Vietnam	Middle	Colombia	Small	Uruguay
LAC	Argentina	Middle	Costa Rica	Small	Venezuela
LAC	Brazil	Middle	Dominican Rep.	Small	Zambia
LAC	Chile	Middle	Ecuador	Small	Zimbabwe
LAC	Colombia	Middle	Honduras	Large	Argentina
LAC	Costa Rica	Middle	Indonesia	Large	Brazil
LAC	Dominican Rep.	Middle	Jamaica	Large	China
LAC	Ecuador	Middle	Jordan	Large	Colombia
LAC	Honduras	Middle	Korea, Rep. of	Large	India
LAC	Jamaica	Middle	Mauritius	Large	Indonesia
LAC	Mexico	Middle	Mexico	Large	Kenya
LAC	Panama	Middle	Morocco	Large	Korea, Rep. of
LAC	Paraguay	Middle	Panama	Large	Mexico
LAC	Trinidad andTobago	Middle	Paraguay	Large	Morocco
LAC	Uruguay	Middle	Philippines	Large	Nigeria
LAC	Venezuela	Middle	South Africa	Large	Pakistan
ECA	Turkey	Middle	Thailand	Large	Philippines
MNA	Jordan	Middle	Trinidad andTobago	Large	South Africa
MNA	Tunisia	Middle	Tunisia	Large	Tanzania
SAR	India	Middle	Turkey	Large	Thailand
SAR	Nepal	Middle	Uruguay	Large	Turkey
SAR	Pakistan	Middle	Venezuela	Large	Vietnam

Source: WDI, Staff assessment.

Note: See note to table D5.1.

Trade-related loan borrower?		**Pace of trade reform**		**Intensity of trade reform**	
No	Brazil	Gradual	Brazil	Low	Argentina
No	Central AFR Rep.	Gradual	China	Low	Brazil
No	China	Gradual	Costa Rica	Low	Chile
No	Ecuador	Gradual	Côte d'Ivoire	Low	Costa Rica
No	Korea, Rep. of	Gradual	Dominican Rep.	Low	Côte d'Ivoire
No	Lesotho	Gradual	India	Low	Dominican Rep.
No	Paraguay	Gradual	Indonesia	Low	Ecuador
No	South Africa	Gradual	Jamaica	Low	Ghana
No	Trinidad andTobago	Gradual	Jordan	Low	India
No	Venezuela	Gradual	Kenya	Low	Indonesia
Yes	Argentina	Gradual	Madagascar	Low	Jordan
Yes	Cameroon	Gradual	Malawi	Low	Kenya
Yes	Chile	Gradual	Mauritius	Low	Korea, Rep. of
Yes	Colombia	Gradual	Morocco	Low	Lesotho
Yes	Costa Rica	Gradual	Nepal	Low	Madagascar
Yes	Côte d'Ivoire	Gradual	Niger	Low	Mali
Yes	Dominican Rep.	Gradual	Nigeria	Low	Mauritius
Yes	Ghana	Gradual	Panama	Low	Mexico
Yes	Honduras	Gradual	Paraguay	Low	Morocco
Yes	India	Gradual	Senegal	Low	Nepal
Yes	Indonesia	Gradual	Tanzania	Low	Nigeria
Yes	Jamaica	Gradual	Thailand	Low	Pakistan
Yes	Jordan	Gradual	Tunisia	Low	Paraguay
Yes	Kenya	Gradual	Turkey	Low	Philippines
Yes	Madagascar	Gradual	Uruguay	Low	South Africa
Yes	Malawi	Fast	Argentina	Low	Tanzania
Yes	Mali	Fast	Cameroon	Low	Thailand
Yes	Mauritius	Fast	Central AFR Rep.	Low	Trinidad andTobago
Yes	Mexico	Fast	Chile	Low	Tunisia
Yes	Morocco	Fast	Colombia	Low	Turkey
Yes	Nepal	Fast	Ecuador	Low	Uruguay
Yes	Niger	Fast	Ghana	Low	Venezuela
Yes	Nigeria	Fast	Honduras	Low	Vietnam
Yes	Pakistan	Fast	Korea, Rep. of	Low	Zimbabwe
Yes	Panama	Fast	Lesotho	High	Cameroon
Yes	Philippines	Fast	Mali	High	Central AFR Rep.
Yes	Senegal	Fast	Mexico	High	China
Yes	Tanzania	Fast	Pakistan	High	Colombia
Yes	Thailand	Fast	Philippines	High	Honduras
Yes	Tunisia	Fast	South Africa	High	Jamaica
Yes	Turkey	Fast	Trinidad andTobago	High	Malawi
Yes	Uruguay	Fast	Venezuela	High	Niger
Yes	Vietnam	Fast	Vietnam	High	Panama
Yes	Zambia	Fast	Zambia	High	Senegal
Yes	Zimbabwe	Fast	Zimbabwe	High	Zambia

Table D5.2a: Real GDP per Capita Growth after Trade Reform

Dependent variable: changes in growth rates of real GDP per capita	**Basic DD estimation**	**Correction for panel sample selection**	
		Bank assistance	**No Bank assistance**
Lagged growth rate of real GDP per capita	–0.68	–1.05	–0.98
	(7.90) ***	(12.38) ***	(18.49) ***
0–2 yrs since trade reform	1.10	1.08	1.06
	(1.57)	(1.33)	(0.64)
3–5 yrs since trade reform	1.24	1.91	1.72
	(2.01) *	(2.60) **	(2.38) **
6–8 yrs since trade reform	0.83	2.40	0.46
	(1.08)	(2.62) **	(0.50)
Inflation reduction	–0.64	1.08	–0.76
	(1.25)	(1.58)	(0.77)
Trade-assistance dummy	–0.50		
	(0.62)		
Inverse Mills ratio to control for selection of trade		–0.36	0.96
assistance and unobserved heterogeneity		(0.86)	(1.90) *
Observations	450	350	100
Adjusted R–squared	0.34	0.53	0.48
Test for homosckedasticity (p–value)	0.11	0.09	0.06
Test for normality of residuals (p–value)	0.00	0.00	0.00

Source: Jinjarak, Salinas, and Tsikata 2005.

Note: * 10 %; ** 5 %; *** 1 %.

Table D5.2b: Growth of Imports after Trade Reforms

Dependent variable: changes in growth rates of imports	Basic DD estimation	Correction for panel sample selection: Bank assistance	Correction for panel sample selection: No Bank assistance
Lagged growth rate of imports	–0.95	–1.00	–1.15
	(20.71) ***	(15.39) ***	(22.16) ***
0–2 yrs since trade reform	9.45	8.26	11.43
	(2.79) ***	(1.90) *	(2.94) **
3–5 yrs since trade reform	14.85	14.37	10.77
	(2.79) ***	(2.25) **	(1.15)
6–8 yrs since trade reform	22.37	23.93	8.56
	(2.79) ***	(2.54) **	(0.66)
REER changes	0.40	0.31	0.53
	(4.44) ***	(2.79) ***	(3.64) ***
Lagged capita GDP growth rates	1.05	1.19	1.32
	(5.37) ***	(4.20) ***	(2.69) **
Time trend	–2.54	–2.92	0.12
	(2.68) **	(2.68) **	(0.08)
Trade-assistance dummy	2.18		
	(1.32)		
Inverse Mills ratio to control for selection of trade assistance		–0.17	–0.33
and unobserved heterogeneity		(0.11)	(0.10)
Observations	450	350	100
Adjusted R-squared	0.51	0.52	0.60
Test for homosckedasticity (p-value)	0.02	0.00	0.78
Test for normality of residuals (p-value)	0.00	0.00	0.00

Source: Jinjarak, Salinas, and Tsikata 2005.

Note: * 10 %; ** 5 %; *** 1 %.

Table D5.2c: Exports Growth after Trade Reforms

Dependent variable: changes in growth rates of exports	Basic DD estimation	Correction for panel sample selection: Bank assistance	Correction for panel sample selection: No Bank assistance
Lagged growth rate of exports	–0.83	–0.96	–1.05
	(13.79) ***	(19.41) ***	(7.37) ***
3–5 yrs since trade reform	1.71	2.59	0.38
	(1.24)	(1.70) *	(0.15)
6–8 yrs since trade reform	1.34	2.59	–0.55
	(1.01)	*(1.97)	(0.22)
REER changes	–0.13	–0.16	–0.08
	(2.04) **	(1.59)	(1.86)
Lagged REER changes	–0.08	–0.12	–0.15
	(1.40)	(1.90) *	(1.20)
Infrastructure	1.70	4.17	–11.16
	(0.70)	(3.82) ***	(0.15)
Trade–assistance dummy	0.23		
	(0.17)		
Inverse Mills ratio to control for selection of trade		–1.70	0.30
assistance and unobserved heterogeneity		(1.46)	(0.29)
Observations	346	270	76
Adjusted R-squared	0.44	0.48	0.50
Test for homosckedasticity (p-value)	0.72	0.65	0.29
Test for normality of residuals (p-value)	0.00	0.01	0.01

Source: Jinjarak, Salinas, and Tsikata 2005.

Note: * 10 %; ** 5 %; *** 1 %.

Table D5.2d: Export Growth and Increased Value Added, 1983–2003 (annual increase, %)

Country	Manufactured exports adjusted for purchasing power 1	Total exports adjusted by purchasing power 2	Value added by manufacture 3	Total value added 4
High export growth	**11.9**	**12.8**	**6.6**	**5.5**
Bangladesh	11.5	10.3	6.3	4.4
China	6.5	12.8	11.9	9.8
Dominican Republic	11.9	13.9	4.0	4.1
India	13.0	11.2	6.7	5.8
Lesotho	..	11.7	7.1	4.1
Mali	25.3	10.2	2.9	3.8
South Korea	12.8	14.2	7.1	7.1
Tanzania	6.3	10.0	3.7	4.1
Thailand	16.9	12.5	8.8	6.1
Turkey	9.8	11.3	5.6	4.2
Vietnam	4.6	22.3	8.7	6.6
Medium export growth	**11.4**	**7.3**	**3.0**	**3.2**
Argentina	9.1	6.9	1.1	1.8
Brazil	9.4	8.9	1.2	2.4
Cameroon	–2.1	5.5	2.5	1.9
Chile	13.9	9.5	4.7	5.7
Colombia	11.2	7.6	1.2	3.1
Costa Rica	13.8	9.5	5.1	4.6
Ecuador	19.3	7.0	0.5	2.3
Ghana	22.0	7.1	2.4	4.3
Indonesia	16.7	6.8	9.2	5.3
Kenya	8.7	5.2	3.1	2.7
Pakistan	9.2	9.6	5.6	4.7
Madagascar	14.0	8.1	1.8	1.8
Malawi	10.0	5.0	0.8	3.0
Mauritius	12.1	8.0	6.8	5.5
Mexico	15.1	9.5	2.8	2.3
Morocco	9.2	6.9	3.6	3.4
Nepal	..	8.4	8.1	4.5
Nigeria	15.2	5.3	2.0	3.3
Paraguay	8.7	8.1	1.6	2.2
Philippines	12.7	6.8	2.1	2.6
Tunisia	9.6	6.5	4.0	4.3
Uruguay	5.0	5.2	–0.3	1.4
Zimbabwe	7.1	6.3	–0.5	1.6

(Table continues on the following page.)

Table D5.2d: Export Growth and Increased Value Added, 1983–2003 (annual increase, %) (continued)

Country	Manufactured exports adjusted for purchasing power 1	Total exports adjusted by purchasing power 2	Value added by manufacture 3	Total value added 4
Low export growth	**7.2**	**3.0**	**2.1**	**1.9**
Central African Republic	..	2.7	1.5	0.8
Côte d'Ivoire	5.7	2.4	2.3	1.1
Honduras	7.0	2.6	4.2	3.1
Jamaica	–0.4	0.4	0.0	1.6
Jordan	7.5	4.9	4.8	3.5
Niger	..	1.1	1.5	1.6
Panama	2.9	2.7	1.4	2.8
Senegal	5.9	4.8	3.9	3.1
South Africa	10.4	4.3	1.2	1.6
Trinidad and Tobago	10.0	4.2	1.8	1.0
Venezuela	14.4	4.1	–0.2	0.8
Zambia	8.3	2.5	3.3	1.4

Source: World Bank, World Development Indicators; IMF, International Financial Statistics, August 2005.

Table D5.3: List of Conflict Countries

Afghanistan	Iraq
Algeria	Lebanon
Angola	Liberia
Azerbaijan	Myanmar
Bosnia and Herzegovina	Nicaragua
Burundi	Peru
Cambodia	Romania
Chad	Rwanda
Congo, Dem. Rep.	Sierra Leone
Congo, Rep.	Somalia
El Salvador	Sri Lanka
Ethiopia	Sudan
Georgia	Tajikistan
Guatemala	Uganda
Iran, Islamic Rep.	Yemen, Rep.

Source: Collier (2000).

APPENDIX D6: SOURCES OF GROWTH DECOMPOSITION

Table D6.1: Sources of Growth Decomposition (Decomposition of GDP Growth by Contribution of Domestic Demand, Import Substitution and Export Expansion, Pre- and Post-Reform)

Country	(Imports+exports)/GDP (percentage)		GDP change (in US$ million)		Contribution in GDP change (As percent of real GDP change): Domestic demand		Import substitution		Export expansion	
	pre	post	pre	post	pre	post	pre	post	pre	post
Argentina	16.4	21.6	105,467	33,000	104.6	84.3	–8.1	–15.0	3.5	30.7
Brazil	–	17.3	–	262,667	–	97.5	–	–1.9	–	4.4
Cameroon	–	49.0	–	760	–	97.4	–	–35.0	–	37.6
Central African Republic	–	–	–	–	–	–	–	–	–	–
Chile	58.7	64.8	2,367	9,967	56.9	76.0	–21.9	–7.9	65.0	31.9
China	31.3	41.3	67,667	106,333	73.2	90.3	–2.2	–21.3	29.0	31.0
Colombia	30.7	34.6	2,333	5,200	70.3	75.3	–17.9	–9.9	47.6	34.5
Costa Rica	71.5	73.9	797	2,350	90.9	78.4	–24.1	–4.2	33.2	25.8
Côte d'Ivoire	75.0	72.4	1,507	737	55.5	75.1	–26.0	12.7	70.5	12.2
Dominican Republic	65.3	66.6	2,297	3,227	73.7	67.8	16.7	4.1	9.6	28.1
Ecuador	55.4	51.9	4,823	6,467	74.1	78.6	13.0	4.5	12.8	16.9
Ghana	41.4	42.1	1,010	580	107.7	111.4	–62.5	–16.0	54.8	4.7
Honduras	74.3	96.6	227	800	134.0	59.8	–54.4	–32.8	20.4	73.0
India	–	22.8	–	103,000	–	94.2	–	–6.7	–	12.5
Indonesia	46.8	51.2	20,167	40,400	75.5	79.2	–4.8	–5.8	29.3	26.7
Jamaica	96.1	–	1,560	–	74.8	–	0.4	–	24.7	–
Jordan	–	123.6	–	1,733	–	60.9	–	21.9	–	17.1
Kenya	70.5	59.4	1,480	2,347	91.9	90.2	–26.7	11.1	34.9	–1.4
Korea, Republic of	66.4	57.8	81,633	108,667	68.6	87.2	3.2	1.4	28.1	11.5
Lesotho	140.5	139.9	163	224	85.2	94.1	3.5	–0.7	11.3	6.6
Madagascar	–	41.8	–	340	–	94.2	–	–3.7	–	9.5
Malawi	54.4	–	643	–	93.1	–	–7.8	–	14.7	–
Mali	52.1	58.5	147	93	98.0	18.6	–11.3	–30.7	13.3	112.2
Mauritius	113.1	133.5	240	863	49.7	74.9	–22.0	–22.6	72.3	47.7
Mexico	–	37.2	–	116,000	–	93.5	–	–7.6	–	14.1
Morocco	–	51.6	–	6,100	–	68.0	–	12.8	–	19.2
Nepal	48.1	60.4	107	827	45.1	95.8	–196.6	–32.1	251.5	36.3
Niger	40.7	41.8	67	60	156.5	98.2	–81.8	–19.7	25.3	21.5

(*Table continues on the following page.*)

Table D6.1: Sources of Growth Decomposition (Decomposition of GDP Growth by Contribution of Domestic Demand, Import Substitution and Export Expansion, Pre- and Post-Reform) (continued)

	(Imports+exports)/GDP (percentage)		GDP change (in US$ million)		Contribution in GDP change (As percent of real GDP change): Domestic demand		Import substitution		Export expansion	
Country	pre	post	pre	post	pre	post	pre	post	pre	post
Nigeria	59.5	81.8	1,033	2,100	–50.6	137.9	–141.4	–146.8	291.9	108.9
Pakistan	36.6	37.5	7,433	8,967	80.1	69.8	–0.5	7.3	20.4	22.9
Panama	67.2	69.3	1,907	1,357	78.8	96.4	–5.8	–16.5	27.0	20.0
Paraguay	69.1	86.1	1,973	1,927	90.1	99.3	–9.5	–35.7	19.4	36.4
Philippines	60.7	69.7	10,500	13,067	96.3	88.0	–22.6	–19.7	26.4	31.7
Senegal	_	70.6	_	70	_	153.2	_	42.1	_	–95.3
South Africa	48.5	40.4	25,433	29,667	77.3	81.1	3.5	11.9	19.1	6.9
Tanzania	62.8	44.1	70	2,843	–2.1	66.8	–303.9	26.9	406.0	6.3
Thailand	48.2	59.0	5,633	11,533	81.8	65.4	10.2	–10.6	8.0	45.2
Trinidad andTobago	78.8	88.6	403	313	92.4	2.4	–31.1	–28.6	38.7	126.2
Tunisia	88.3	91.7	3,667	2,433	84.6	65.3	–14.5	–4.2	29.9	39.0
Turkey	31.0	39.4	59,000	5,667	91.1	90.4	1.1	–101.3	7.8	110.9
Uruguay	40.9	39.1	2,743	4,320	77.5	91.5	6.0	–3.2	16.6	11.7
Venezuela	55.6	53.2	7,300	10,667	117.4	32.4	–27.1	28.9	9.6	38.7
Vietnam	88.1	103.6	10,943	4,967	79.3	52.8	–13.3	–20.1	34.0	67.2
Zambia	_	70.2	_	283	_	67.3	_	33.5	_	–0.8
Zimbabwe	_	81.3	_	717	_	81.3	_	–41.5	_	60.2
Middle income	52.3	60.4	15,699	30,182	72.2	72.9	–6.4	–9.7	23.9	34.2
Low income	44.6	57.9	1,299	6,786	48.3	80.0	–41.6	–10.4	68.8	23.3
Africa	48.5	61.7	1,874	2,453	48.8	80.2	–35.9	–9.2	63.6	21.1
East Asia and Pacific	56.9	63.8	32,757	47,494	79.1	77.2	–4.9	–12.7	25.8	35.5
Europe and Central Asia	31.0	39.4	59,000	5,667	91.1	90.4	1.1	–101.3	7.8	110.9
Latin America and the Caribbean	53.5	54.1	8,948	30,551	77.2	69.6	–9.4	–7.6	23.4	33.6
Middle East and North Africa	36.8	89.0	1,230	3,422	35.6	64.7	2.6	10.2	17.4	25.1
South Asia	32.0	40.2	2,517	37,598	45.4	86.6	–62.0	–10.5	94.3	23.9
Non–intense reformers	52.0	63.6	10,542	23,493	60.9	77.8	–24.5	–12.4	49.9	34.7
Intense reformers	39.9	46.1	6,768	10,445	65.9	70.1	–11.4	–2.4	21.2	14.1
Slow reformers	49.9	58.4	6,905	22,530	55.9	82.1	–30.6	–11.3	58.7	23.8
Fast reformers	48.0	60.5	13,012	17,521	69.9	68.1	–9.6	–8.3	23.0	36.9

Source: IEG staff calculations.

APPENDIX D7: CASE COUNTRY PROFILES

Table D7.1: Trade Portfolio in Case Study Countries (Bank operations, 1987–2003)

	SAL*	SIL/FIL	SECAL	ESW	TA	Grant
India	1	4	1	15		
Indonesia	2	2	2	10		
Morocco	2	4	4	6	1	
Mozambique	4	1		3	1	1
Senegal	3	1	2	1	1	
Zambia	5	3	2	1		

Source: IEG Trade Assistance Evaluation Project Database.

Notes: Structural Adjustment Loans (SALs), Sector Investment Loans (SILs), Financial Intermediary Loans (FILs), and Sector Adjustment Loans (SECALs); Economic and Sector Work (ESW); Technical Assistance Loan (TA).

India: A Gradual Reformer

The period between 1988 and 1991 was marked by an economic growth spurt of 7.6 percent in India. The growth appears to have been underpinned by a recovery in agriculture, response to industrial liberalization during the previous decade, and increased imports of critical machinery and inputs facilitated by earlier trade liberalization that helped to boost productivity. Despite this growth, underlying economic fundamentals were misaligned. In June 1991, a confluence of these factors (growing external debt, high fiscal deficits, and dwindling foreign exchange reserves) precipitated a crisis that led India to the IMF and the World Bank. The Bank's structural adjustment loan in 1991 helped initiate a process of gradual trade liberalization that continues today. In the intervening years, India's policy regime and economy have been considerably transformed, trade has responded strongly to the reforms, and the growth rate has stabilized at about 6 percent per annum.

The Bank's assistance program has consisted of a regular series of economic reports (often with extensive trade analysis), the SAL in 1991, and other supporting investment loans. With the exception of the 1991 SAL, these loans were marked by relatively low conditionality; therefore much of the Bank's influence has been through policy advice and research.

Indonesia: Home-Grown Liberalization Short-Circuited by Crisis

At least until the time of the Asian financial crisis, Indonesia had been seen as a model of successful adjustment. Among the most pressing problems facing Indonesia in the late 1970s and early 1980s was an excessive and dangerous dependence on income from oil. Indonesia did a remarkable job of facilitating adjustment to positive and negative oil shocks. A combination of prudent macroeconomic policies and trade and regulatory reform supported a rapid growth and diversification of non-oil exports in the 1980s and early 1990s, an acceleration of FDI inflows, and substantial poverty reduction. In the early 1980s, oil and other fuel products accounted for over 70 percent of merchandise exports and manufactures for only 2.3 percent. By 1996 the share of manufactures had risen to over 50 percent. Among the greatest achievements of Indonesia's economic performance over this period was a substantial reduction in the incidence of poverty, from 40 percent in the late 1976 to 11 percent in 1995. The high rates of growth and the rapid expansion of investment and of labor-intensive manufacturing over the period were major contributing factors.

Despite two major oil crises, Indonesia sustained an average real growth rate of 7 percent between 1980 and 1996. Trade policy reforms were an integral part of successful adjustment in the 1980s, and the problems arising in 1997 were certainly not connected with trade policies. The economic problems were related to weaknesses in domestic financial regulation and contagion effects in global financial markets. These were aggravated by political and social disturbances that had serious short run impacts on the investment and business environment.

Trade and investment policy reform played a key role in helping Indonesia to come through several major external shocks relatively unscathed, transforming its economy away from dependence on oil and laying the foundations for two decades of extraordinarily rapid growth and poverty reduction. The Bank's role in Indonesia's trade reforms has been defined less by individual programs and projects than by what has been described as a long-term 'policy dialogue' with Indonesian policy makers, donors, and other stakeholders. Conditionality played almost no role in most of the Bank's work in Indonesia. Its research and reports complemented the work of the Government of Indonesia (GOI) and was appreciated. The Bank's work and its advice were generally of high quality. But it was not in a position to play a significant direct or even supervisory role in trade reform. The GOI chose to use its own resources to get external technical assistance elsewhere. The Bank was quite supportive, and did assist in making the Indonesian government's work more generally known and accepted.

Viewed as a sympathetic monitor of the Indonesian trade-related reforms, the Bank's overall performance can be rated as satisfactory to highly satisfactory. The GOI made good use of the Bank's assistance in this regard, and most of the senior Bank personnel who worked in Indonesia recognized and accepted this important but nevertheless limited role in the area of trade and other related regulatory policies. This helped to support a long and mutually trusting relationship between the GOI and the Bank's Indonesia mission. As an independent monitor of the process, the Bank performed a valuable role in certifying the value of the reforms for other members of the donor and international lending communities. The lending support provided by several trade-related loans was useful in itself and as an encouraging signal to other donors. Technical support in export promotion (Export Development Loan initiated in 1986) and in the design of export incentive programs was not particularly useful. Serious questions will however remain about the value of the Bank's role on the one occasion, during the financial crisis, that it allowed itself to be drawn into detailed trade-related policy prescriptions at a time when many other issues were of more pressing importance.

The Indonesian experience provides confirmation of a number of general lessons about trade reform:

- Trade and regulatory reform appears to be an important contributor to growth and poverty reduction.
- Trade reform is certainly not sufficient for promoting development.
- Trade facilitation is important. Indonesia's bold moves in port and especially Customs reform resulted in large reductions in the cost of trade. Failure to lock in the reforms has led to a resurgence of old problems.
- The institutions for the design, implementation, and monitoring of trade policies are important. This was recognized and acted on in a number of innovative ways by the GOI, sometimes very successfully and other times less so.
- Import and export licensing schemes and other NTBs are far more costly than tariffs.

- Reforming tariffs according to some simple formula is easier and more effective than negotiated rate changes.
- Freeing exporters from the burdens of import substitution regimes can be an effective short-term measure, politically and economically, but needs to be followed up with the more fundamental reform for which it is a temporary substitute.
- Trade reform is easier and more effective when the exchange rate is right.
- Fiscal incentives for investment can be costly and they are not necessary.
- Recent developments suggest that the battle for trade reform is never truly and completely won.

Morocco: Crisis Precipitates Reform, Fiscal Concerns Dampen the Pace

Morocco's economy is heavily dependent upon agriculture, with that sector's share in gross domestic product fluctuating between 14 and 24 percent in the period 1982–2002. This dependence has led to pronounced swings in growth of gross domestic product over the period. Droughts and the consequent negative effects on agricultural output are correlated strongly with this economic growth record. The public sector has historically played a dominant role in the economy as producer and employer as well as regulator. This has resulted in persistent central government budget deficits over the years. The budget challenge is related to another: the need to induce more rapid labor absorption. Urban unemployment was estimated in 1995 to be roughly 15 percent and rising, and the public sector has played the role of employer of last resort

The Government of Morocco (GOM) has been consistent in its economic-development goals over the last 30 years. Its priority is to accelerate the economic growth of the economy, both to increase incomes and to create jobs for unemployed citizens. Beginning with the economic crisis in 1982 and continuing through to the present, the GOM concluded that one strategy to address these problems is export-led growth. Morocco chose to change its trade policy from import substitution to export promotion in 1983. The World Bank was a close partner with government policy makers in the beginning of this period, and provided both financing and technical support to assist the government in introducing this strategy. In recent years it has focused on trade-facilitation and private sector–development projects. The government has moved forward slowly, and with little World Bank assistance, in negotiating and implementing free-trade agreements with the European Union (EU), the U.S., Turkey, and its Mahgreb neighbors.

The World Bank has made a positive contribution to trade policy reform in Morocco over the last 25 years. It was an irreplaceable contributor to the initial architecture of trade liberalization in the early 1980s, through its lending, its technical support, and its high-level advice. In more recent years the Bank's focus has turned to trade facilitation and infrastructure development, and its contributions here also have been well-appreciated. The World Bank played a critical role in 1983 in assisting in the formulation of the export-promotion strategy of structural adjustment. While the stabilization policy supported by the IMF would have gone forward, the initial steps toward trade liberalization would have been less sure. From that time on, however, there has not really been World Bank support for trade liberalization.

Morocco's implementation of trade liberalization has been less profound since 1988 than in the period prior to that. This slowing of reform is at its heart a product of the negative consequence of tariff reform for achieving fiscal balance: the policy of macroeconomic balance has in the past taken precedence over the trade liberalization agenda. It also coincides with the Bank's decision to place more emphasis on trade facilitation issues in this area, and on poverty, and social expenditure more generally.

The World Bank's policy goals have been largely in line with those of the government. Its focus has been upon structural adjustment rather than macroeconomic stabilization. Over the last 15 years, however, the World Bank has shifted its focus more tightly to the alleviation of poverty and social concerns in Morocco. This has led to some criticism among Moroccan policy makers: they claim (rightly or wrongly) that the Bank rejected the value of social spending in Morocco in its support for the stabilization program of the

1980s. As a result of that stabilization program, in their view, social spending was cut and poverty rose. Now, the World Bank calls on the GOM to reverse the consequences of that earlier austerity through social spending. The evolution of Bank ESW on the impact of trade liberalization in Morocco illustrates this shift. A major contribution of Bank ESW throughout the trade policy–reform process in Morocco has been the quantification of the benefits and costs of freer trade. While the basic channels of benefits and costs remain the same, current ESW focuses exclusively on the impact on poverty while earlier ESW focused upon the potential aggregate gains from trade.

There is a paradox in World Bank activities in Morocco. Individual projects when considered in isolation are almost always considered successful by the Moroccan counterparts. However, the overarching goal of accelerated economic growth has not been achieved, and so Bank interventions in aggregate are not viewed so positively by Moroccan officials and private observers. Tariffs on industrial goods remain rather high. Tariffs and quantitative restrictions on agricultural products remain in force. The share of exports in GDP in the Moroccan economy has climbed only slightly since 1983. While the government has negotiated a system of free trade agreements (with the EU, the U.S., its Arab neighbors, and Turkey), the commitments under those agreements are backloaded, and have yet to cause large efficiency gains within the economy.

The most important lesson for the World Bank from the Moroccan experience with trade policy reform is the immense value of creating the preconditions of policy reform among GOM officials. Another important lesson is the need to balance structural adjustment with fiscal reform. The Ministry of Commerce and Industry may be solidly in favor of tariff reduction. If the Ministry of Finance is reliant upon trade taxation for budget balance, however, the reforms will not go through. The trade policy compromises associated with budget shortfalls in the late 1980s, continuing up to the present, are a reminder that these reforms can not be considered in isolation of macroeconomic balances. Further progress in trade liberalization in Morocco will be contingent on the identification and exploitation of sources of fiscal revenue separate from that of tariffs and trade taxes.

Mozambique: Cashew Controversy Overshadows Post-Conflict Gains

As is to be expected in an economy devastated by war and then by extensive structural change, GDP values and growth rates have fluctuated sharply over the last two decades. Gross national income per capita is now just above $200 per annum, compared to more than $300 in 1986. Before 1993, peaks of more than 10 percent growth and troughs of -8 percent were experienced, though more recently greater stability has been observed, except in 2000 when GDP growth faltered because of widespread flooding. In the mid-1980s Mozambique's economy was virtually closed and the metical was grossly overvalued. Along with the elimination of import licensing and the reduction of import tariffs and export barriers, real devaluations have allowed the export sector to begin its recovery. They have helped attract new investment into the tradables sector, enhancing the country's prospects for sustained growth and external viability.

With the emphasis on macroeconomic stabilization, trade policy per se did not become a priority until the 1990s. In the late 1980s exchange rate rationalization was a more pressing priority and took the form of progressive devaluations. By 1992 a free currency market was in place. This reform had the deepest impact on Mozambique's trading environment, as it set the stage for the tariff reforms and the elimination of export and import licenses and quantity restrictions that followed. Market liberalization became a high priority, particularly the liberalization of the cashew export. Here the Bank took the initiative in the trade reform process in Mozambique, but was preceded in this by equally important government reforms that had received Bank support and advice, particularly in the area of tariff reform. It was the predominance of cashews in national exports that gave such significance to the reforms, which have been largely beneficial to the cashew sector, though much remains to be done in field production and processing. Given the far-reaching overall impact on the economy, the long-term support that the Bank Group has provided to trade liberalization constitutes the most significant trade-related Bank activity in Mozambique. The Bank and other donors also supported customs reform and institutional strengthening. Here the government was proactive in adopting an aggressive and highly successful modernization process that has allowed the country to welcome major new investments such as the Mozal aluminum smelter, which currently contributes 10 percent of GDP. Trade volume has also grown because of the Bank's technical and financial assistance supporting the development of transport infrastructure to South Africa, Zimbabwe, and Malawi, regional integration through trade agreements, and private sector capacity building.

Under structural adjustment, from 1985–95, the World Bank Group provided ample financial resources to aid Mozambique in the adoption of rational and sustainable economic policies. However, it is not uncommon to find precise and detailed policy analysis and recommendations in Bank Economic and Sector Work publications from the early 1990s that were not fully discussed with government, but were reflected in World Bank country strategies. But, beginning in 1997, the Bank addressed this problem adequately through much fuller consultation. Consequently, the country assistance strategies in the late 1990 and 2000 are joint products of the Bank and the government. The PARPA, or poverty reduction strategy, provides a neutral and highly relevant focus for these consultations that was lacking in the early stages of Bank work in Mozambique.

While the process of providing trade assistance to Mozambique has encountered difficulties, the assessment concludes that the impact, relevance, efficiency, and sustainability of the reforms advocated by the Bank are generally satisfactory. Given the overall success of Bank activities in the areas referred to it can be concluded that both quality at entry and quality of supervision were adequate. With the exception of some minor aspects of the cashew study, and the predominance of the highly prescriptive advice of the early 1990s that presaged the export tariff reforms, the Bank's advice was in the main forward-looking and helped Mozambique establish itself as democracy with good prospects of sustainable economic development in a multilateral trading environment. Without it, there is no question that the national economy would have suffered major difficulties when COMECON (the Eastern bloc's free market) closed its doors to Mozambique in 1984. However, Mozambique's continued development at high rates of growth will require a more concerted effort to overcome some major constraints, including the further removal obstacles to private sector development, including in the financial sector. Improving financial sector performance, which is hampered by limited supervisory capacity, poor accounting practices, and a weak judicial system, would improve the lending environment and facilitate access to bank credit, the greatest constraint to private sector growth.

In addition, there is a continued need to reduce the cost of doing business, notably by improving infrastructure, especially transport, and reducing labor rigidities, which hinder external competitiveness.

Major lessons learned from the Bank's work in Mozambique include:

- Borrower ownership and commitment to the reform program is a key factor of success. The fact that the Economic Management Reform Operation supported reforms that were clearly defined, previously agreed upon, and fully owned by the authorities facilitated implementation and contributed to program sustainability.
- Appropriate sequencing and complementarities between macroeconomic policies and structural reforms reinforce program outcomes. The simultaneous implementation of indirect tax reform, gradual trade liberalization, and rationalization and simplification of import procedures, shielded the budget from a potential decline in revenue that could have endangered fiscal adjustment, at the same time as it reduced distortions in the allocation of resources and supported a strong supply response. When combined with prudent fiscal and monetary policies, a favorable external environment and the high level of foreign as-

sistance, this resulted in strong GDP growth, low inflation, and high private investment.

- Political economy considerations can derail technical analysis, especially where the poor do not have a voice.
- Faced with capacity constraints, a smaller number of selective reforms results in greater impact. The focused nature of the operation, which concentrated on a limited number of areas, enabled the government to concentrate on actions considered critical for the success of the overall reform process, and helped implementation in the face of acute capacity constraints.

Senegal: The Limits of Advice and the Importance of Domestic Constituencies for Reform

The economy of the Republic of Senegal—a semi-arid West African country with a fragile natural resource base and just over 10 million people—is more open to trade than on average in Sub-saharan Africa or among least developed countries. Along with some of its neighbors, Senegal joined in a special monetary agreement with France that established a currency (CFA franc) that was both fixed and convertible against the French franc (and against the euro after 1999). While Senegal benefited from monetary stability and low inflation for an extended period of time, the sustained deterioration of the CFA zone's terms of trade and the increasing overvaluation led to a stagnation of exports, a deterioration of public finances, capital flight, and a deep recession in 1993. By mutual agreement, the CFA franc was devalued by 50 percent against the French currency. Concurrently, a program of macroeconomic and structural reforms was announced. In Senegal, the devaluation and accompanying reforms produced robust results in terms of growth and poverty reduction, particularly in the years immediately following the devaluation.

The World Bank has not pursued a trade assistance program per se in Senegal. Rather, it has pursued an economic liberalization program, of which increased openness to trade has been one expected intermediate outcome. The Bank's message to Senegal's economic policy makers has consistently emphasized decreased intervention by the state in markets and increased trade integration in order to achieve the goal of increased competitiveness, increased economic growth, and improved welfare for all Senegalese. Along the way, mixed messages have sometimes been given by the World Bank with respect to trade. When quick-disbursing adjustment lending was at its peak, trade liberalization was seen as part of a broader structural adjustment policy reform package and trade was folded into the Ministry of Finance's portfolio. As adjustment lending has yielded to the return of more traditional investment projects, trade flows and trade capacity building are once again seen as important topics in their own right and trade is again managed by a separate ministry. Yet the Bank's tepid embrace of trade as a unique area of operation, perhaps out of respect for the primary authority of Joint Integrated Technical Assistance Program to Selected Least Developed and Other African Countries (JITAP) organizations in this area, means that trade capacity support from the Bank in terms of financial and human resources has been somewhat limited.

Given the economic context in which Senegal found itself in the 1980s, the World Bank clearly pushed the right reform priorities at that time. Senegal's biggest constraints to economic growth stemmed from the pervasive involvement of the state in most aspects of economic activity. Disengagement of state-owned enterprises and reform of state-run market functions at all points in the value chain, from input distribution to price-setting, collection, storage, processing, trade, and distribution, were crucial if the Senegalese economy was to become more competitive. Unfortunately, given the institutional context in which the World Bank found itself, it was unable to address the single-most critical constraint to trade development in Senegal by the late 1980s, which was overvaluation of the CFA franc. The design of structural adjustment in Senegal up until 1994 was inappropriate because its second-best nature forced it to follow a path of fiscal compression that ultimately caused more harm than benefit.

Since 1994, the Bank has provided assistance in areas that address key constraints to trade development. Immediately after the devaluation, the Bank supported more comprehensive structural adjustment in both industry and agriculture, including tariff reform, elimination of import reference prices, and withdrawal of the state from many production and marketing activities. Since the late 1990s, trade infrastructure (e.g., sea and airports, rail, airlines), trade promotion (for horticulture), trade institutions (exporters' associations in horticulture), further tariff reform, trade institutions (e.g., Customs Service), and investment promotion have been the focus of privatization, reform, and/or modernization with support from the World Bank.

The World Bank's advisory, analytic, and lending services have provided a consistent message in support of the big picture of trade openness and global integration as the key to economic growth. Since the "big push" on structural adjustment following the 1994 devaluation, the Bank's efforts have focused on trade policy reform and privatization and modernization of trade-related infrastructure. Other forms of trade capacity building, such as the development of trade institutions, have received more limited attention from the Bank. At times the Bank has sharply disagreed with the government (or other donors) on policy or institutions, as with the longstanding stalemate over the National Oilseed Marketing Company's (SONACOS) privatization and more recent dispute regarding the future institutional home of export promotion assistance. Topics such as trade finance, trade negotiations, or the development of trade-related skills at the microeconomic level, have received far less attention in Senegal. Where Bank assistance has been targeted at the private sector, as with the Agricultural Export Promotion Project (AEPP), the effects on export supply response and institutional capacity have been quite positive, albeit limited in scope to specific product categories.

In Senegal the experience of the World Bank over the last 17 years with trade-related assistance suggests a number of lessons, recommendations from which may have wider applicability to Bank operations in other countries:

- The effect of exchange rates on export competitiveness cannot be overlooked in a debate over conflicting international institutional mandates.
- Trade and enabling environment reforms are necessary but insufficient conditions for inducing export diversification and global market penetration.
- Although the West African financial crisis of the late 1980s was addressed through a financial sector adjustment program, Senegal's commercial banking sector remains cautious and overly liquid.
- Future diagnostics of trade prospects and delivery of trade advice must also consider the factors shaping trade from a global demand perspective.
- Given that the private sector is often weak in developing countries, appropriately structured public-private partnerships are needed in a wide range of trade-related areas, including trade negotiations, trade-related investigations and legal actions, trade-related research and extension, compliance with norms and standards, local market regulation, export-oriented investment promotion, and export market linkages.

Zambia: Political Change Opens Window of Opportunity Leading to Economic Change

Following the declaration of unilateral independence by Rhodesia in 1965, new trade routes had to be found for Zambia. Energy supplies were most affected and the upshot was that Zambia adopted a policy of self reliance. The copper mines and a large proportion of industrial and commercial concerns were nationalized and placed under holding companies which were controlled and operated by the ruling party. Economic policies were inward-looking. Countering a persistently overvalued exchange rate, industry was heavily protected by a combination of quantitative restrictions, high tariffs, and administered allocation of foreign currency. In the aftermath of the 1973 global oil crisis, the price of copper collapsed, but the government assumed that low copper prices would be a temporary phenomenon and did not therefore seek to fundamentally change the patterns of consumption and production in the economy. Zambia began to accumulate the significant levels of external debt which soon became a major restraining factor in macroeconomic policy making. To resolve the tension between the necessity to service the debt while at the same pursuing development objectives, Zambia became heavily dependent on external assistance, particularly from the International Monetary Fund and the World Bank. Throughout the 1980s and 1990s, Zambia has had a series of significant loans from the Fund and the Bank, as well as a mix of substantial grants and loans from bilateral donors. However, the period from the downturn in copper prices to the present has been characterized by poor economic performance, and income and social indicators have deteriorated dramatically.

Between 1987 and 2002 there was only one project which was exclusively devoted to trade. This was the seven-country Regional Trade Facilitation Project, which was approved in 2001 and involves establishing a trade insurance facility. Zambia's direct share of the Bank's contribution to this project is small ($15 million). The Bank's main trade assistance to Zambia over the period was incorporated in a series of structural adjustment lending operations. However, given the primary trade objective of assisting the country to diversify its export base, other Bank projects in agriculture, private sector development and the like also have to be considered when evaluating the Bank's trade assistance.

As expressed in successive adjustment operations, the main trade objectives were to remove biases against exports, major aspects of this being liberalizing imports and the foreign exchange market. The operational objectives were initially to remove NTBs and administrative control of imports and foreign exchange and thereafter to reduce tariffs and narrow spreads, strengthen export promotion institutions, and improve the duty drawback system. These predominantly trade regime issues were to be complemented by a favorable macroeconomic regime, including a competitive exchange rate and access to finance for exporters. These changes were intended to encourage nontraditional export growth so as to reduce the country's dependence on copper. This would then contribute to the overall country assistance strategy goals of sustainable economic growth and poverty reduction.

The relevance of these objectives in the Bank's adjustment operations and the complementary projects is not in doubt. In 1991, Zambia's economy was in a deep economic crisis which the new government recognized could not be effectively addressed except via a clean break with the past. What is, however, controversial is whether the approach to meet the basic trade objectives, particularly the objective of export diversification, was relevant. Two related concerns are raised in this connection: firstly, that the liberalization of imports was too rapid and secondly that insufficient attention was paid to supply side constraints. Zambia was therefore left overly exposed to import competition (particularly from regional trading partners, such as Zimbabwe and South Africa), while not being in a position to respond adequately to the improved export incentives.

The reforms undertaken in Zambia since the Movement for Multi-Party Democracy (MMD) came to power in October 1991, including rapid trade liberalization, have not produced anything like the results which had been hoped for. At the same time, they have not been completely ineffective, not least in respect of the growth of non-traditional exports. Nonetheless, it remains the case that without much higher levels of growth of both GDP and exports, Zambia will remain highly indebted and will not disentangle itself from its extraordinarily high level of donor dependence, nor make any sustainable reductions in poverty. The country needs to have much greater commitment to developing a viable and competitive economy capable of enhancing incomes and generating jobs and wealth. Trade policies need to be integral to any growth strategy, but it will only be through a conscious effort to develop linkages and maximize employment growth that the result will be sufficiently inclusive for it to reduce, rather than exacerbate, inequalities and poverty.

More specific recommendations on the design of the trade components of economic reform and development strategies are as follows:

- Sequence enhancement of trade with increased employment.

- Buttress the sequencing of liberalization with an explicit strategy to maintain commitment and support.
- Cushion the impact on the losers.
- Take account of the regional and international trade environment.
- Provide the lead on good governance.
- Create a macroeconomic environment conducive to private sector growth.
- Maintain a real exchange rate that provides a strong incentive for nontraditional export growth.
- Ensure effective institutions.
- Invest in infrastructure.
- Develop human resources and technological capabilities.

Lessons from ESW in Case Study Countries

The main lesson for the examination of economic and sector work and its impact in the case studies is that high-quality analytical work (or its absence) matters for project design and the overall country relationship.

In Morocco, a 1993 study (Alavi 1993) reported the results of a private sector survey and highlighted the role of customs administration and the issue of corruption (previously taboo). Private sector associations used the study as backing to urge intervention by the king (which happened), and customs officials have been complimentary of Bank (and Fund) technical assistance provided in the early stages of customs reform.

In India, ten sector studies carried out from 1985 to 1991 laid the foundation for dialogue. A 1987 country report offered a detailed set of policy reforms in various areas, including trade. A substantial part of the trade reform in the 1990s and the remaining agenda can be found in this early report. However, key Bank staff members from that period are modest in drawing causal links between the study and the reforms, instead drawing attention to Indian policy makers from that time who shared similar views. Given that this comprehensive report was discussed with the authorities, however, it is likely that it contributed to changing some minds within the bureaucracy and also influenced Bank staff involved in negotiations on a trade loan three years later. The 1990 economic report took a more pragmatic approach, allowing more scope for state intervention and formed the basis for the SAL the following year. In agricultural trade, Pursell and Gulati (1993) systematically documented the anti-agricultural bias of the policy regime and offered recommendations and this report significantly influenced agricultural policy changes in India.

In Mozambique, the controversy over the liberalization of the cashew nut industry that was based on analytical work commissioned by the Bank subsequently spanned eight years. It generated ex-post several assessments by Bank staff, the Bank president, the Mozambicans, and academic researchers. Assumptions in the original ESW fueled the cashew debate. The study was too willing to assume that traders would pay more for the nuts and that farmers would hasten to improve the state of their trees. Critics said that the study underestimated the free on board price of exported kernels and overlooked the complexity of the marketing structure where the Indian industry and its representatives played a decisive role. Excessive faith was placed in market structures and processes to ensure the transmission of price incentives to highly dispersed producers in remote rural areas. These criticisms, political economy dynamics (resistance by those who gained from the prevailing system), and the subsequent debate led by NGOs kept the issue alive. Thus, even though three ex-post assessments as well as McMillan, Rodrik, and Horn (2002) concluded that the reforms recommended yielded many of the benefits they were intended to, McMillan et al. note that "even under the most favorable assumptions, the magnitude of the benefits generated by these effects were quite small [$12 million]—both in economic terms and in relation to the amount of time and energy ... spent on this question over the years."

In Zambia, an intense and relatively rapid trade liberalization starting in 1991 and stretching out to the end of the decade was heavily biased toward lending with little detailed ESW on trade. A narrowly focused tariff study was done in 1992. The country economic memorandum in early 1990 stated that further (trade) reforms should be made only after careful revenue and protection analysis. A better idea is needed of the effective protection structure, given the linkages between production and imports, before designing further changes in structure. The last effective protection study done in Zambia by the Bank was in the mid-1980s. The Bank was undoubtedly preoccupied in the early 1990s with macroeconomic stabilization and privatization; it was also attempting to take advantage of a "window of opportunity" for reforms. Regardless of the reasons why the Bank failed to conduct analytical work, the absence of trade ESW gave some Zambian observers the impression that the Bank's commitment to liberalization was based not on analysis but on a doctrinal "belief that resources were misallocated as a result of price distortions" (IEG, 1996c, p. 60). It may also have failed to prepare the authorities adequately for the potential risks and costs associated with trade liberalization.

Trade has always been an important component of the Bank's policy dialogue with Indonesia and since the early 1980s the Bank's Jakarta office has always had a resident trade economist. Starting in the early 1980s up to the mid-1990s, the Bank consistently produced a series of economic reports that included a focus on trade for donor meetings. The contribution of Bank analytical work has been influenced by Indonesian political sensitivities, government ability to carry out its own research, and the existence of alternative sources of advice. By the mid-1980s, the Indonesian government was clearly in charge of its reform program.

The IEG case study on Indonesia concludes that the Bank's annual reports, which were widely read, were useful in providing support and recognition for the government's trade-related reforms in the investment and donor communities. Their impact on policy was not as great as might have been expected given their quality and frequency for at least three reasons. First, to be seen to be bowing to the wishes of the Bank was perceived as reducing policy makers' credibility with the president. There was a precedent for this—the 1983 tariff reform was aborted after claims it was being forced on the country by the Bank. Second, the government had built up its capacity to conduct its own analysis on trade and industrial policy. Third, up until the late 1990s, the authorities could also draw on the advice of outside consultants, the most prominent of which were the economists from the Harvard Institute for International Development. The Bank was highly supportive of the reform process in Indonesia and conducted a large amount of analytical work and a relationship of considerable mutual respect existed between the two parties. But the greatest contribution of the Bank's analytical work may have been its value as a signaling device to other development partners on the state of Indonesian reform, rather than actual policy changes.

APPENDIX E1: ORGANIZATIONAL CHART FOR THE INTERNATIONAL TRADE DEPARTMENT

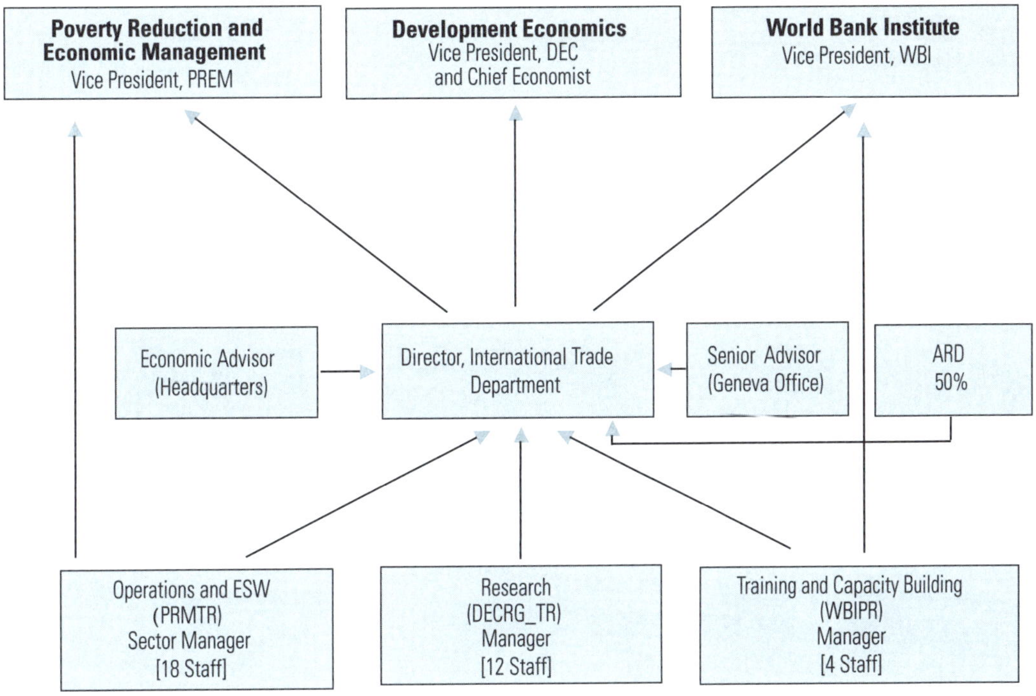

APPENDIX E2: ESTABLISHMENT OF THE TRADE DEPARTMENT

Director, Trade Department, PREM/DEC/WBI

Concurrent with the launch of the Doha Development Agenda, the Bank's trade work has grown dramatically in the last year, and trade was identified as one of the Bank's priorities at the Strategic Forum in January. At the same time, the Bank's work on trade at the center is dispersed across DEC, ESSD, PREM, and WBI. To improve our capacity to respond to the growing demand for Bank services on trade and to manage more effectively the expanded resources in this area, we have decided to create a Trade Department.

The Trade Department, headed by a Director for Trade, will provide a single venue for accountability for trade-related work. This work will include global advocacy on trade-related development issues based on research findings, support to the Regions on trade strategies at the regional and country levels and on trade operational work (including that carried out by the research team in DEC), and capacity building on trade issues. Although the Department will be housed in PREM, the Director will report jointly on trade strategy issues to the VPs for DEC, PREM and WBI, underscoring efforts to strengthen collaboration among our VPUs. The new Department will combine the relevant policy and analytic work, and capacity building on trade within a coordinated budget envelope, which will also include resources from trust funds, such as those supporting the Integrated Framework.

The Trade Department will address global trade issues through analysis and advocacy, and support regional and country work on trade. Agricultural trade issues are central to the current round of negotiations, and agricultural trade work on the global trade agenda currently housed in ESSD will also be aligned with the new Trade Department. Moreover, to ensure synergy between the Trade Department and work on global economic prospects (which includes a large trade component), the Director will also be responsible for managing the Development Prospects Group in DEC.

The Trade Department will be subject to a major review after 3 years using criteria based on an assessment of the services provided and the level of demand for services. Clear outputs and outcomes will also be reviewed annually.

[...]

Gobind Nankani
Vice-President
PREM

Nicholas Stern
Senior Vice-President DEC,
and Chief Economist

Frannie A. Leautier
Vice-President
World Bank Institute

APPENDIX E3: WORLD BANK ADVOCACY ON INDUSTRIAL COUNTRY TRADE POLICIES

Table E3.1: World Development Reports 1980–2002 (Main Themes on Trade)

World Development Report 1980	World Development Report 1981	World Development Report 1982	World Development Report 1983
Some agricultural products remain constrained by heavy protection in Japan and Western Europe—textiles and clothing elaborate mechanism to control imports have become more entrenched, reducing the chance of their earlier removal. In some industrialized countries, imports on footwear and some consumer electronic goods are still subject to fairly stringent quotas. Tariff escalation inhibits exports of processed products from developing countries.	Tariffs remain high in some sectors—particularly those of interest of developing countries exporters. Tariff escalation—removing the tariffs on processed varieties of eight agricultural products. Disturbing development in trade restrictions. MFA, safeguards, antidumping, and countervailing duties. Many subsidies were overtly protectionist.	Protections have taken the form of NTB, quotas, voluntary restraints, antidumping, countervailing duties, safeguards and the increase of subsidies. Unlike tariffs, many of those are bilateral outside the scope of the GATT. Today's institutionalized restrictions were yesterday's temporary measures. In contrast to the situation in most developing countries, agriculture in the developed world is heavily protected and supported. European Economic Community (EEC), USA, and Japan have high protection levels and subsidies. Little progress was made in the Tokyo Round in reducing agricultural protection	High protectionism in agriculture. Tariff and NTB against clothing and textile imports from developing countries grew. Recession rose protectionist pressure.
World Development Report 1985	**World Development Report 1986**	**World Development Report 1987**	**World Development Report 1989**
Increased protectionism in industrial countries against developing countries' exports reduces the export earnings that developing countries would otherwise obtain. Detrimental to their capacity to import and to service their debt. Protectionism can adversely affect the developing countries terms of trade. New protectionism: escalation, NTB in agriculture, steel, footwear, MFA, quotas, voluntary export restraint (VER).	NTBs on developing countries' exports are higher than industrial countries' exports. MRN should focus on NTB and effective system of safeguards. Agricultural trade policy has been excluded from multilateral negotiations. Protectionism in agriculture: variable imports levies, exports restitutions, high tariffs, imports quotas Preferences: Lome. Caribbean Basin Initiative (CBI). Generalized System of Preferences (GSP): limited benefits, partly because they are restric-	Developing countries subject to NTB, VER, tariff escalation. Demands to combat "unfair" trade are protectionism and attack the basis of trade—comparative advantage. GSP limited gains—sectors excluded. Urged more open trading system: include agriculture, MFA to be phased out, safeguards amended to assure access to developing countries' exports. CVD-AD reform.	Specific safeguards actions taken by industrial countries increasingly discriminate against developing countries. VER, MFA, and quotas have their greatest effect on the exports of developing countries The share of developing countries exports that face NTB is roughly 20 percent, about twice the share of industrial countries exports. Protection in agriculture. Increase in bilateral trade agreements. Uruguay Round (UR) need to take care of those issues.

(Table continues on the following page.)

Table E3.1: World Development Reports 1980–2002 (Main Themes on Trade) (continued)

World Development Report 1985	World Development Report 1986	World Development Report 1987	World Development Report 1989
	tive, exclude or place limits on precisely those products in which developing countries could be most competitive.		
World Development Report 1991	**World Development Report 1999/2000**	**World Development Report 2000/2001**	**World Development Report 2002**
Trade reform in developing countries is much more likely to go ahead if success in trade is not punished. Use of quotas, subsidies, VER, CVD, and AD has risen alarmingly since the 1960s. Subsidies in agriculture increased by 80 percent in the U.S., and 69 percent in Canada between 1980 and 1985. It remains to be seen if regional blocs will support or hinder the goal of more open global trading system. UR must be revived to eliminate quantitative restrictions, open agriculture, and restrict the use of the so-called fair trade legislation.	Trade sanctions, which may be little more than a cover for the introduction of protectionist measures, may be implemented in ways that have little to do with child labor.	Agricultural trade grew only 1.8 percent from 1985 to 1994. One reason for this slow growth is the continuing protection of agricultural products by developed countries—protection not only through tariffs and quotas but also through subsidies. High tariffs in products of interest in developing countries. High income countries' agricultural tariffs and other distortions, such as subsidies, have been stimulated to cause annual welfare losses of $19.8 billion for developing countries—equivalent to about 40 percent of the development assistance given to developing countries in 1998. For manufactured goods, tariffs facing developing country exports to high-income countries are, on average, four times those facing industrial country exports to the same market. Tariff escalation can discourage industrialization efforts in developing countries.	The benefits of trade liberalization for developing countries would be significantly enhanced if industrial countries also reduced their tariff and nontariff barriers, especially on agriculture and textiles. Industrial country support to agriculture rose from 31 percent of gross farm receipts in 1997 to 40 percent in 1999. Much of the liberalization under the MFA has been on products that were not under restraint to begin with. The initiatives of industrial countries to liberalize exports from LDC needs to be extended to all products. Even after the elimination of MFA, developing countries still face high tariffs.
Global Economic Prospects (OECD and other Trade Themes)			
Global Economic Prospects 1991	**Global Economic Prospects 1992**	**Global Economic Prospects 1993**	**Global Economic Prospects 1994**
High tariffs in products of interest of developing countries. NTB-VER, AD, 24 OECD economies are on balance, more protectionist now than they were ten years ago. NTB in sectors of interest of developing countries. Escalation on processed commodities.	Restrictive trade policies in industrial countries affect prospects for developing countries exports of manufactures. AD—CVD—VER—MFA—Domestic subsidies MFA	Protectionism in OECD markets is particularly vexing for aid-receiving countries. Exports of developing countries would increase in the OECD tariff and NTB were removed. "Trade not Aid"	A disappointing result of the recent UR is that tariff escalation will continue for agricultural products. NTB, quotas, variables levies, exports subsidies, AD, CVD in agriculture. The total transfers provided to agriculture in OECD countries amounted $350 billion in 1992 or about six times the official development finance provided to developing countries

Global Economic Prospects 1995	Global Economic Prospects 1996	Global Economic Prospects 2001	Global Economic Prospects 2002
Escalation remains. The UR appears to have done little to constrain the use of AD. Trade policies are not suited to deal with labor and environmental standards.	Important and real external obstacles to growth in trade remain, including the spread of anti-dumping practices, agricultural protection, and the MFA phase-out will likely to be delayed until 2005. *The importance of tariff escalation has been exaggerated given the special relations and conditions of market access of developing countries in OECD markets.	NTB in agriculture—high tariffs in sectors where the developing countries have comparative advantage. Agricultural subsidies. Tariff escalation. Quotas	Extend duty free access to all LDC exports in Quad countries. Removal of distortions in agriculture: reduce most favored nation (MFN) tariffs, peaks, quotas, subsidies. Expand access in labor-intensive manufactures, phase out remaining quantitative restrictions, MFA, reduce escalation, tariffs, and peaks.

Source: Rajapatirana (2003).

APPENDIX E4: DISTRIBUTION OF TRADE CAPACITY BUILDING COMPONENTS, 2001–04

Table E4.1a: Objectives of TCB Assistance by Region, 1998–2003 (number of components)

	Africa	East Asia and Pacific	Europe and Central Asia	Latin America and the Caribbean	Middle East and North Africa	South Asia
Trade liberalization	2	3	0	1	0	0
Export development promotion	7	1	1	1	1	0
Export development finance	3	0	3	3	1	1
Export development competitiveness	4	1	1	1	1	1
Trade facilitation: customs	4	0	35	14	1	2
Trade facilitation: logistics	1	1	0	1	1	0
Trade facilitation: other	2	0	2	8	3	1
Standards	3	5	6	2	1	0
International negotiations	1	0	0	2	0	1
Total	27	11	48	33	9	6

Source: Trade Assistance Evaluation Trade Capacity Building Database.

Note: Please see Chapter 5, box 5.2, for a detailed definition of trade capacity building.

Table E4.1b: TCB Lending: Linkages to Bank TCB Objectives (2003–04)

Country /Region	Project name	Fiscal year of approval	Obj. 1	Obj. 2	Obj. 3	Obj. 4	Other	Description of TCB components and activities per project[a]
Philippines	Diversified Farm Income and Market Development Project	2004					X	Support Implementation information systems in SPS and standards.
Vietnam	Poverty Reduction Support Credit II	2003	X					Support actions in the trade liberalization arena.
Moldova	Trade and Transport Facilitations in Southeast Europe Project	2003					X	Technical assistance for customs control and information systems.
Russian Federation	Customs Development Project	2003					X	Customs control and clearance, trade facilitation, regulation of custom activities, organizational structure and management, training, IT.
Yugoslavia	Export Finance Facilitation Project	2003					X	Political risk insurance facility, working capital loan facility, exporter performance insurance facility, technical assistance to Yugoslav exporters. Technical assistance will be provided to the Serbia and Montenegro Export Credit Agency (SMECA) for institutional strengthening.
Turkey	Anatolia Watershed Rehabilitation Project	2004				X		Support for implementing the EU Nitrates Directive, development of a Code of Good Agricultural Practices, support of producing and marketing organically produced farm products.
Honduras	Trade Facilitation and Productivity Improvement Project	2004					X	Support for the creation of centers to support textile, wood and artisan crafts industries to reach new markets. Analysis of standards and labeling. Assessing of the Technical Barriers to Trade (TBT) Enquiry Points, staff training on enquiry points and standard-related information. Creation of the National Quality Council.
Peru	Programmatic Decentralization and Competitiveness SAL	2004					X	Improvement of trade logistics, support to the issuing of new technical standards.
Ecuador	Institutional Reform Project	2004					X	Support for the re-design of the Audit and Internal Affairs Unit, foster agency coordination to supervise foreign trade

Country /Region	Project name	Fiscal year of approval	Obj. 1	Obj. 2	Obj. 3	Obj. 4	Other	Description of TCB components and activities per project[a]
Ecuador (cont.)								activities, training and evaluation for Customs Administration Staff, customs valuation.
Argentina	Economic Recovery Support Structural Adjustment Loan	2004					X	Actions to issue new regulation to reduce TBT in the transport sector, link private sector enterprises and public sector agencies to enhance export and import substitution, program to support SME's to develop export business plans. Accreditation of the National Institute of Industrial Technology and international accreditation.
Tunisia	Second Exports Development Project	2004					X	Support to export initiatives and diversification of markets, pre-shipment export finance, technical barriers inquiry point, standards and technical regulations, customs procedures, information system on trade logistics performance.
Yemen, Rep. of	Port Cities Development Program	2003					X	Support in automating the Customs administration.
Afghanistan	Emergency Customs Modernization and Trade Facilitation Project	2004		X				Actions to help build the capacity of intermediary entities to support groups of firms linked to export plans; strengthen the Pre-Shipment Export Finance Guarantees Facility, improve information access about TBTs through the establishment of the WTO Technical Barriers to Trade Enquire Point, support for the streamlining of procedures and automation of processes of exporters and importers.
Sierra Leone	Economic Rehabilitation and Recovery Credit III	2003				X		Study on the economic and fiscal impact of the adoption of the Common External Tariff. In the mining sector, harmonizing policy with those of competing and neighboring countries to discourage smuggling and foster trade through official channels.
Ethiopia	Public Sector Capacity Building Program Support Project	2004					X	Reforming and modernizing customs.

Source: World Bank data.

Note: Objective 1: Formulate and implement sound trade policy to enhance growth and reduce poverty; Objective 2: Manage the adjustment cost of trade reform and external trade shocks; Objective 3: Participate effectively in international negotiations; Objective 4: Develop appropriate regional trade policies.

a.The description refers to TCB elements included under the project's component category.

Table E4.2: Stand-Alone Trade Technical Assistance Loans, 1987–2004

Region	Country	Project name	Fiscal year of approval	Amount approved (US$m)	Amount disbursed (US$m)
Africa	Senegal	Development Management Project	1988	17	15.9
Africa	Angola	Economic Management Capacity Building Project	1991	23.0	22.1
Europe and Central Asia	Romania	Technical Assistance & Critical Imports Project	1991	180.0	179.2
Latin America and the Caribbean	Argentina	Public Sector Reform Technical Assistance Project	1991	23	23.0

	Implementation completion report project ratings				
Objectives	**Outcome**	**Sustain-ability**	**Institutional development impact**	**Bank perform-ance**	**Borrower perform-ance**
The primary objective of the project was to assist the government to build up the internal capabilities for strategic planning, financial management, and personnel management in the relevant agencies within the Ministries of Planning and Cooperation, Economy and Finance, and Civil Service and Labor. In particular, the project was to support action programs prepared by these agencies to carry out the tasks related to the implementation of the ongoing structural adjustment program.	HU	U	N	HU	HU
The project will help finance (a) a program of training to build up local skills in economic and financial management, accounting, procurement, project analysis, and statistics; (b) technical assistance, studies, and logistical support to improve economic management and facilitate the transition, including a pilot program for the privatization and liquidation of parastatals; and (c) supervision and project management to closely monitor project implementation. The project consists of the following components: (a) human resource development; (b) economic statistics; (c) legal assistance; (d) public resource management; and (e) liberalization policies.	U	U	M	U	U
The Technical Assistance & Critical Imports Loan Project is expected to support the ongoing economic reform program. The project will provide (i) technical assistance to support the ongoing economic reform process in the formulation and implementation of macroeconomic and sectoral policy programs and (ii) foreign exchange for the import of essential spare parts and equipment to the irrigation, telecommunications, power, lignite, petroleum, gas, and transportation sectors. The project includes a technical assistance (TA) and an import component. The TA component will support (a) national macroeconomic management to prepare fiscal and legal reforms; (b) strategy formulation and pricing reforms in the energy sector, sectoral restructuring programs in the industrial sector and support for the privatization of industrial enterprises, services, and housing; (c) establishment of an efficient service to administer unemployment benefits, improve labor market information; (d) strategic studies and assessments for computer requirements for commercial banks; and (e) sector studies in the irrigation and energy sectors. The imports component will provide spare parts and equipment financing for the transportation sector, two major power plants, the lignite mines, petroleum and gas wells, the telecommunications system, irrigation system and agricultural machinery.	MS	U	N		
The Public Sector Reform Technical Assistance Loan Project will support (a) modernization and computerization of the Customs Department; (b) administrative reform and modernization of the central government; (c) establishment of a new framework and development of systems for comprehensive public sector financial management; (d) reorganization and modernization of the Central Bank; and (e) implementation of a program for a complete restructuring of the Superintendency of Financial Entities (SEF). The project will strengthen the capacity of the Ministry of Economy by providing	S	L	S	S	HS

(*Table continues on the following page.*)

Table E4.2: Stand-Alone Trade Technical Assistance Loans, 1987–2004 (continued)

Region	Country	Project name	Fiscal year of approval	Amount approved (US$m)	Amount disbursed (US$m)
Latin America and the Caribbean	Argentina	Hydrocarbon Engineering Project	1992	28	8.3
Africa	Burundi	Agribusiness Promotion Project	1993	3.1	0.1

Objectives	Implementation completion report project ratings: Outcome	Sustain-ability	Institutional development impact	Bank perform-ance	Borrower perform-ance
consultant services, computer equipment and software, and logistical support to (i) manage economic reforms; (ii) allocate and control public resources; and (iii) administer customs by the establishment of new administrative procedures and related computerized information systems. It will strengthen the central government ministries and the presidency by providing consultant services, computer equipment, and software to modernize its internal administration by developing new uniform procedures and information systems for personnel, financial resources, and facilities management. Last, it will strengthen the Central Bank through the provision of consultant services, computer equipment and software to improve its organizational structure and administrative procedures, develop key information systems and enhance staff capabilities, with special emphasis on the SEF.					
The Hydrocarbon Engineering Project aims to (a) help the YPF Sociedad Anonima (YPFSA) make an effective transition to its new commercial role; (b) expand opportunities for mobilizing greater private enterprise investment in the sector; (c) strengthen the government's hydrocarbon policy making and regulatory capabilities; and (d) support energy conservation and bolster the government's efforts in developing and enforcing environmental and safety standards. Technical assistance will be provided to prepare engineering designs and specifications to support YPFSA's and the government's investment program in the areas of: (a) enhancement of primary, secondary and tertiary hydrocarbon recovery in YPFSA fields; (b) natural gas processing and storage facilities expected to be put in place by private investors; and (c) improvement of YPFSA's petroleum processing and marketing in terms of dispatch centers and export infrastructure The institutional strengthening component will provide technical assistance to: (a) design and implement YPFSA's financial information, procurement, taxation and accounting systems to function as a private corporation, define environmental policies, and provide related staff training; and (b) develop in the Combustibles Subsecretariat of the Ministry of Economy the capability to oversee sector policy and regulatory activities and negotiate contracts for exploration and production.	S	L	M		
The Agribusiness Promotion Project is designed to accelerate a private sector supply response to the government's more liberal policies in the area of agro-processing. Its objectives are to increase and diversify agricultural exports and induce greater efficiency in agricultural production, processing and marketing. The project will include (i) the privatization of government-owned agro-industries in the tea, sugar, cotton, and rice subsectors and (ii) the establishment of an agri-business development fund, which will finance professional training and commercial services to private entrepreneurs and professional organizations, for market development, on a matching fund basis.	HU	U	N		

(*Table continues on the following page.*)

Table E4.2: Stand-Alone Trade Technical Assistance Loans, 1987–2004 (continued)

Region	Country	Project name	Fiscal year of approval	Amount approved (US$m)	Amount disbursed (US$m)
Europe and Central Asia	Albania	Tax Administration Modernization Project	1995	4	3.3
Africa	Cameroon	Transport Sector Technical Assistance Project	1995	10.2	9.3
Europe and Central Asia	Turkey	Baku Ceyhan Oil Export Pipeline Technical Assistance Project	1997	5	2.9

Objectives	Implementation completion report project ratings				
	Outcome	Sustain-ability	Institutional development impact	Bank perform-ance	Borrower perform-ance
The Tax Administration Modernization Project's objective is to assist the authorities to sustain and enhance revenue collection in the short term and to improve tax and customs administration in the long run. This objective is to be achieved by institutional and technological strengthening of administrative units in charge of national taxes. The strategy includes defining the roles of the various entities, the collection and taxpayer auditing areas, the improvement of taxpayer services for the current tax structure, preparation for the implementation of the value added tax (VAT), as well as measures to improve the efficiency of the Customs Directorate. The project has five major components: (a) technical cooperation to implement the short/medium-term measures to sustain revenue collection, and to reorganize the tax and customs administrations; (b) technical cooperation for the development and implementation of a VAT that would replace the current turnover tax in 1995; (c) technical cooperation for the setting up of two pilot units to implement a computer-based system for monitoring compliance with basic tax obligations; (d) training for both tax and customs officers; and (e) purchase of vehicles, equipment and materials and any necessary refurbishing of buildings to accommodate the equipment for both tax and customs directorates.	S	L	S	S	S
With the assistance of the Transport Sector Technical Assistance Project, the government intends to (a) launch the transport sector reform program, which would result in the creation of a new private civil aviation company, private operation of rail services, liquidation of the urban bus company, sale of public in CAMSHIP and CAMTAINER, restructuring of the Ministere des Transports (MINT), and reform of the regulatory framework for air, urban, and maritime transport; and (b) continue preparation of the subsequent phases which will result in (i) restructuring of Ministere des Travaux Publics (MINTP); (ii) restructuring and downsizing of the port authority; implementation of an efficiency-driven organization for dredging; and (iii) improved customs institutional framework, overhaul of customs computerized information system, and implementation of a new international transit system.	S	L	S	S	S
The objectives of the Baku-Ceyhan Oil Export Pipeline Technical Assistance Project are to (a) identify and evaluate technically viable and environmentally sustainable pipeline route options for the export of crude oil from Baku in Azerbaijan to the international markets throughout Ceyhan in Turkey, under various throughput assumptions; (b) conduct optimization studies of the routes so identified to arrive at the most robust pipeline route and configuration which merits further and more detailed technical financial and economic evaluations; and (c) recommend a realistic commercial structure for building, constructing and operating the selected pipelines. The project will be carried out by one or more consultants and will consist of the following components: (a) review and update existing studies by Boru Hatlari ile Petro Tasima A.S. (BOTAS) on the various pipeline routes; (b) preliminary design, route survey, implementation plan; (c) economic and financial analysis on various throughput assumptions to be agreed with BOTAS; (d) commercial structure and development of Tariff models; and (e) an environmental audit.	S	L	M	S	S

(Table continues on the following page.)

Table E4.2: Stand-Alone Trade Technical Assistance Loans, 1987–2004 (continued)

Region	Country	Project name	Fiscal year of approval	Amount approved (US$m)	Amount disbursed (US$m)
Africa	Côte d'Ivoire	Private Sector Development Capacity Building Project	1998	12	
South Asia	Bangladesh	Export Diversification Project	1999	32.0	
East Asia and Pacific	Papua New Guinea	Gas Development and Utilization Technical Assistance Project	2000	7	

	Implementation completion report project ratings				
Objectives	**Outcome**	**Sustain-ability**	**Institutional development impact**	**Bank perform-ance**	**Borrower perform-ance**
The objective of the Private Sector Development Capacity Building Project is to help Côte d'Ivoire achieve a sustainable growth rate of at least 6 percent per annum through increased levels of investments and exports. Specifically the project will contribute to (a) reducing the dependency of traditional exports and increasing the share of high value added products in the nation's export structure; (b) attracting foreign investors and promoting domestic investment by foreign direct investment (FDI) targeting, simplifying investment procedures; and (c) creating a more secure legal and judicial environment for new investors and existing mechanisms. The project components include: (a) export promotion; (b) investment promotion/ simplification of investment procedures/ small and medium-size enterprise (SME) support/ public/private consultation; (c) strengthening of legal and judicial system (implementation of regional business law reform under the OHADA (Organisation pour l Harmonisation du Droit des Affaires en Afrique—Organization for the Harmonization of Business Laws in Africa) Treaty; and (d) project preparation facility (PPF) and contingencies.					
The Export Diversification Project's main goal is to accelerate Bangladesh's integration into the world economy by expanding net export production value through product and market diversification, including increased value added. Important subsidiary goals are to improve the business environment for industry and commerce generally. The project is divided into three broad components. The first, product and market development support, emphasizes entrepreneur capacity building and promoting markets in export support services. It consists of administration and advisory services as well as funding to operate a matching grant facility and smaller subprojects to strengthen selected public, private, and public/private support service providers not amenable to matching grants. The second component, trade management capacity building, focuses on key aspects of the policy and institutional environment for export and other business. It includes more rapid clearance for exports and their imported inputs, better bonded warehousing and duty drawback schemes, a management information system, the piloting of modern auditing and risk management methods, taxpayer education, and staff training. Another subproject strengthens capacity in the tariff commission for trade data and protection policy analysis and in the commerce ministry for international and regional trade cooperation. A coordination and development unit will undertake analysis of export constraints and institutional change needs.					
The Gas Development and Utilization Technical Assistance Project will strengthen the government's capacity to efficiently manage the gas sector development in Papua New Guinea. The components call for (1) enhanced skills within the Petroleum Division's expertise in gas resource evaluation, market assessment, processing, and distribution. Skills will be upgraded through a needs-based training program, consisting of on-the-job training, short courses, industrial know-how, and post-graduate studies.					

(*Table continues on the following page.*)

Table E4.2: Stand-Alone Trade Technical Assistance Loans, 1987–2004 (continued)

Region	Country	Project name	Fiscal year of approval	Amount approved (US$m)	Amount disbursed (US$m)
Africa	Malawi	Fiscal Restructuring and Deregulation Program Technical Assistance Project (03)	2001	3	
South Asia	Pakistan	Trade and Transport Facilitation Project	2001	3.0	

Objectives	Implementation completion report project ratings: Outcome	Sustainability	Institutional development impact	Bank performance	Borrower performance
Management training will be provided to cover project management and implementation, while other government departments will also participate in relevant courses and training assignments to promote coherent policies and understanding of the petroleum industry to enable consistent sector management practices within the government; (2) studies, to be undertaken in-house, by the Petroleum Division staff, under expert supervision, covering liquid petroleum gas (LPG) policy and utilization; gas-based industrial development and power generation opportunities, and gas transportation and export, as well as gas pipeline and facility regulations. Institutional studies will address the transition of the Petroleum Division into a Statutory authority; (3) promotion of investment opportunities for gas export, and domestic utilization, through seminars, and public awareness campaigns.					
The Third Fiscal Restructuring and Deregulation Program Project and the Third Fiscal Restructuring and Deregulation Program Technical Assistance Project are made in support of policy reforms designed to accelerate economic growth and reduce poverty and to help deepen structural reforms launched in 1995 to improve public sector management, promote private sector growth, and strengthen the social safety net, and to help Malawi implement policy reforms, especially in the area of financial management, supported by the Credit. The Credit will also assist the government in maintaining macroeconomic stability by meeting financing requirements (gap) in the balance of payments. In the fiscal accounts, the Credit will enable the government to maintain an overall non-interest expenditure level at about 24 percent of GDP. This will allow the government to protect outlays in key social sectors, while reducing domestic borrowing, thereby helping to reduce inflation and interest rates.					
The Trade and Transport Facilitation Project will establish a public/private sector collaborative institutional framework to develop the first phase of Pakistan's medium-term trade and transport facilitation program; that is, to modernize trade practices and procedures based on international best practices. The project components call for (1) establishment and operation of the National Trade and Transport Facilitation Committee (NTTFC) Secretariat. The component comprises technical assistance (TA) provided by the United Nations Conference on Trade and Development (UNCTAD); incremental costs of the Secretariat's professional staff; selected and agreed reimbursable operating costs of the Secretariat and the Ministry of Commerce, while local support staff, office space, utilities, and cash contributions, among others, will be provided by the Pakistan Shippers Council; (2) TA to draft modern trade and transport facilitation procedures, documents, and legislation; (3) human resources development, by providing training to NTTFC Secretariat staff, as well as to the public/private staff directly involved in project implementation; and (4) development of the third-year program, to be detailed at the mid-term review, which should cover the above-mentioned components.					

(*Table continues on the following page.*)

Table E4.2: Stand-Alone Trade Technical Assistance Loans, 1987–2004 (continued)

Region	Country	Project name	Fiscal year of approval	Amount approved (US$m)	Amount disbursed (US$m)
Latin America and the Caribbean	Panama	Public Policy Reform Technical Assistance Project	2002	10.5	
Latin America and the Caribbean	Peru	Peru Trade Facilitation and Productivity Improvement Technical Assistance Project	2003	20.00	

Source: IEG staff estimation.

	Implementation completion report project ratings				
Objectives	**Outcome**	**Sustain-ability**	**Institutional development impact**	**Bank perform-ance**	**Borrower perform-ance**
The Public Policy Reform Technical Assistance Project aims at consolidating and deepening the reforms needed to accelerate growth, and reduce poverty, by strengthening the government's economic monitoring and planning, policy formulation, and execution capacity. The components will (1) support trade reform and institutional capacity by (a) implementing the competition, consumer protection, and unfair trade policy law and (b) strengthening the trade negotiating capacity of the Vice-ministry of International Trade, so as to conclude market opening trade agreements, develop capacity to prepare—with the private sector participation—international competitiveness diagnostic and negotiating strategies, and by building management capacity in specialized trade policy areas; (2) improve the quality and timeliness of macroeconomic data through technical assistance (TA) focused on accurate calculation methodologies of economic activities, and modernization of computer systems. Capacity building and advisory services will be provided to strengthen economic management, to draft legislation, and to implement economic proposals. It includes the management of the debt reduction scheme and implementation of the Economic Recovery and Public Expenditure Rationalization Plans; (3) improve social spending and reduce poverty through TA provision, focused on monitoring and evaluation of tools, targeted toward poverty reduction; (4) strengthen the public procurement system, by improving the procurement legal framework, and building institutional capacity, supported by the development of an electronic system; and (5) support project management, namely to oversee project design, implementation, and coordination among implementing agencies.					
The Trade Facilitation and Productivity Improvement Technical Assistance Project development objectives are to assist the GOP in (a) establishing a more streamlined, integrated, and effective institutional, and policy framework to increase nontraditional exports and (b) developing and implementing initiatives designed to foster the entrance of new export market participants, especially small and medium producers.					

APPENDIX E5: GENEVA SURVEY RESULTS

Interviews with Geneva-Based Organizations

Princeton Survey Research Associates International was retained by the Independent Evaluation Group of the World Bank to conduct in-depth interviews to assist in the assessment of the Bank's work in the area of global trade and trade negotiations. Twenty-eight interviews were conducted with individuals associated with negotiations of the World Trade Organization in Geneva and Bern, Switzerland, between March 17 and March 24, 2005. The one-on-one interviews took place with high-level WTO officials, ambassadors to the WTO, and professional staff members from country delegations and ancillary organizations. Those interviewed represented a good distribution of people from developing and industrial countries.

The objectives of the interviews were to:

(i) Assess perception of the World Bank's work on trade, in view of its advocacy objectives.
(ii) Obtain views on the World Bank's strategy for trade.
(iii) Capture the most effective Bank products and sources of information for advocacy.

Background

Almost without exception, those interviewed had a detailed and thoughtful knowledge of trade and trade negotiations. Most believe trade has been and will continue to be an engine of economic improvement. They point to global trade growing at a faster rate than the world economy overall. However, there is some fear among the least-developed countries as they see preferences eroding, and a push to get them to liberalize their trade policies without sufficient help in transforming their economies.

Everyone associated with the WTO realizes the critical stage of the negotiations with important benchmarks over the summer, a crucial meeting at the end of the year in Hong Kong, and final talks next year. There is a great deal of uncertainty on whether the goals will be achieved, and opinions range from very optimistic to very pessimistic.

Perceptions of the World Bank

The Bank is seen as a key organization that has the resources and the standing to generate necessary research relating to the talks. The Bank's increased attention to trade in recent years is also viewed positively. High praise is given to the Bank office in Geneva, which is viewed as accessible and responsive.

On a more critical note, most of the people interviewed talked of a disconnect between the Bank's work and its practical application. There is fairly wide agreement that the Bank's research often lacks a strong correlation with current negotiations, and with what is actually happening within countries. As part of the criticism, it was often mentioned that the Bank only works "top-down" and does not consult or partner with others while producing research.

Almost all assume that the Bank has a role in trade and trade negotiations. The type of research currently being conducted is seen as a primary role of the Bank. In addition, a larger role in applicable and topical research is desired, and most would like to see the Bank's lending practices more tied to their trade work. Infrastructure and transitioning costs in countries attempting to modernize their trade economies were frequently mentioned as areas where Bank resources could be of great assistance.

The Bank is viewed as having an agenda that pushes trade liberalization. This is generally seen as positive by industrial countries and WTO officials, but somewhat negatively by developing countries and some nongovernmental organizations that work with the developing world. Despite the perceived predisposition, just about everyone still appreciates Bank research.

Several individuals mentioned the need for the Bank to recognize the importance of regional trade agreements. With the length of time it takes to produce a global trade pact, they say it is natural that countries will seek regional agreements. They wish the Bank would give more time and effort to researching the impact of these agreements, and help countries determine whether these regional agreements are to their benefit or detriment.

The Bank is seen as too often taking a "one-size-fits-all" approach to trade. Developing countries wished to be seen as full partners, to be included at every stage of the Bank's research and lending policy.

Two ambassadors to the WTO had little to no knowledge of the World Bank's work on trade in Geneva. They assumed that the Bank's work in trade was tangential at best, and was only evident in Bank lending policies. These individuals were not only unaware of the Bank's office dealing with trade in Geneva, but were largely unaware of the research and data developed by the Bank on trade. It is not possible to extrapolate how many ambassadors might have the same low level of knowledge, but it is a cautionary note: there is a segment of delegations that is unaware of the Bank's work on trade.

The World Bank Strategy

The Bank's stated strategy on trade—as supporting development—was generally applauded by those interviewed. Only a small minority believe that trade does not have a role in development. Their position is that the WTO is an organization whose mission is to liberalize trade, which will help the economy overall, but there is no guarantee (nor should there be) that trade will help developing countries. For most, their only criticism of the strategy is a perceived disconnect between the stated strategy and a push toward liberalization that does not always account for the interim stages developing countries go through, or the transitional adjustment they may face.

Integration of trade as a core aspect of country development strategies is seen as being on point. The importance of making trade work with all the other aspects of development within a country is seen as critical to a successful, comprehensive approach. In line with the Bank's strategy of integration, most give the Bank a great deal of credit for developing and taking the lead on the Integrated Framework for Trade-Related Technical Assistance. They see the Integrated Framework approach of having all of the major organizations working together toward one policy for a given country as a major advance. However, the high expectations accompanying the Integrated Framework leave some fearful that the Bank will stop at the stage of diagnosis, and not follow through with actions to fix the problems identified.

The vast majority believes that, taken together, the Bank's strategy of promoting changes in the world trading system to make it supportive of development on a global level, especially for the poorest of the developing countries, and integrating trade at the country level are exactly the correct focus areas for the World Bank. Most often the only suggestion for making the strategy stronger is to add the inclusion of countries as partners in the process, and realize the uniqueness of each country in developing their specific strategy.

In the current world of trade preferences, tariffs, and internal subsidies, many worry that while the Bank says it is supportive of development, the least developed countries will suffer from the Bank's push toward liberalization. They want to see the Bank work with these countries on strategies—tailored for the specific country—that provide contingencies for the inevitable dislocations their economies will experience as they move more into a world of lower trade barriers.

Many understand the Bank's reluctance to get into areas viewed as political, and they see the possibility of the Bank losing standing in the trade and development community if it attempts to tackle all of the areas that are criticized. Nevertheless, most often mentioned is the need for work on ad valorem tariffs. This work is seen as critical in the current negotiations, and the

Bank is viewed as a neutral source with the resources to work on this issue. While some view the ad valorem issue as too political for Bank involvement, others say that *because* the issue has become so political, the World Bank is needed to step in and provide an impartial formula to cut through the current complexity.

Products and Information

A theme heard throughout the interviews and relayed in this report is the high quality of the research done by the Bank. The Bank is viewed as having some of the most respected people in the area of trade and trade negotiations working on its staff. Trips to Geneva to discuss recent research are appreciated by all. For the most part, the work produced by the Bank is well regarded by the trade community in Geneva. There is wide diversity of opinion regarding which reports are of the most use.

The annual *Global Economic Prospects* reports that focus on trade were mentioned more than any other Bank report. These reports are viewed as long-term reference material. Beyond this series, there is a range of opinion on what specific studies are particularly useful. There is a consensus that in their busy lives, a strong summary of the document is particularly helpful. Also, many continue to point out they would like to see the Bank move beyond its analytical, one-step-removed mode of operating to a mode that includes countries early in the process of deciding which topic to research, doing the actual research, and the write-ups and implementation of the research.

Most appreciate both the longer in-depth research that they use as reference material and the shorter, more focused reports. Most are overwhelmed with paperwork, and a short, focused, area-specific report is viewed by many as ideal. Again, work that is not country-specific and practical enough is an often-heard criticism. A role partially filled by the Bank, and seen as critical, is helping individuals identify the specific Bank research that would be helpful to them.

It was often mentioned that it is appreciated when trade information is written into individual country reports. A fairly frequent criticism is that the Bank charges for reports. Many would like to be able to access this information on the Internet, or receive the reports/data for free. The Bank is seen to be working at cross-purposes: that it attempts to disseminate its findings, yet charges for those findings.

There is uneven use of the World Bank's Web site as a means of accessing trade information. Several say it is the first place they would go if they needed trade data and that they find the site easy to navigate. Others profess a lack of time or ability to wade through the information.

Meetings and seminars are viewed as important tools for the trade community in Geneva to keep abreast of the Bank's work. Those interviewed are particularly grateful when reports still in development are discussed with them. These meetings are seen as one of the few opportunities for those outside the Bank to have a small influence on its work. A minority say they are usually too busy to attend these meetings.

A sizeable number of those interviewed have personal contacts within the Bank. These individual contacts are seen as very useful in accessing Bank resources. Bank personnel are generally viewed as helpful, with more assistance seen as coming from staff directly involved in trade, and slightly less from the operational side.

APPENDIX E6: STAFF SURVEY RESULTS

Introduction

This appendix, prepared by Princeton Survey Research Associates International, summarizes findings of Bank staff views on the effectiveness and quality of the Bank's trade work, based on survey results from 141 staff members drawn from among operational country economists, economic advisers, private sector development (PSD) task team leaders of trade-related projects, trade economists Bankwide, and country directors. The responses constitute about 37 percent of the total numbers of the target groups.

Evaluation Survey on the Bank's Analytical Work and Operational Linkages

n = 141 Bank Staff
Field Dates: 03.17.2005—05.25.2005
Margin of error based on full sample = = +/– 8% (5% based on PREM)

Sample Type One

Total	141
Regional	74%
Non-regional	26%

Sample Type Two

Total	141
Bank staff—trade	16%
Bank staff—not trade	84%

Sample Type Three

Total	141
All Bank staff	100%
External (not Bank staff)	—

Q1. In general, how much do you follow trade issues?

Total	141
A great deal	28%
A moderate amount	34%
An average amount	25%
Only a little	13%
Not at all	1%
No response	—

Q2. And how knowledgeable are you about trade issues?

Total	141
Very knowledgeable	23%
Moderately knowledgeable	45%
Average knowledge	28%
Not too knowledgeable	4%
Not knowledgeable at all	—
No response	—

Q3. Now thinking about the World Bank, how much do you follow the Bank's work on trade?

Total	141
A great deal	18%
A moderate amount	38%
An average amount	28%
Only a little	15%
Not at all	1%
No response	—

Q4. And how knowledgeable are you about the Bank's work on trade?

Total	141
Very knowledgeable	17%
Moderately knowledgeable	40%
Average knowledge	32%
Not too knowledgeable	10%
Not knowledgeable at all	1%
No response	—

Q5a. Overall how would you rate the Bank's performance on:

- (Percent of respondents rating it good or very good)
- Promoting changes in the world trading system to benefit poor countries?
- Promoting trade as a means of growth, competitiveness and poverty reduction in country development strategies
- Promoting policy reforms that influence trade integration
- Promoting institutional reforms that have a positive effect on trade
- Promoting a multi-sectoral approach to trade development
- Strengthening borrower capacity-building in trade
- Considering trade-poverty linkages such as potential adjustment costs of trade or labor market channels

Q6. Do you agree or disagree with this Bank strategy —To promote changes in the world trading system so that it is supportive of development especially for the poorest countries and for poor people across the developing world.

Total	141
Strongly agree	72%
Somewhat agree	20%
Neither agree nor disagree	6%
Somewhat disagree	1%
Strongly disagree	1%
No response	1%

Q7. And how likely is it that this goal will be achieved in the next decade?

Total	141
Very likely	2%
Somewhat likely	50%
Neither likely or unlikely	19%
Not too likely	26%
Not likely at all	1%
No response	1%

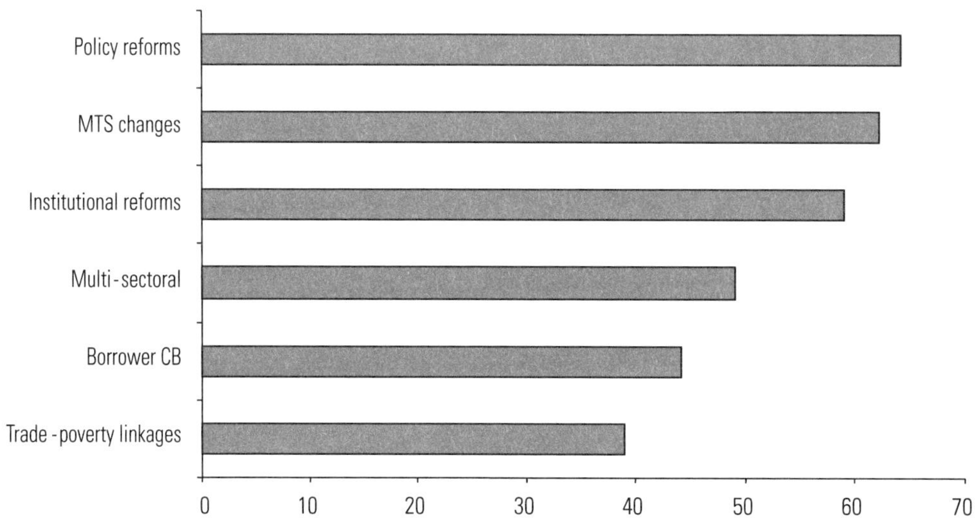

Q8. The second goal is to promote integration into the world economy through trade as a core aspect of a country's development strategy. Do you agree or disagree with this Bank strategy?

Total	141
Strongly agree	63%
Somewhat agree	31%
Neither agree nor disagree	4%
Somewhat disagree	1%
Strongly disagree	—
No response	1%

Q9. And how likely is it that this goal will be achieved in the next decade?

Total	141
Very likely	13%
Somewhat likely	60%
Neither likely or unlikely	17%
Not too likely	9%
Not likely at all	—
No response	1%

Q17. What recommendations, if any, do you have to improve the Bank's analytical work on trade whether from Networks or Regions?

Open end response please see World Bank IEG Verbatims.xls

- Increase operational relevance
- More practical how-tos
- Better integration between regions and TD and other networks (PSD, ESSD mentioned most frequently)
- More empirical research to bolster Bank's case
- More practical work on regional/bilateral FTA issues

Q18. Have you ever used the World Bank's trade website—www.worldbank.org/trade?

Total	141
Yes	58%
No	41%
No response	1%

Q19.1 Which of the following best describes why you haven't used the Bank's trade website

Asked if never used website

Multiple Mentions

Total	58
It isn't relevant for my current assignment	29%
I wasn't aware of it	47%
It is hard to navigate the website	3%
The information on the website isn't current	—
The information on the website isn't useful or informative	2%
I'm too busy	14%
Other reason	3%
No response	2%

Q19.2 Which of the following best describes why you haven't used the Bank's trade website

Asked if never used website

Total	9
It isn't relevant for my current assignment	—
I wasn't aware of it	44%
It is hard to navigate the website	11%
The information on the website isn't current	—
The information on the website isn't useful or informative	—
I'm too busy	44%
Other reason	—
No response	—

Q19.3 Which of the following best describes why you haven't used the Bank's trade website

Asked if never used website

Total	4
It isn't relevant for my current assignment	—
I wasn't aware of it	—
It is hard to navigate the website	—
The information on the website isn't current	—
The information on the website isn't useful or informative	25%
I'm too busy	25%
Other reason	50%
No response	—

Q19.4 Which of the following best describes why you haven't used the Bank's trade website

Asked if never used website

Total	1
It isn't relevant for my current assignment	—
I wasn't aware of it	—
It is hard to navigate the website	—
The information on the website isn't current	—
The information on the website isn't useful or informative	—
I'm too busy	100%
Other reason	—
No response	—

Q20. On average how often do you use the Bank's trade website?

Asked if used website

Total	82
A few times a week	10%
Weekly	6%
At least once a month	26%
Once every few months	40%
At least once a year	13%
Less often	5%
No response	—

Q21. Is there one particular trade-related topic that should receive more attention from Bank trade specialists, whether from Networks or Regions, than it is currently receiving?

Asked if Bank Staff

Total	141
Yes	51%
No	40%
No response	9%

Q22. What one area should receive more attention?

Open end response

- Adjustment/transitional costs from liberalization and the links between trade and poverty at the operational level were most frequently cited
- Next: market access, political economy, regional integration, trade facilitation, behind the border constraints, trade and growth (country-specific)

Q23. What is the most important aspect of the ongoing work of the Bank's Trade Department?

Open end response

- Advocacy of the TD on industrial country policies by a landslide — mentioned five times as frequently as the next issue (TA to developing countries)

Q24. What is the least important aspect of the ongoing work of the Bank's Trade Department?

Open end response

Q26. What aspect of the ongoing trade work of the Bank, whether from Networks or Regions, is most in need of improvement?

Open end response

- Multi-sectoral linkages
- More short notes, lessons, best practice pieces
- New empirical evidence that can be used to convince governments and skeptics outside the Bank
- More country-specific support on the linkages between trade, growth and poverty
- Integration of work between network and regions

Q27. Is there any activity or topic that the Bank's Trade Department should drop?

Asked if Bank Staff and not in Trade Department

Total	118
Yes	5%
No	56%
No response	39%

Q28. What is it and why should it be dropped?

Open end response

Q29. Over the last three years, how many projects or ESW activities have you worked on with Bank staff who are trade specialists?

Asked if Bank Staff and not in Trade Department

Total	118
Zero	27%
One	25%
Two	27%
Three	12%
Four	2%
Five	2%
Six	—
Seven	1%
Eight	1%
Nine	—
Ten	3%
No Response	1%

Q30. How knowledgeable were they in the areas you required assistance?

Asked if worked with Bank Staff who are trade specialists

Total	85
Very knowledgeable	55%
Moderately knowledgeable	29%
Average knowledge	12%
Not too knowledgeable	2%
Not knowledgeable	—
No response	1%

Q31. In your opinion, is expertise related to international trade under-represented in your region?

Asked if Bank Staff and not in Trade Department

Total	118
Yes	46%
No	47%
No response	8%

Q32. What expertise related to international trade is under-represented? Please list from most important to least important expertise.

Open end response

- Trade facilitation, customs, trade finance, EPZs, trade promotion institutions most frequently mentioned (equal weight)

Next in order of frequency:

- Regional integration; analysis of bilateral, regional FTAs
- Practical how-tos; implementation experience; best practice
- Agriculture commodity markets
- Standards
- Trade and growth linkages

Demographics

D1. What is your primary network affiliation?

Total	141
PREM	79%
Private Sector Development	8%
Infrastructure	1%
Environmentally and Socially Sustainable Development	9%
Operational Core Services	2%
Other	1%
No response	—

D1_1. What is your primary network affiliation?

Open end response

D2. What is your current regional affiliation?

Total	141
Africa	19%
East Asia & the Pacific	13%
Europe and Central Asia	18%
Latin America & the Caribbean	11%
Middle East & North Africa	9%
South Asia	6%
PREM Anchor	7%
DEC	12%
WBI	1%
OPC	1%
Other	1%
No response	2%

D3. Where are you based?

Total	141
Headquarters	65%
Field	34%
Other	1%
No response	—

D4. For approximately how many years have you worked at the Bank?

Total	141
Less than 5 years	28%
5 to 10 years	38%
More than 10 years	33%

D5. Please indicate which of the following best describes your current functional position.

(percent of respondents)

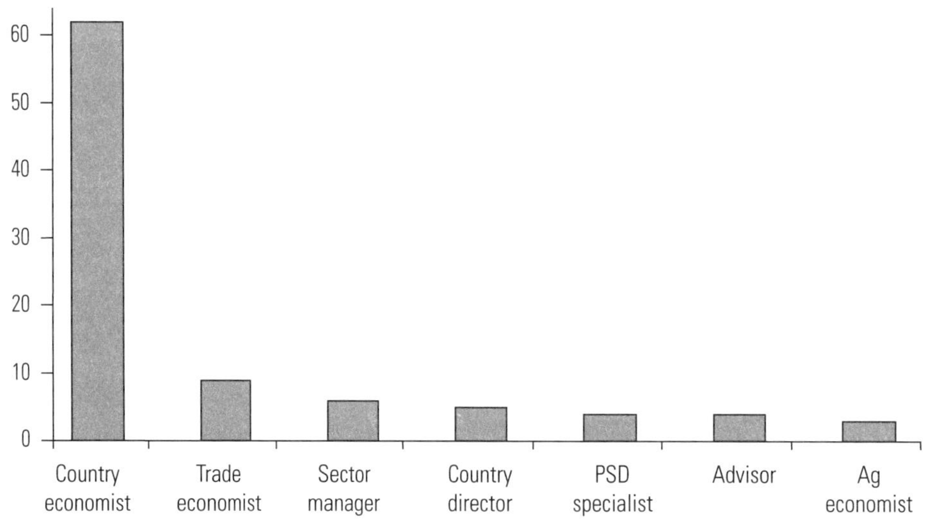

APPENDIX E7: TRADE IN COUNTRY ASSISTANCE STRATEGIES

Fiscal Years 1998–2000

Country	Extensive analysis	Specific measures proposed
Tanzania		Simplify tariff structure.
Ghana		Gateway project. Complete review of tariff regime.
Mozambique		Continue liberalization of trade regime. Main ports under concession.
Nigeria		
Zambia		Maintain liberal exchange and trade regime. Resolution of ZCCM reform. Remove oil import restrictions.
South Africa	Subsection on regional trade integration.	Maintain competitive exchange rate. Commitment to future trade liberalization. Reduction of regional trade barriers.
Gabon	Subsection on exports diversification	Deepen trade liberalization.
Kenya		
Gambia, The	Section on export oriented growth	Tariff reduction. Establish free trade zones. Gateway project. Establish export promotion agency.
Malawi	Section on trade and investment	Improve administration of EPZs. Tariff reforms and better exchange rate management.
Lesotho	Section on integrating into the regional and global economy.	Eliminate remaining exchange controls.
Mali		Privatize international railway.
Rwanda		Promote development of high value added crops for exports. Tariff reduction. Duty drawback for exports.
Senegal	Section on regional integration	Implement Common External Tariff (CET) reduction. Trade reform adjustment credit (2000).
Cape Verde		Reduction of NTBs and reform of foreign exchange system.
Guinea	Section on exports diversification	
Mozambique		Tariff Reform. Cashew impact monitoring.
Niger		Road rehabilitation.
Ethiopia		Liberalize trade regime. Develop exports promotion strategy. Liberalization of foreign exchange regime.
Côte d'Ivoire		Implement Common External Tariff.
Ghana	Subsection of diversifying agricultural exports	Promote agricultural exports harnessing private sector participation (trade facilitation studies). Increase availability of working capital credit to exporters.
Pacific regional strategy		Trade liberalization.
Cambodia		
Bhutan	Section on trade diversification.	Increase horticultural exports.
Papua New Guinea		
Philippines		Simplify customs procedures.
Laos		Improve accessibility to neighboring countries.
Malaysia		Lifting of temporary import tariffs.
Belarus		Adoption of a unified market exchange rate.
Vietnam		Trade liberalization program. Exports competitiveness study.
Thailand		Competitiveness study.
Mongolia		Upgrade freight corridor through China. Reduce infrastructure costs for exports sectors.
Bosnia and Herzegovina		
Russia		Customs strengthening. Accession to WTO.
Azerbaijan		Support for trade liberalization in agriculture.
Croatia		Improve customs procedures.
Lithuania		
Moldova		Simplify customs policies.

Main objective	Only briefly mention trade
Subobjective of promoting agricultural exports.	
Subobjective of expanding non-traditional exports.	
	Oil exports
Subobjective of raising exports and regional trade integration.	
Subobjective of promoting trade.	
	U.S. trade initiative toward Africa
Subobjective of further trade liberalization.	
Subobjective of promoting nontraditional exports.	
Main objective to promote private sector trade and investment.	
Trade liberalization in the context of West African Economic and Monetary Union (WAEMU).	
Main objective of promotion of open economic policies.	
Promoting export expansion is part of one main objective.	
Coordinate enhanced IFC and MIGA lending and nonlending assistance in the areas of financial sector, exports and infrastructure.	
	Commodities exports
	Mining exports
Objective of liberalization of the exchange rate mechanism.	
Subobjective of promoting agricultural exports.	
Subobjective to facilitate trade infrastructure.	
Main objective to develop infrastructure to support to contribute to global integration.	
	Importance of exports performance
Objective of supporting EU accession.	

(*Table continues on the following page.*)

Fiscal Years 1998–2000 (continued)

Country	Extensive analysis	Specific measures proposed
Macedonia		Lowering tariffs level and dispersion.
Albania		Maintain low and uniform tariffs.
Tajikistan		Move to a market denominated exchange rate. Eliminate export restrictions.
Latvia		Strengthen customs administration.
Kyrgyz Republic		Implement automated customs system.
Bulgaria		Support EU accession program. Elimination of exports taxes and QRs to imports. Develop clear objectives regarding Free Trade Areas.
Uzbekistan		Gradually remove trade and exchange rate restrictions.
Hungary		
Georgia		Strengthen customs administration.
Turkey		One of the actions is to strengthen customs. Also port reform. Supports oil exports. Rationalize trade barriers in agriculture.
Armenia		Trade and Transport Project.
Bosnia and Herzegovina	An overview section entitled "Recovery of Trade Important for Medium-Term Growth."	
Kazakhstan		
Uruguay		Adoption of technology to diversify exports.
Brazil		Ports restructuring.
Honduras		Improve business climate to promote export sectors.
Dominican Republic	Subsection on trade liberalization and agricultural sector reform	Trade reform bill.
Mexico		Seek to improve linkages between large exporters and small firms.
Trinidad and Tobago		Strengthen customs administration.
Panama		Eliminate NTBs and issues WTO regulation. Lowering NTBs and tariffs on food items.
Guatemala		Support for regional infrastructure development.
Bolivia		Infrastructure for international trade.
Nicaragua		
Colombia		
Tunisia	Section on increased international competition.	Support export promotion, trade liberalization, customs strengthening.
Jordan	Subsection on Private Investment, Export Development and Tourism	Establish standards system for agriculture exports. Promote linkages between farmers-exporters. Aqaba Freeport development.
Yemen		Reform of customs administration. Establishment of exports zones. Non-Lending Services: Institutions for exports promotion.
Lebanon		Export Promotion Project (nonlending FY98).
Nepal	Section on Foreign Trade and Investment	
Bangladesh		Concrete program to reduce tariffs and NTBs. Project supporting export diversification. Trade institutional strengthening. Exports matching grants. Promoting agricultural exports.
India	Section on Trade and regulatory reforms	

Main objective	Only briefly mention trade
Subobjective of ensuring environment conducive to exports growth	
Subobjective on trade and price policies.	
Improvement of incentives for private investment by further liberalizing trade.	
Main objective of liberalizing trade and exchange rate regimes.	
	Completion of trade liberalization.
One of the explicit goals of improving infrastructure is to promote exports.	
	Previous trade liberalization.
Subobjecitve of increasing agroexports and exports diversification through private sector participation.	
Subobjective of liberalize trade and agriculture.	
Subobjecitve of exports diversification.	
Subobjective of trade reform.	
Subobjective to increase trade.	
	Trade policy regime.
	Trade policy regime.
Subobjective to promote Tunisia's integration in the world economy.	
Objective of reviving growth through export development.	
Subobjective of export development.	
Main objective to support an outward-oriented private sector driving economic growth.	

(Table continues on the following page.)

Fiscal Years 2001–03

Country	Document	Extensive analysis	Specific measures proposed
Algeria	CAS	(1) The movement to a market economy and the liberalization of trade represented two things simultaneously to many enterprises: a shock but also a scope for extraordinary development opportunities. Many enterprises struggle in the face of foreign competition, for which they are ill prepared.	As of April 20, 2002, International Finance Corporation (IFC) net committed portfolio in Algeria is $558.6m, of which $20m is guarantee of a trade enhancement facility.
Ethiopia	CAS		
Gambia	CAS	Section on strategy describes an export promotion strategy.	
Guinea	CAS		The PRSP envisages that policy reforms in customs, tax administration, transportation and the like will be implemented to foster regional integration and to remove bottlenecks constraining trade. The results of a 2003 integrated trade framework diagnostic will support the government's actions in this area.
Malawi	CAS	A section is devoted to the analysis of the trade sector.	Mentions the implementation of the Regional Trade Facilitation Project.
Mauritania	CAS		
Niger	CAS		Mentions that the Agro-Pastoral Export Promotion Project is helping producers of exportable crops and animal products collectively invest in production and marketing so as to allow them to increase sales by putting tools of transport, market information, storage and credit in their hands.
Rwanda	CAS	The PRSP identifies export production as an important source of growth and the transformation of the economy.	The ongoing Regional Trade Facilitation project is mentioned. New trade-related loans.
Senegal	CAS		Refers to the DTIS and supports its implementation. These include reforms in fisheries policies, to be implemented under the planned Coastal and Marine Biodiversity Project (FY04—base case, with GEF support). Further efforts will be made to improve food safety, as identified in the current regional AAA on food safety, so as to meet world trade standards. The proposed PIPP will continue promotion of tourism.
China	CAS		A set of studies addressing the effects of China's WTO accession on trade and investment in Asia is nearing completion.
Philippines	CAS		

Main objective	Only briefly mention trade
Part of key development challenges are: (1) Reducing Algeria's vulnerability to export revenues from oil. (2) Enhancing the efficiency of infrastructure, trade-related services, streamlining customs procedures, and upgrading product standards to international norms to improve Algeria's attractiveness of export-oriented investment and to reap the benefits from a free-trade zone for industrial products with the EU and the requirements of WTO accession.	
Trade is identified as a key sector / cross-cutting issue and promoting higher export growth is part of one of the core objectives of the CAE.	
Within the PRSP framework, Mali's trade policy aims to reduce existing handicaps by pursuing and consolidating the trade liberalization policy that has been implemented since the 1990s (comprising openness to external trade, promoting the development of modern information and communication technologies, and accelerating and strengthening the regional integration process within WAEMU and ECOWAS by implementing an export promotion strategy.	
As part of the First Pillar of the strategy on Poverty and Growth "Actions will be taken to improve the environment for trade. Guinea's trade environment is one of the main impediments to economic growth."	
Part of the PSD strategy is "(v) improving trade facilitation for existing and potential exporters; and (vi) helping exporters meet product and phyto-sanitary standards to export."	
Trade is a significant part of the wealth creation pillar of the CAS, aiming at the development of export-oriented manufacturing, especially garments; in part stimulated by the African Growth and Opportunity Act (AGOA); provision of trade services, in particular based on Senegal becoming a Gateway to West-Africa; and support to ports infrastructure. The strategy also supported reform in the groundnut sector.	
Accession to WTO is a major part of the country strategy.	
Part of the growth objective is to enhance competitiveness through trade and regulatory reforms, especially in the agriculture, services, and small and medium enterprise sectors.	

(*Table continues on the following page.*)

Fiscal Years 2001–03 (continued)

Country	Document	Extensive analysis	Specific measures proposed
Thailand	CAS	One paragraph mentions that China's WTO accession provides export opportunities to Thailand, even as it poses new challenges in third-country markets. There is considerable scope for increasing exports to a more open China.	An in-depth report on Thailand competitiveness will be undertaken in the CEM, in order to sustain higher private investment, to benefit from the rapidly expanding Chinese market and to compete with Chinese exports in the global marketplace.
Vietnam	CAS		
Albania	CAS		(1) The Bank is supporting the port sector through the ongoing Durres Port Project. The ongoing Trade and Transport Facilitation in Southeast Europe Project-part of a regional program joining eight Balkan countries-aims to reduce non-tariff costs of trade and transport and reduce corruption and smuggling at border crossings. A planned Transport Strategy (FY05) will take stock of overall transport sector issues and needs, especially in the context of Albania's alignment with EU structures.
Azerbaijan	CAS		
Belarus	CAS	(1) Belarus' creditworthiness for IBRD lending is poor. This reflects the country's weak liquidity position (reserve coverage is currently only about 2 weeks of imports), fairly substantial external payments arrears that could represent contingent claims on the government, heavy dependence on barter trade, heavy dependence on Russia for trade and finance, and lack of progress on the key reforms required to underpin sustainable growth in the medium term.	(1) The Bank will conduct a financial sector review (2003), which might provide the basis for further policy advice, particularly in the context of the envisaged currency unification with Russia. Under the improvements stipulated in the base case, IFC may be able to attract foreign banks to partner with Belarusian financial institutions, especially in the area of trade financing. (2) In the financial sector, the EBRD is planning to expand the trade facilitation program with local banks and the development of a micro-lending facility.
Bulgaria	CAS		
Kyrgyz Rep.	CAS		
Latvia	CAS		

Main objective	Only briefly mention trade
Among the 5 main objectives of the strategy is to enhance competitiveness through trade reforms.	
(1) A 1998 Country Assistance Evaluation (CAE) by OED assessed IDA assistance to Albania from 1992 to 1997. The CAE concluded that IDA assistance was largely effective, especially in supporting agricultural growth, small- and medium-scale enterprise privatization, tax reform, and price and trade liberalization.	
As a part of strategic goal to generate jobs and sustainable non-oil growth: (a) improving the trade policy regime and market access by creating a more export-friendly tariff structure, accelerating Azerbaijan's accession to the WTO, increasing access to regional markets and the EU, (b) enhancing trade facilitation by streamlining customs procedures and improving the quality and capacity of transportation infrastructure.	
is despite of recent developments in and trade, thus offering better business opportunities for Bulgaria, any setback in the security situation in the region could have a severe impact on Bulgaria's external position and slow down economic growth.	(1) One of the risks in CAS implementation Yugoslavia augur well for regional stability
Trade and Investment is one part of the strategy, with specific attention to exports standards, regional integration. The document mentions an upcoming DTIS as well as the Trade and Transport Facilitation Project as part of this strategy.	

(Table continues on the following page.)

Fiscal Years 2001–03 (continued)

Country	Document	Extensive analysis	Specific measures proposed
Poland	CAS		
Russia	CAS		(1) Improving financial intermediation by IFC and MIGA will extend to trade finance.
Tajikistan	CAS	(1) World Bank's regional study on trade and transportation (FY03).	(1) While export-led growth will be needed to pull Tajikistan's people out of poverty, serious infrastructure deficiencies, unfavorable geography and difficult regional trade environment mean that Tajikistan will have to pay increased attention to the development of its internal markets, that is, on improving local economies during the CAS period. At the same time, it will continue implementation of export diversification programs, but the pay-offs from these programs are likely to come only in the long run. (2) The Analytic and Advisory Activities (AAA), to be undertaken by the World Bank, will include trade and transport facilitation.
Uzbekistan	CAS		(1) Trade liberalization should include the most urgent measures related to import contract registration, foreign currency access, commodity exchanges and the cotton trade. Competition could be addressed by strengthening the Anti-Monopoly Committee (AMC) as proposed in Bank staff's policy note on competition policy reform.

Main objective	Only briefly mention trade
	(1) Another risk to Poland's growth may be imposed by further economic slowdown in Europe. Although exports as a percent of GDP are not that high, 29% in 2001, export's contribution to GDP growth has greatly increased in recent years. Hence, a protracted slowdown in Europe would have a more pronounced impact on Poland's economy than just a few years ago. The indirect effect of the diminished opportunities for Poland's exports to the West would be reduced output and profitability of those firms engaged in export activities and those linked to it.
	(1) Recently, the factors that have driven Russia's economic growth have changed. In 1999, the first year after the crisis, the trade balance provided the single largest contribution to economic growth, reflecting ruble devaluation and oil price improvements. (2) Rail represents a major challenge. Freight rates are high and discriminatory, and the financial transactions of many non-core activities and ancillary companies are not transparent. The cross-subsidy to passenger services forces rail freight rates well above costs, damaging remote locations and potential export trade. (3) At the federal level, the most serious policy issues in agriculture are not with pricing or trade policy, but rather with the legal framework, continued state domination of some markets.
(1) One of the key CAS objectives is to improve the policy framework for liberalization of the foreign exchange and trade regime.	

(*Table continues on the following page.*)

Fiscal Years 2001–03 (continued)

Country	Document	Extensive analysis	Specific measures proposed
Chile	CAS	(1) Trade liberalization helped efficient resource allocation, ensuring a rapid and sustained growth in mining and natural resources. This growth has been export led: export have averaged 9.6% growth per year since 1984 and trade now accounts for about 75% of GDP. While copper remains a key part of Chile's exports (37%), there has been significant diversification into forestry, fishing, wines, fruits, and other agro-based products. (2) Chile is collaborating with its MERCOSUR neighbors and is currently advancing in trade discussions with the USA for a possible bi-lateral trade agreement. It expects the on-going trade talks with the EU to be completed as early as mid-2002. These efforts continue the path that Chile has followed for the past two decades, in liberalizing its trade relations on a bilateral basis, making Chile the most open economy in Latin America.	(1) As a part of the challenge of enhancing investment climate, a reduction in logistics costs would result in the highest welfare gain for Chile due to the importance of trade in the economy.
Colombia	CAS	(1) With regard to the fiscal sector, trade liberalization led to a fall in tariff revenues and negatively affected fiscal balance.	(1) Core CAS monitoring benchmark includes progress implementing Doha, increased number of free trade agreements with developed and developing countries. This is a part of the Global partnership for development. The strategy of is improved coordination of national strategy, maintenance of strong relationship with international financial institutions, negotiation of free trade agreements at regional and global levels. The instruments are competitiveness plans, open trade policy, and international trade negotiations.
El Salvador	CAS	(1) Maquila exports and employment could be affected by WTO rules on removing special tax incentives and the WTO agreement to phase out trade barriers on textiles and clothing. Projected to continue growing at double digits in the medium-term, as a result of an expanded benefit of the Caribbean Basis Initiative, Salvadoran maquila exports could be hit by the global trade agreement scheduled to enter in full effect in January 2005.	(1) As a part of structural growth prospects, preserving productivity gains is essential to remain competitive in world trade. (2) In addition to prudent macroeconomic management, the government's program included a number of critical structural reforms: (i) completing trade reform with enhanced Caribbean Basin Initiative (CBI) access and free trade agreements with Mexico, Canada, Panama, Dominican Republic, and others.

Main objective	Only briefly mention trade
(1) As a part of facilitating the rebirth of the rural economy, the government embarked on a comprehensive reform program for the sector called la apertura. It essentially aimed at (a) trade liberalization and lower tariff reforms, (b) the promotion of market-oriented approaches, and (c) the reduction of state intervention in marketing and licensing activities.	

(Table continues on the following page.)

Fiscal Years 2001–03 (continued)

Country	Document	Extensive analysis	Specific measures proposed
Guyana	CAS		
Mexico	CAS		
Nicaragua	CAS		
Peru	CAS		An export competitiveness and trade facilitation project is planned.
Jordan	CAS		
Yemen	CAS		(1) Yemen's Second Five Year Plan (SFYP), launched in 2001 and the recently completed PRSP provide the basis for this CAS. It benefits, as well, from recent extensive joint work between Yemen and IDA on poverty, public expenditures, trade-enhancement and the investment climate. (2) A multi-donor, Bank-led diagnostic study under the Integrated Framework for Trade Development (FY03) has helped Yemen identify the policy and technical assistance needs. (3) WBI would also provide advice on trade strategy; help develop the Development Research Forum.
Pakistan	CAS		
Pakistan	CAS	(1) Had Pakistan encouraged global production sharing in the textile industry by easing imports of raw materials, its textile and clothing exports would probably both have performed significantly better. (2) The private sector is exposed to international competition, but the anti-export bias and nontransparent trade regime remains. Tariff reductions and rapid devaluation of the currency since 2000 are probably behind the improvements in export performance in recent years.	(1) The Bank will continue to encourage the federal and provincial governments to pursue the trade liberalization that is already under way. To build the knowledge base to underpin the policy dialogue on private sector development, the Bank plans to carry out a significant program of analytical work. An analysis of the trade regime will also be undertaken in FY03. (2) The government also intends to reduce maximum tariffs to 25% by 2003 and the number of tariff slabs to three, to rationalize duty drawback and export-financing schemes for exporters, and to comply with the WTO trade regime and standards.
Benin	PRSP		
Ethiopia	PRSP	A section discusses export development within the strategy, focusing on the agricultural sector and promotion of industrial zones.	

Main objective	Only briefly mention trade
	(1) Trade deficit averaged about 8% of GDP during 1998–2000, lower than the level for 1991–1997. However, this was achieved at the cost of a contraction in trade in real terms.
(1) As a part of consolidating macroeconomic stability objective, with "Promoting Trade FY04" as a non-financial instrument framework ($81,000 for FY03-05).	
Part of the strategy is to support Nicaragua in the CAFTA process.	
A central part of the strategy is to support exports development and increase its linkages to the rest of the economy, through enhanced logistics, support to fertilizer exports, and IFC supporting other export-oriented sectors.	
	Strategy considers the need for "supportive trade polices" as part of the macroeconomic and competitiveness environment, without further detail.
(1) The essence of Pakistan's poverty reduction strategy is to maintain an environment conducive to trade and investment, including foreign investment.	
As part of the macroeconomic framework objective, the strategy supports the implementation of a WAEMU common trade policy and overall integration process.	
One of the major objectives is to improve the environment for exports and private sector growth.	

(Table continues on the following page.)

Fiscal Years 2001–03 (continued)

Country	Document	Extensive analysis	Specific measures proposed
Gambia	PRSP	A section of the strategy analyses external trade.	A strategy for the development of Free Zones under the Trade Gateway Project is an important part of the growth strategy.
Ghana	PRSP	Section on analysis and actions to develop nontraditional exports.	Specific policies include improving the export/import regime, minimize incidence of dumping, promote areas with competitive advantage, make full use of preferential areas, and promote agro-export business.
Guinea	PRSP	A section of the strategy is devoted to regional integration. Sections are also devoted to the development of handicrafts exports and tourism.	
Malawi	PRSP	A section discusses access to national, regional and international markets.	The strategic actions towards access to markets will include developing an efficient and effective Market Information System (MIS).
Mali	PRSP		The staffs are working with the authorities on deepening the analysis of the potential sources of growth and export diversification. The outcome of the analysis would be the elaboration of a program to overcome the oft-cited challenges to growth in Mali. The growth analysis will be complemented by the Integrated Framework for Trade activity supported under the World Trade Organization and being conducted in 2003. The PRSP progress report would need to incorporate the updated growth and trade strategies.
Mozambique	PRSP	Analysis of some trade-related sectors including fisheries and tourism.	
Niger	PRSP		The strategy translates into the following actions and measures to be implemented during the period under consideration: (i) better monitoring the flow of imports by involving additional customs offices; (ii) managing re-exports more closely with the use of escorting missions; (viii) identifying new customs revenues.
Rwanda	PRSP	The macroeconomic section includes one paragraph discussing the external sector.	Privatization of the key state enterprises such as in coffee and tea is expected to provide immediate stimulus to exports.
Senegal	PRSP		
Zambia	PRSP	Analysis of evolution of Zambian exports.	The government has established a high level task force to prepare an effective response to the copper sector crisis.
Cambodia	PRSP		
Vietnam	PRSP		A World Bank study carried out with a local economic research institute shows that the recently-adopted trade reforms, when implemented, will increase the employment, incomes, and consumption of all income groups.

Main objective	Only briefly mention trade
The growth strategy focuses on export diversification, transit trade, and tourism.	
Part of the objectives of Macro economy and Increasing Production and Gainful employment is the promotion of non-traditional exports.	
Regional integration is part of growth pillar of the strategy.	
A major part of the pro-poor growth pillar of the strategy is to "Improve Access to Domestic. Regional and International Markets."	
The macroeconomic framework objective includes export diversification and increased processing of agricultural products.	
The growth strategy includes the facilitation of access to external markets by enhancing the transport infrastructure.	
As part of one of the main objectives, the PRSP recognizes that exports will be an important source of growth for Rwanda. Given the importance of export development, the staffs would encourage an integrated discussion of the ongoing initiatives for export development and the policies and prospects in a future annual report or PRSP update. The importance of regional cooperation/integration was recognized but staff noted that there was little discussion in the PRSP of how this can be achieved and the role Rwanda might play in achieving it.	
Part of the objective of is a more vigorous promotion of exports and better distribution of production in order to reduce the proportion of imports, and integration to WAEMU. Agricultural, craft activities, and fisheries sector strategy have export promotion in mind.	
A key part of the macroeconomic strategy is export diversification, and some sector strategies are related to exports.	
Part of the diagnosis and strategy deals with the need for export diversification, improvements in customs administration, and EPZs.	
Trade liberalization is a major part of the strategy. Policies that support retraining and job search will help displaced workers find new employment and mitigate the near-term transitional costs.	

(*Table continues on the following page.*)

Fiscal Years 2001–03 (continued)

Country	Document	Extensive analysis	Specific measures proposed
Albania	PRSP	(1) One of the objectives is to increasing openness and improvement of external position of the economy. (2) The liberalization of the foreign trade is one of the first measures taken by the Albanian government in the transition to market economy. Albania became member of the WTO in 2000. Nevertheless, the situation of the trade balance has worsened. The import/export relation is nearly four to one. The volume of exports remains at low levels and export products are not diversified.	
Azerbaijan	PRSP		(1) The government also plans to undertake several measures in order to promote exports. Several initiatives are currently being considered, including the creation of a database to increase marketing opportunities for local products, arrangement of trade fairs, establishment of exhibition centers and bonded warehouses as well as opening trade representations in potential partner countries and establishing an Export Promotion Fund. (2) It is planned to continue the process of applying for admission to the WTO. Bilateral and multilateral trade negotiations will be held for this purpose. (3) Rehabilitation of the port will emphasize minimizing the negative environmental impact of the operations on the Caspian Sea. Improvement of transportation will help to promote trade and economic growth, and will help to spread the extent of growth to include regions outside of Baku.
Kyrgyz Rep.	PRSP	(1) As a part of promoting sustainable economic growth, it is evidence that of all the components of GDP, the largest increase has been registered in net exports (from -14.7% of GDP in 1999 to -0.3% of GDP in 2001). This has reflected stagnation of exports of goods and services and a sharp decrease in imports volume. The reasons for problems in the area of exports were restrictions in trade with neighboring countries and transition of exported goods through their territory, as well as	

Main objective	Only briefly mention trade
(1) As a part of long-term objectives, considerable progress has been made in the liberalization of trade. Albania has no quantity restrictions on imports, and almost no restrictions on exports. Tariff rates have been continuously reduced.	
(1) As a landlocked country, the Kyrgyz Republic's export promotion potentially depends significantly on the easing of trade barriers in the region, particularly by its neighbors, over whom it has little leverage. Improved regional cooperation will, therefore, be critical to achieving PRSP objectives. (2) There is a need to develop a comprehensive rehabilitation plan for Kyrgyz's railroad sector in order to increase the share of cargo transportation in the structure of external trade.	

(Table continues on the following page.)

Fiscal Years 2001–03 (continued)

Country	Document	Extensive analysis	Specific measures proposed
Kyrgyz Rep. (cont.)		the composition of exports and their concentration on a few raw materials the prices of which fluctuate in international markets. The decline in imports is connected with a decrease in imports of capital goods, but to a major extent, is a consequence of import substitution.	
Tajikistan	PRSP		(1) In 2002, there was a measure to promote creation of Commodity Credit Corporation (CCC) on procurement and sale of agriculture production and trade and delivery for processing enterprises.
Guyana	PRSP		(1) Given Guyana's limited market, the objective of the government export promotion program will be to create conditions for the export sector to be an instrument for sustaining rapid and broad-based growth. This will require maintaining a competitive exchange rate, eliminating trade barriers, and providing more effective export promotion services for Guyana's export. In addition, government, through Guyana Office for Investment, will a) provide information and company matching services; b) support local companies to participate in overseas trade fairs and domestic exhibitions; and c) coordinate industrial cooperation. (2) Macroeconomic, trade, and investment framework are in the I-PRSP strategy issue.
Honduras	PRSP	This document evaluates the impact of trade liberalization among other structural reforms, providing a positive assessment of them and suggesting the acceleration in their implementation.	
Nicaragua	PRSP	(1) Liberalization of foreign trade was on reform with a substantial impact on the Nicaraguan economy. The abolition of government-owned export trading monopolies encouraged private production for export.	
Yemen	PRSP		
Sri Lanka	PRSP		

Note: PRSP = Poverty Reduction Strategy Paper.

Main objective	Only briefly mention trade
	Strategy supports liberal trade policies, regional integration efforts and WTO accession.
	The strategy supports reducing trade policy barriers.

APPENDIX E8: TRADE NOTE SERIES

Trade Note 1 (5/29/03)	World Bank Activities on Trade
Trade Note 2 (5/29/03)	From Singapore to Cancun: Investment
Trade Note 3 (5/29/03)	More Favorable Treatment of Developing Countries and the Doha Development Agenda
Trade Note 4 (5/29/03)	Rules of Origin in Free Trade Agreements
Trade Note 5 (5/29/03)	Implementing the Doha Mandate on TRIPS and Public Health
Trade Note 6 (9/10/03)	Market Access: Agricultural Policy Reform and Developing Countries
Trade Note 7 (9/10/03)	Domestic Support for Agriculture: Agricultural Policy Reform and Developing Countries
Trade Note 8 (9/10/03)	Export Subsidies: Agricultural Policy Reform and Developing Countries
Trade Note 9 (9/10/03)	Trade for Development in Latin America and the Caribbean
Trade Note 10 (9/10/03)	Cotton and Developing Countries: A Case Study in Policy Incoherence
Trade Note 11 (9/10/03)	Services in a Development Round
Trade Note 12 (12/8/03)	Trade Facilitation: New Issues in a Development Context
Trade Note 13 (12/17/03)	After Cancún: Continuation or Collapse?
Trade Note 14 (3/3/04)	Sugar Policies: Opportunity for Change
Trade Note 15 (5/10/04)	Trade Facilitation: Ways WTO Disciplines Could Promote Development
Trade Note 16 (7/13/04)	Brazil vs. U.S.: Cotton Subsidies and Implications for Development
Trade Note 17 (7/22/04)	Market Access in Agriculture: Beyond the Blender
Trade Note 18 (9/27/04)	Mexican Corn: The Effects of NAFTA
Trade Note 19 (11/5/04)	Agricultural Negotiations: Recent Developments in the Doha Round
Trade Note 20 (02/07/05)	Tightening TRIPS: The Intellectual Property Provisions of Recent U.S. Free Trade Agreements
Trade Note 21 (05/16/05)	The Value of Trade Preferences for Africa
Trade Note 22 (06/06/05)	WTO Accession: Lessons from Experience
Trade Note 23 (06/27/05)	Agricultural Market Access: The Key to Doha Success

APPENDIX F: MANAGEMENT RESPONSE

Introduction

Management expresses its appreciation to the Independent Evaluation Group (IEG) for the constructive suggestions to improve the effectiveness of the Bank's assistance on trade put forward in *Evaluation of World Bank Support for Trade, 1987-2004*. Among the review's important contributions are (a) its characterization of the different dimensions of the Bank's work on trade, (b) its observation that the Bank still faces an important challenge in better incorporating trade as a part of growth and poverty reduction strategies in country programs, and (c) its set of recommendations, notably on ways to better address the challenge of mainstreaming trade. Management agrees with the thrust of most of these recommendations, but notes that they must be placed in the context of competing priorities in a constrained budget environment (while recognizing that better use can also be made of available resources). Management's specific responses are noted in the attached Management Action Record. The comments set out in Section II should not be taken as detracting from the overall appreciation management has for the quality and completeness of the IEG review.

Management Comments

Overall, management appreciates the quality and timeliness of this review, in the context of its recent and ongoing work to rebuild its capacity in the trade area. The Trade Progress Report discussed by executive directors in March 2005 reported on the increase in staffing in the Regions and within the Trade Department, the considerable improvement in the quality and coverage of trade-related diagnostic analytic work at the country level, and increased trade-related lending. The Trade Report also highlighted remaining challenges, including (a) addressing the cross-cutting nature of many trade issues; (b) helping countries integrate trade issues into their national planning exercises (notably, Poverty Reduction Strategies in low-income countries); and (c) helping country teams better integrate these issues into Country Assistance Strategies (CASs). The IEG review similarly highlights these issues and suggests where progress is needed. Rather than dwell on the many areas of agreement, the comments below focus on matters where Management thinks the IEG analysis might have gone further or treated topics in a different manner.

Greater Differentiation across Review Periods

The review could have provided a greater differentiation across three periods—1987-95, when trade policy dialogue and adjustment lending was intensive; 1995-2000, during which the Bank was significantly less active in this area; and 2001-04. A more refined assessment of performance in each period would have been valuable, not least because in the "middle" period the resource envelope and trade capacity (knowledge base) of the Bank declined importantly. As a result, the re-launch of trade work in 2001 started from a very narrow base and was highly constrained as regards budget. In particular, 2001-04 seems a short period in which to evaluate the success of the new trade strategy, especially in the areas of capacity building and mainstreaming, which by their nature are gradual processes, requiring changes in long-term country strategies and steady management attention and increased resource flows over time at the Regional level.

Budget Constraints

A stronger emphasis in the review on "value for money" or productivity would have been useful, given that post-2001 resources allocated to trade (both at the center and in the Regions), while growing, are still quite limited and are likely to remain so in the context of overall flat budgets and many important competing demands. The review's recommendations have important implications on resources. Having a more explicit focus on what IEG sees as lower-value activities that could be reduced or eliminated in a resource constrained environment would help management allocate resources.

Focus on the Trade Department

The thrust of the focus of the review, especially for 2001-04, is on the Trade Department. However, management thinks that greater recognition might have been given to the fact that implementation of many of the recommendations proposed in the review would be undertaken at the Region/country level. Greater clarity on the locus of actions would have been helpful. An important part of the institution's response to trade issues and to support for mainstreaming trade needs to take place at the Regional level (as contemplated, for example, in the new Africa Action Plan).

Poverty and Distributional Issues

At the country level, the review recommends that all new projects with trade policy components include a discussion on poverty and social impact analyses (PSIAs) drawing on the cross-sectoral expertise from economic policy, poverty, gender, private sector development (PSD), and (as appropriate) agricultural and rural development units, as well as existing research in the country. Management believes that this issue can be important, but that the message should be nuanced. First, Operational Policy (OP) 8.60, *Development Policy Lending,* already requires documentation of the expected contribution of development policy operations to sustained growth and poverty reduction. Second, there is a range of guidance for staff and more is being put in place. The Bank has developed methodologies to analyze these issues, including PSIAs and PRMPR's work on analyzing the distributional impact of reforms, which has a chapter on how to analyze the distributional implications of trade reforms. Recent examples of the application of this guidance are available from the Trade Department and other work is in draft and will be available soon. However, management sees PSIAs as being mainly a tool for use by partner countries and much more effective when led by the country itself, rather than imposed from the outside.

Mainstreaming in Country Programs and Adjustment

The review also recommends that more attention be paid to adjustment to trade liberalization as part of increased efforts to mainstream trade in country programs. There is a continuing effort on the part of Regions to provide trade information and analysis in support of the country-owned Poverty Reduction Strategy (PRS) processes and to increase attention to trade in CASs, most notably as reflected in the Africa Action Plan. Going forward, the Trade Department will work with the Regions through the Regional trade representatives to prepare brief country-specific Guidance Notes for all countries where trade integration remains a major opportunity and challenge. The criteria for this engagement have already been articulated in the aforementioned March 2005 report to the Board on trade policy. The Guidance Note will include assessments of (a) trade policy and performance; (b) major supply-side constraints; (c) external environmental impacts on a country's trade prospects; and (d) possible issues requiring specific adjustment needs.

Aid for Trade

An additional important element of the Bank's response to the review recommendations relating to mainstreaming, as well as to the concerns expressed regarding the functioning of the Integrated Framework, is the Aid for Trade initiative as outlined in the joint Bank-Fund paper discussed at the Development Committee in September. This initiative is expected to result in an enhanced Integrated Framework (with larger and more predictable funding as well as improved governance mechanisms) and to increased attention to trade in both bilateral and multilateral trade programs as announced by several major donors around the Hong Kong Ministerial.

Conclusions

Notwithstanding the issues cited above, management finds this review to be a solid overview of the Bank's experience in the trade area. It will be a reference document for the ongoing work to strengthen the Bank's trade advocacy work at the global level and its work to help countries address trade issues as part of their strategies to increase growth and reduce poverty. Management's response to IEG's specific recommendations are given below in the Management Action Record.

Management Action Record

Major Monitorable IEG Recommendations Requiring a Response	Management Response
Recommendation 1: Address Poverty-Distributional Outcomes and External Shocks in a Balanced Approach This evaluation found that despite the increasing volume of research on poverty issues in the Trade Department and of poverty and social impact analysis more generally, trade-related projects do not consistently or systematically address poverty and distributional outcomes. While much import liberalization has already occurred, further liberalization appears possible for some developing countries, notably within agriculture. With that in mind, three actions are critical: a. IEG recommends that at the country level all new projects with trade policy components include a discussion of this issue that, at a minimum, draws on the cross-sectoral expertise from economic policy, poverty, gender, PSD and (as appropriate) agricultural and rural development units, as well as existing research in the country. Identification of possible transitional costs, an assessment of the existing institutional framework for cushioning shocks and actions to mitigate or minimize shocks would be important considerations in the discussion. Placing trade in a broader discussion of the determinants of poverty will help ensure that this is not a mechanical exercise but rooted in its expected importance. b. At the institution-wide level, and following the Bank's statement at the Cancun Ministerial in 2003, IEG recommends that a concrete program of adjustment assistance be developed more rapidly to respond to trade-related shocks that developing countries may face. To the extent that such a program is no longer deemed relevant, it would be helpful for management to clarify this. c. IEG recommends a more systematic program of research on micro level adjustment to trade policies, looking at firms, individuals and households.	Management agrees that it is important to use available research tools to assess the poverty and distributional impacts of trade reforms. The extent and depth of the analyses should be consistent with the depth and pace of projected reforms. Recent examples of how this is being implemented at the country level include the analyses for the Central America Free Trade Agreement and Vietnam's accession to the World Trade Organization (WTO). The planned Guidance Note for the preparation of Country Assistance Strategies (CASs) in Recommendation 2 can be a useful vehicle to highlight the need and appropriate scope for this analysis. The Note will stimulate consultations by country economists across Networks on the need to identify possible transitional costs, the institutional framework for cushioning shocks, and actions to mitigate shocks. Having said that, management would like to stress that a focus on adjustment costs/managing shocks from possible trade reforms is too narrow. There is a broader need for Bank economic and sector work (ESW) related to growth to continuously assess policies that will facilitate adjustment and reallocation of labor as well as capital in response to changes in the environment–which could come from changes in trade policies, technology, other domestic reforms, and the like. This is essential to facilitate growth and also to support economic reforms. This analysis should not be triggered by just trade reforms, which for the most part today are implemented gradually and are not as deep as those undertaken in the 1980s and early 1990s. Management agrees on the importance of being prepared to assist countries face adjustment challenges that could potentially stem from a successful Doha Round. The joint Bank-Fund paper on Aid for Trade, which was endorsed by the Board of the Bank and the Development Committee in September 2005, recognizes this need and outlines a process to address this issue by strengthening the capacity of the Bank and the Fund to do the diagnostic work needed to evaluate the adjustment needs and to work with donors

Major Monitorable IEG Recommendations Requiring a Response	Management Response
	in bringing together packages of financing. Bank management is of the view that existing Bank instruments are adequate to address this potential issue. In some cases, there may be an issue of availability of concessional funding from IDA, given the limits to IDA resources. Management will continue close coordination with donors to help IDA countries find appropriate concessional financing. Management is of the view that the Bank already has the tools that are needed to assess impact effects at the micro level. Research in this area has been increasing significantly during the last three years (see for example the recently published studies on trade and poverty, collected in a volume by Hertel and Winters) and is planned to continue.
Recommendation 2: Revisit the Balance between Global and Country Agendas and Strengthen Operational Links on Trade Issues IEG recommends that management revisit the balance between its activities at the global level on the one hand, and on the regional and country agenda on the other. Given the multi-sector nature of trade issues, a participatory process that involves operational sector colleagues, other networks and the Trade Department is likely to yield the greatest benefits. Operational linkages need to be strengthened between different units of the Bank and greater emphasis placed on country and field operations. Three actions are necessary: a. Greater strategic and intellectual guidance is needed from the Trade Department with respect to the conceptual framework within which country teams should consider trade issues. The design of a guidance note and upstream support on a pilot basis to country teams planning country assistance strategies would be practical first steps and would help determine those cases in which trade is logically a priority element in the country dialogue. b. In three thematic areas of focus, a more formal set of arrangements between operations, networks and the Trade Department is needed to maximize synergies—agricultural trade and policies, services liberalization, and distributional outcomes associated with trade policies. c. As has been done between the Transport and Agriculture units on the one hand, and the Trade Department on the other, IEG recommends that working arrangements with the Private Sector Department Vice-Presidency be established to highlight the interface between the two areas and bring the global dimension to bear more precisely. This cross-fertilization of trade and the need for better integration of trade and the FPSI work program is	Management agrees with the recommendation and with its implication—and is working to strengthen Regions to cope with the growing growth and trade agenda. Given the small size of the center and the need to continue to stay engaged at the global level, strengthened operational linkages can only be achieved through better use of resources devoted to trade at the country level. Needs will vary by Region, but the Africa Region has already committed, in the context of the Africa Action Plan, to increasing resources devoted to trade issues at the country level. Management agrees with the need to strengthen the support from the Trade Department to country teams to help integrate trade into the growth and poverty reduction in CASs. The September 2005 Development Committee paper on Aid for Trade outlines a plan for significantly increasing resources dedicated to trade in country programs through the enhanced Integrated Framework and other instruments. The main bilateral donors have announced major increases in Aid for Trade around the Hong Kong Ministerial. The Trade Department will work with Regional trade representatives to prepare brief country-specific Guidance Notes for all countries where trade integration remains a major opportunity and challenge. The criteria for this engagement have already been articulated in the Report to the Board on Trade Policy of March 2005. The Guidance Note will include assessments of (a) trade policy and performance; (b) major supply-side constraints; (c) external environmental impacts on a country's trade prospects; and (d) possible issues requiring specific adjustment needs. Management agrees that further efforts to formalize arrangements between operations, networks, and the Trade Department to address services liberalization and distributional outcomes associated with trade policies

Major Monitorable IEG Recommendations Requiring a Response	Management Response
especially evident in the work on trade in services. Greater interaction between the Trade Department staff specialized in trade in services and the sub-sectoral expertise in transport, power, finance, telecoms and so on located in FPSI is needed.	could yield benefits. However, the area of services covers roughly 15 sectors, and this would entail very substantial coordination costs in areas of work where the trade angle is narrow. Accordingly, management proposes to explore more formal arrangements between the Trade Department and operations in one or two "backbone" services, namely finance, telecommunications, and transport. On the relations with the Private Sector Development (PSD) Vice-Presidency, there is already good coordination in the area where the synergies in competencies are the highest: trade logistics and trade facilitation. Coordination exists already for the preparation of performance indicators as well as analytic tools (notably, logistics value chain analyses from PSD and trade and transport facilitation audits from PREM/INFR). Dissemination of these tools is carried out jointly for Bank staff training and they are often used in a complementary fashion in Bank ESW and project preparation. However, additional progress can be made by strengthening the linkages at the country level. In that context, the planned Guidance Note for trade in preparing CASs will help by stressing the links between trade and PSD issues as they relate to supply-side constraints and by guiding country teams in that direction. In order to reach decisions on how best to coordinate across the Bank on trade issues and how best to operationalize trade issues within country programs, the Trade Department will prepare a note for discussion among Operational Vice Presidents (OVPs). The note will include staffing and budget issues. Any budgetary implications coming out of the OVP discussion will be highlighted in upcoming budget and work program documents. Management will consider the agreed action related to Recommendations 1 and 2 complete with (1) the launch of the Guidance Notes; (2) the OVP discussion and decisions on the Trade Department note, (3) the launch of the trade related work identified through fiscal year 2007 in the Africa Action Plan (see *Strengthening the Development Partnership and Financing for Achieving the MDGs: An African Action Plan* (DC2005-0021), September 16, 2005, commitments on growth diagnostics on page 22 and on creating an export push on page 23); and (4) the creation of an active thematic group on trade and competitiveness (see below). Progress will be monitored in the context of periodic progress reports on the Africa Action Plan for Sub-Saharan African countries and for all countries in the next two CAS Retrospectives. The CAS retrospectives will assess the appropriate integration of trade issues into CASs.

Major Monitorable IEG Recommendations Requiring a Response	Management Response
Recommendation 3: Strengthen Knowledge Management Efforts Two actions are important. a. A concerted effort to bring all country economists up to date with the main features and application of the WITS software would enhance their awareness of the global trade issues and implications for the countries they work on and enable them to supervise research assistants/ consultants and seek further training if and when needed. b. Knowledge management efforts could reflect greater cross-fertilization with other networks and better integrate trade work done in the center and country-level work on agriculture, economic policy, labor markets and private sector development. As part of these efforts, the possibility of joint thematic groups with other networks should be explored.	Training on WITS is being offered twice a year and open to all Bank staff. Management endorses the suggestion that the WITS tool will help country economists address trade issues. The country guidance note for the CAS will raise awareness on this tool and encourage its use. However, Management's view is that WITS will not be enough to enhance the awareness of global trade issues and implications for specific countries staff work on. For that reason Management will continue to strengthen its overall program of trade-related training in line with what has been done over the last two years. A thematic group focusing on one or more selected aspects relating to Trade and Competitiveness will be launched with strong participation from other groups important for the trade agenda, most notably PSD. The suggestion to increase feedback from operational staff on relevant trade related topics is a good one. To that end, management plans to strengthen the dialogue with operational staff through the Trade Notes series, the establishment of a new thematic group, and the establishment of an ideas line. Management will consider the agreed action on this item complete within six months of the launch of the new thematic Trade and Competitiveness group; the establishment of an ideas line, and the strengthening of the discussion series on Trade Notes.

APPENDIX G: CHAIRMAN'S SUMMARY: COMMITTEE ON DEVELOPMENT EFFECTIVENESS (CODE)

On January 11, 2006, the Committee on Development Effectiveness (CODE) considered the report *Evaluation of World Bank Support for Trade, 1987-2004* prepared by the Independent Evaluation Group (IEG), together with the Draft Management Response.

Background. During the 1980s and early 1990s, the Bank was an important source of trade policy advice and financial assistance to support trade-related activities. Following a lull in the late 1990s, the Bank intensified its focus on trade following the Doha Trade Ministerial Meeting in 2001. In 2002, the Trade Department was created from elements from DEC, PREM, and WBI. Over the course of 2005 there were several Board meetings focused on trade issues, including a March 2005 review of the *Trade Progress Report: Focus on Country Trade Policy*; and a September 2005 review of the Development Committee paper *Trade Progress Report: Doha Development Agenda and Aid for Trade.*" In these and other meetings, many Executive Directors have stressed that the Bank is well-placed to play a global advocacy and advisory role to facilitate trade. They have also encouraged the Bank to: focus more on country-level trade work; mainstream trade diagnostics into its operations; provide trade-related capacity building; and provide financial assistance to help bridge potential short-term costs associated with adjustment to trade liberalization.

Highlights of the Report. The IEG report focuses on Bank assistance between fiscal years 1987 and 2004. IEG found Bank support for trade reform from 1987 to 2001 to be generally consistent with the 1987 WDR on trade, Operational Directive 8.60, and the literature on trade reforms. It also recognized the important contribution and high quality of Bank research on international trade over the period. IEG found that country reforms with Bank support since the 1980s have been instrumental in reducing distortions and relaxing import constraints. IEG also found that Bank interventions over this period have been less successful in achieving structural improvements in export performance and diversification, notably in Africa. During the same period, IEG determined that overall conditionality associated with trade has declined. However, it noted four concerns: (i) the Bank sometimes supported trade reforms in countries without due consideration to macroeconomic issues; (ii) compliance with complementary measures/conditions crucial to trade reforms tended to be the lowest of all conditions, underscoring difficulties associated with their implementation; (iii) trade-related projects did not adequately attend to the analysis of potential poverty and distributional outcomes; and (iv) the Bank did not take the external environment into account sufficiently. As for the Bank's trade advice, IEG found little evidence of a generic approach to trade reforms in client countries, but it was too narrowly focused and too optimistic about the benefits of trade liberalization for growth in the short-run.

The Bank's interventions on trade since 2001 have had two objectives: make the world trading system more supportive of development, through a reciprocally open trading system; and make trade an important part of country development strategies. IEG considered these objectives relevant, timely, and responsive to the changing global environment on trade issues. Nevertheless, it also noted that more attention was needed to strengthen analytical tools, processes, and systematic interactions between the Trade Department and operational colleagues. Three IEG recommendations are: (i) address poverty-distributional outcomes and external shocks; (ii) revisit the balance between global and country agendas and strengthen operational links on trade issues; and (iii) strengthen knowledge management efforts.

Highlights of the Management Response (MR). Management welcomed and appreciated IEG's review which they felt was a solid overview of the Bank's experience in the trade area. However, given the Bank's very different emphasis with regard to trade issues during the review period, a greater differentiation of the different phases of the review period would have provided valuable insights. Specifically, given the scaled back emphasis on trade issues on the part of the Bank during the mid 90s to 2000, the reinvigorated interest in trade in 2001 was started from a much reduced resource base and constrained budget envelope. On the latter, a more explicit discussion would have been helpful to management in allocating resources. Lastly, management felt the focus of the review for 2001-04 was on the Trade Department. Management also felt that much of the implementation of the review's recommendations would take place at the region/country level. Hence, greater clarity on the locus of actions would have been helpful. Also, management believes that three years (2001-04) is too short a period in which to evaluate the new trade strategy, especially in the areas of capacity building and mainstreaming. Management is of the view that existing instruments to address adjustment and distributional effects are adequate, especially given the reduced role of trade conditionality and the fact that liberalization is usually gradual. Adverse shocks resulting from changes in trade policy are, by and large, a small part of the story of the adverse shocks affecting the poor. In the few instances where shocks deriving from trade policy changes are large (e.g., due to preference erosion) the Bank is adequately equipped and ready to provide assistance.

Overall Conclusions. The Committee noted with favor that the report was comprehensive and well-written, covering most of the relevant issues both retrospectively and prospectively. There was unanimous support among both CODE members and management for the main recommendations of the review, particularly on mainstreaming and knowledge management. Indeed, the Committee appreciated the positive and constructive MR and noted it was helpful in clarifying practical implementation issues, particularly mainstreaming trade in country assistance strategies and operational work. Regarding the recommendation for more attention to distributional impact and adjustment opinions were mixed. The discussion focused mainly on some aspects of the evaluation framework; under what external conditions and policy environment the Bank can maximize the efficacy of the its assistance; how the Bank should respond to adjustments that developing countries face, such as those induced by trade-related shocks; and how the Bank can enhance its current organizational capacity and effectiveness. Members appreciated staff comments about trade integration into country programs in Central America and East Asia.

Next Steps. Some speakers requested that management prepare a paper linking the approach for mainstreaming and integrating trade work, including a business plan, accountability matrix, staff incentives and budgetary issues. Management agreed to a discussion among Operational Vice-Presidents on the issue of operationalizing trade issues within country growth strategies. Some members requested further elaboration in the revised MR on areas such as mainstreaming of trade-related work and its resource implications, distributional assessment, and country-specific Guidance Notes (GN). They also stressed the importance to consider an appropriate communication strategy for the public disclosure of IEG report and MR. Members look forward to receiving a paper on "shocks".

Members raised the following issues during the meeting:

Evaluation Framework. Some speakers stressed the need to explore comprehensively the impact of trade liberalization including unilateral reforms in developing countries giving greater attention to adjustment and transitional costs, sequencing, distributional effects, and micro-level implications. They agreed that compliance with complementary measures was crucial to trade reforms. This evaluation could include the causes underlying the weak performance of many Bank-assisted countries (notably in Africa and to some extent the Middle East and North Africa) especially with respect to lack of progress in export growth and economic diversification, which had been noted by several members. IEG responded that the report examines the causes of weak performance at the country level. Speakers also noted the need to distinguish between short and long-term impacts.

Distributional Impact. Many speakers encouraged more analysis of distributional impacts, although such work should not be mandatory. Moreover, a few suggested that such assessments should be done not just in terms of poverty and growth, but also with reference to fiscal and trade balances, and mitigation measures. Management noted that recently the Bank had done a lot of work on some distributional aspects of poverty; however, this was a new area of research. There is a toolkit but management informed CODE members that it is very difficult to forecast the precise distributional impact of (trade stimulated) growth so that addressing potential poverty and distributional outcomes could not be done with any high level of confidence.

Focus and Priorities. Mainstreaming trade effectively into poverty reduction strategies, country assistance strategies and operations, and implementation of IEG recommendations garnered attention from many speakers. They stressed the need for a more country-specific approach, including institutional strengthening and capacity building needs. In this regard, a member highlighted that Aid for Trade has become an important component of the Doha Development Round discussions. Several participants welcomed management's proposal to work on country GN; members sought more elaboration in the MR regarding monitoring of GN. The Integrated Framework for Trade-Related Technical Assistance should have a sharper focus on results.

Response to Adjustment. For adjustment to trade-related shocks, management noted the distinction between terms of trade shocks (e.g., induced by oil prices) and policy or reform transitions. Speakers had diverse views, however, on the adequacy of currently available Bank instruments for assisting adjustment or the need for a separate lending window for trade-related shocks. Some of them felt that the current challenge was the effective implementation of instruments. Some speakers encouraged more support for strengthening business climate and competitiveness, and investment in infrastructure. Some expressed the opinion that support for trade facilitation, regional integration, and South-South trade and investment also needed more attention.

Strengthening Knowledge Management. Some speakers encouraged more training on trade and extensive "cross-fertilization" between trade and other areas such as agriculture, economic policy, labor market, and private sector development. Speakers recognized the important Bank's contribution through its research work although one member sought staff's and IEG's views on the Bank's dependence on donor trust funds to finance this activity. Speakers felt that knowledge created outside the Bank should enhance and substitute for in-house research (see below on the use of external resources). One member suggested two areas of research: non-tariff barriers—including standards and dumping measures; and study of complaints filed by affected countries with the WTO's appellate body such as the recent experience in cotton and sugar.

Bank's Advocacy Role. Though there was broad support for the Bank playing an active advocacy role in trade, opinion was divided regarding the Bank's posture. Some speakers stressed neutrality and even-handedness. Several speakers pointed at the fact that the Bank had overestimated the benefits of trade liberalization and subsequently had to revise them downwards. Others interpreted the Bank's mandate for poverty reduction to mean a more activist role in putting forward the interests of the poorest borrowing countries. Management emphasized that it views its role as advocating changes in the world trading system that promote development, and not necessarily the position of any group. Nevertheless, there was broad agreement to maintain overall balance between global advocacy and local programs. Speakers also noted the role played by Bank partners including Regional Development Banks.

Organizational Capacity and Effectiveness. In addition to coordination across units, better knowledge management, and budgetary implications, several speakers suggested strengthening staff incentives, development of a business plan and accountability matrix, and perhaps an approach paper on integration of trade issues. Many members encouraged more formal arrangements between the virtual Trade Department and Regions, operations, and networks, and sought additional information on the role of Regional Trade Coordinators. Management informed the formation of a new Trade and Competitiveness Thematic Group. A few members asked for greater coordination within the World Bank Group. Another specific suggestion included making better use of external resources and analyses.

Pietro Veglio, Chairman

ENDNOTES

Chapter 1

1. Refers to either free-standing trade projects or projects with trade components exceeding 10 percent of total project costs.

2. The findings of several large multicountry comparative studies prepared during this period reinforced this message: Choksi and Papageorgiou (1986), Michaely and others (1991), Thomas and Nash (1991), Cooper and others (1991), and Krueger, Schiff, and Valdes (1991).

3. World Bank (1987). The WDR of 1986, which focused on agricultural development and liberalization, also covered a number of important trade issues, such as the distortions inherent in the policy-induced anti-trade biases in developing countries, as well as those arising from industrial country agriculture subsidies.

4. Operational Directive 8.60, which provides guidance *inter alia* on trade policy, was only issued at the end of 1992, when lending for trade adjustment was already declining. Sixty-one percent of all adjustment lending with trade content between fiscal years 1987 and 2004 had been approved by June 1992.

5. The Bank's work on commodities (which largely consists of market outlook and price projections) is not part of this review, except where it overlaps with market access considerations. In addition, links between trade and the environment, while important, are beyond the scope of the evaluation as outlined in the Approach Paper.

6. Previous IEG evaluations have looked at trade liberalization experience in nine countries, adjustment in Africa, support for industrial activities, agricultural sector adjustment loans, and lending for port development. In addition, the World Bank summarizes the Bank's conclusions from its dialogue with NGOs under the Structural Adjustment Participatory Review Initiative (SAPRI) and focuses on, among other things, the results for trade liberalization. Thomas and Nash (1991) provide a comprehensive overview of lessons from trade reform up to the late 1980s.

7. The Approach Paper for this study (IEG 2004c) provides more detail on the evaluation methodology.

8. The criteria for selection were: (i) countries in which the Bank had a large and diversified trade portfolio; (ii) a geographically mixed group with diversity in country experience and performance; (iii) variation in the countries' approach to trade reform; (iv) variation in country size; and (v) availability of microeconomic data. In addition, desk reviews were conducted for other countries in the portfolio. IEG (2004c) includes the detailed terms of reference for the case studies.

Chapter 2

1. This evaluation is not a research project to analyze major questions such as whether integration into the world economy is good for development. It is mainly a study of the relevance and effectiveness of Bank trade assistance, but, in the process, it sheds light on issues such as desirable speed of adjustment, sequencing, and complementary policies.

2. The experience of the East Asian "tigers" that moved the furthest away from the import-substitution model was simplified and generalized to support the export-led growth model. See Amsden (1989), Wade (1990), Lall (1992), Rodrik (1995), and UNCTAD (2003) for differing and nuanced interpretations of East Asia's experience.

3. See, for example, Shafaeddin (1995).

4. Hall and Jones (1999) and Rodrik and others (2002) suggest that institutions are an important determinant of growth, while Acemoglu and Johnson (2003) and Chang and others (2005) delve more deeply into which institutions are most important.

5. Several studies carried out in the 1990s, such as Dollar (1992), Sachs and Warner (1995), Krueger (1998), Edwards (1998), and Frankel and Romer (1999), suggested that countries that are more open

grow faster. These studies typically measured openness to trade with what is more accurately described as a trade intensity index—defined as the ratio of trade (imports plus exports) to GDP. As Collier, Greenaway, and Gunning (1997) show, however, the trade intensity index may not be an appropriate indicator of a country's trade policy stance. The index may instead reflect an increase in aid flows or an improvement in a country's terms of trade rather than the extent of trade liberalization. Rodriguez and Rodrik (2000) criticize this literature, arguing that methodological problems with the empirical strategies used make interpreting results more ambiguous than the various authors assert. In particular, they criticize the use of the "openness" dummy variable in Sachs and Warner (1995) and used by several researchers subsequently. In their view, the dummy variable that aims to characterize the restrictiveness of a trade policy regime is often correlated with other measures of poor economic performance. Additional challenges to a simple link between growth and openness have come from Stiglitz (2002).

6. This section draws on Salinas (2003).

Chapter 3

1. Analysis of trade-related assistance is made difficult by the fact that until recently, "trade" did not constitute a formal sector (unlike economic policy, education, rural, or transport, for example) in the Bank's sector classification system. Earlier Bank definitions of "industry and integration" excluded several projects that trade economists would define as trade-related and included others that, while supporting economic integration, were not necessarily trade-related. Building on the original database, since 2002 the Trade Department has updated and maintained a database of trade-related projects. The 2002 OPCS reclassification of sector and thematic codes rectifies this difficulty for post-2000 projects.

2. Bank trade lending rose rapidly in the 1980s because: (i) the Bank underwent an ideological shift from bottlenecks as presented in the two-gap models of growth developed by the Bank in the 1970s to a more market-oriented view of the world; (ii) in line with this, trade was seen as a way out of the debt problems of the 1980s.

3. Defined as lending operations whose trade components accounted for 50 percent or more of total commitments.

4. This trend is consistent when comparing the amount of lending spent for each component. Lending for the institutional and infrastructure aspects increased from 9 percent and 10 percent, respectively, for the period between 1987 and 1994, to 18 percent and 71 percent, respectively, for the period between 2000 and 2004.

5. Technical assistance is a subset of trade capacity building and focuses on enabling a client to implement reform or strengthen institutions.

6. Unless otherwise noted, this section draws on Tsikata (2005), which reviews trade conditionality in World Bank projects between 1987 and 2004.

7.The trade share in an adjustment loan is approximated by the proportion of actions in the policy matrix that are trade-related: that is, the trade share is the number of trade-related actions divided by the total number of actions included in the policy matrix of the Project Appraisal Document. The total trade cost is thus the trade share multiplied by the total project cost.

8. In some Regions, such as Africa, other policy aspects historically have been intertwined with trade, such as marketing. For example, government parastatals often controlled key exports (such as groundnuts in Senegal, cocoa in Côte d'Ivoire and Ghana, tobacco in Malawi, and tea in Tanzania), taxing them inefficiently and constraining entry into the sector by others.

9. *Conditions* refer to both legally binding conditions and "desired" conditions as spelled out in the president's report of the project.

10. The "Concordat" refers to the joint memorandum from the President of the World Bank and the Managing Director of the Fund entitled Bank/Fund Collaboration in Assisting Member Countries (SM/89/54, Revision 1 and R89-45), March 31, 1989.

11. In four cases, reference was made to a reform program detailed in the letter of development policy.

12. Because in the long run all countries face a balance of trade constraint, import liberalization is in effect export promotion (economists call this "Lerner symmetry").

13. This approach is analogous to IEG 1997, which focuses on adjustment lending in Sub-Saharan Africa. As that report notes, if the recommended reforms were implemented, but results were not achieved, then the quality of conditionality and exogenous factors have to be examined as potential explanations.

This approach also enables the implicit construction of a control group (countries that did not implement the agreed upon conditionality).

14. A caveat is in order. By the nature of the process, "grading" implementation inevitably includes an element of subjectivity. For trade conditionality, however, this assessment is often easier than other elements of adjustment due to a combination of the quantitative requirements in some cases, and the need for legislation in others.

15. In addition to the more formal and legally binding conditions, IEG also assesses the evolution of other "conditions" included in the policy matrix of lending operations. While these lack the legal standing (and associated "sanction") of the more formal conditions, these nonbinding "matrix" conditions represent policy agreements and benchmarks (albeit informal) between the Bank and its client countries, which the Bank views as desirable for the country to meet. The ambiguity of their standing notwithstanding, clients often viewed them as part of the Bank's conditionality. As such, they are useful in understanding the evolution of the policy dialogue and agreements between the Bank and its clients. Together the legally binding and matrix conditions allow an overview of aggregate conditionality.

16. "From Adjustment Lending to Development Policy Lending," OPCS, August 2004 and the "Adjustment Lending Retrospective," OPCS, June 15, 2001 illustrate the evolution of Bank views on conditionality toward single-tranche operations as part of a series of development policy loans. The new OP 8.60 on Development Policy Lending codifies the move away from prescription, toward country-owned conditionality.

17. The Bank's nonlending inputs are more typically defined by analytical and advisory activities (AAA) which in addition to ESW include policy dialogue, nonlending technical assistance, and donor coordination. While policy dialogue is a particularly important part of Bank advice to clients, it is difficult to measure. The other two components of AAA are dealt with under the broader rubric of trade-related capacity building, which is a more relevant and commonly accepted classification for client country officials and donors working in trade than is AAA.

18. The discussion in this section focuses on reports that are almost exclusively focused on trade. Bank Country Economic Memoranda almost invariably include a chapter on trade, but our interest lies in more extensive trade analysis that merits an entire report. Thus, the figures for trade-related ESW presented here are an underestimation.

19. Developed in mid-2001, the Diagnostic Trade Integration Study is a major economic report focused on trade. It is essential to the Integrated Framework process and used to identify trade-related capacity building needs. While final content varies among countries, the core template comprises: brief macroeconomic overview; review of trade performance; regional and global context for country's trade; institutional framework for trade policy and development; trade logistics; constraints to competitiveness including standards; subsector competitiveness analysis; and links between trade and the country's poverty reduction strategy.

20. Gelb and others (2000), which focuses on growth more broadly, includes a chapter on trade. Hinkle and others (2003) carries out a review of first-generation trade reforms.

21. EAC refers to East African Community; ECOWAS refers to Economic Community of West African States; UMOEA refers to West African Economic and Financial Union.

Chapter 4

1. IEG rates every completed project against its objectives as stated in the Project Appraisal Document in terms of its relevance, efficiency, and efficacy. A project's outcome is rated as "satisfactory" when the project achieves or is expected to achieve most of its major relevant objectives efficiently, with only minor shortcomings. The rating "moderately satisfactory" applies when the project achieves or is expected to achieve most of its major relevant objectives efficiently, but with either significant shortcomings or modest overall relevance. A project is rated as "unsatisfactory" when it fails to achieve and is not expected to achieve most of its major relevant objectives and delivers only minor development benefits.

2. Following an initial divergence, the performance of adjustment and investment loans has converged in the past five years. After initially performing well in the first decade of their introduction, trade adjustment loans performed poorly between 1995 and 1999 (in part because of crises-related loans in Asia, Brazil, and Russia). In contrast, trade investment loans improved steadily over the same period, reflecting the

reduction in poorly performing state-led and public sector–driven projects.

3. While some of these actions may be subsequently reversed, this is not evident at the time that closed projects are reviewed, as these are often relatively quick–disbursing loans. Overall, the evaluation did not find significant evidence of policy reversal in trade liberalization.

4. The full set of loans approved after 1995 had appreciably better outcomes (statistically speaking) than those before 1995. They were also more likely to be sustainable and to have had a greater institutional development impact. Given the Bank's extensive experience with lending for trade and the switch in the portfolio toward operations with more and financially larger institutional components, these are not surprising results. The estimation also found that projects in middle-income countries were more likely to perform better, exhibit greater sustainability, and have more institutional development impact than those being implemented in low-income countries. In the Regions, trade projects in Europe and Central Asia were more likely to have unsatisfactory performance outcomes than those in other Regions. The estimation also found that conditionality was associated with worse project outcomes—that is, more poorly performing projects were associated with greater trade conditionality. This may reflect that higher conditionality was, in essence, an attempt to enforce implementation in situations where doubts may have existed about country commitment. Higher than average conditionality thus may be a red flag.

5. The CPIA index assesses how conducive a country's policy and institutional framework is in that year to fostering sustainable, poverty-reducing growth and the capacity of the country to effectively use development assistance. This exercise is done annually for all IBRD and IDA borrowers. Operationally, it is based on a set of 20 unweighted indicators in four categories: economic management, structural policies, policies for social inclusion and equity, and public sector management and institutions. Countries are rated on their current status in each of these performance criteria, with scores from 1 (lowest) to 6 (highest). The index is only available for a complete set of countries starting in 1998, but the index is available for a smaller set of countries prior to 1998.

6. Between 1987 and 2000 only a fraction of trade adjustment loans introduced social safety net components or other measures to cushion transitional adjustment arising from liberalization.

7. Mexico's Second Trade Policy Loan Project (FY88).

8. The NTB frequency ratio is defined as the percentage share of import tariff lines covered by nontariff barriers.

9. By Region, the highest levels of import duties prevailed in South Asia. Nontariff barriers were exceptionally high in Europe and Central Asia (97 percent) and South Asia (74 percent).

10. Considerable Regional differences lie behind these aggregate numbers. High and persistent inflation was clearly a Latin American (and thus largely middle-income) problem. External imbalances were most pronounced in Africa, where current account deficits, terms of trade deterioration, and external debt difficulties were pervasive. Economic growth was largely modest for all but East Asian economies. With average investment rates below 20 percent, meager foreign direct investment inflows, and anemic trade performance, GDP growth averaged below 3 percent for the sample (even including the fast-growing East Asian economies). This relatively low growth rate barely kept up with population growth in Africa, the Middle East, and Latin America.

11. Good historical overviews of trade regimes can be found in Oyejide, Ndulu and Gunning (1999) and Hinkle, Herrou-Aragon, and Kubota and others (2003) for Africa, Nogues and Gulati (1992) and Ganuza and others (2004) for Latin America, and Michalopoulos and Tarr (1994) and Kaminski and others (1996) for the transition economies.

12. Many of the nonreformers would consist of countries in crisis or where economic data are difficult to obtain. More appropriate would be a comparison of gradual versus less-gradual reformers.

13. While trade protection in Tunisia remains rather high on a most favored nation (MFN) basis, the trade regime with its largest trading partner, the European Union, is being liberalized more significantly under an association agreement signed in 1995.

14. Countries were classified as rapid reformers if their trade reform process was completed in three years or less (20 countries). All other countries were classified as gradual reformers. This classification was based primarily on the qualitative description provided in economic reports and on the evolution of average tariffs and NTB coverage. Appendix D5 in-

dicates the classification for individual countries in the sample.

15. See Haque and Khan (1998) and Jinjarak and others (2005) for a detailed exposition of the approach discussed here.

16. The methodology used is a "diference-in-differences" approach, which compares changes in various target variables before and after Bank-supported trade reform with changes in those same variables with countries that did not reform with Bank support. This approach further corrects for any potential sample selection bias by using a Heckman selection procedure to model the decision that results in a Bank loan. The correction replaces the presence of a Bank loan with the predicted likelihood of a Bank loan based on some observable characteristics of the country (such as balance of payments difficulties).

17. Assuming constant prices, the following equation is used: $\Delta Y = \Delta DD + \Delta IS + \Delta EE$, where y is real GDP, DD is total domestic demand, EE is export expansion and IS is import substitution. Assuming constant prices, the following detailed equation was used:

$$Y_t - Y_{t\text{-}1} = a_{t\text{-}1}(D_t - D_{t\text{-}1}) + (a_t - a_{t\text{-}1})S_t + a_{t\text{-}1}(X_t - X_{t\text{-}1})$$

GDP increase = Total domestic demand contribution + Import substitution contribution + Export expansion contribution, where,

Y = GDP

D = Total domestic demand (or availability) = $Y + M - X$

S = total supply $= Y + M$

X = total exports of goods and services (free on board [FOB])

M = total imports of goods and services (CIF)

a = GDP as share of total supply (Y/S)

t = final year of period

t-1 = initial year of period

18. If s_{ij} is the current share of product i in county j's exports, and R_i is the rate of growth of the product in world trade. The export prospects index (Pj) is defined as, $Pj = [\Sigma sijRi]/R_w$, where R_w is the rate of growth of world trade in all products. An index value of 0.50 indicates that country's exports grow at one-half the rate of world trade. A value of 1.50 suggests that the country's exports should grow 50 percent faster (see Ng and Yeats 2005 for the application and caveats).

19. This approach based originally on General Agreement on Tariffs and Trade - GATT (1966), used extensively by Ng and Yeats in Africa (2002, 2005) and East Asia (2003).

20. See Tybout (2000); Paus, Reinhardt, and Robinson (2003); Amiti and Konings (2005); Muendler (2004); Topalova (2004); and Van Briesbock (2005). These gains are maintained even after institutional quality and geography are controlled for; see Alcala and Ciccone (2004).

21. This analogy is due to Hill and McPherson (2004), as cited in the Zambia Country Case Study.

22. The 1988 and 1990 Country Economic Memoranda, in particular, made cogent arguments about the links between the two and the risks of additional industrial liberalization in a highly protected environment.

23. According to Bank staff, this may reflect a misunderstanding by Senegalese policy makers. Senegal reformed its tariff within the UMEOA customs union process, not under any WTO negotiating process, which could have provided for a "more lenient tariff reduction schedule."

Chapter 5

1. The Articles of Agreement of the International Bank for Reconstruction and Development (World Bank 1989) call for the Bank to promote the "long-range balanced growth of international trade" (Article I).

2. Around the Doha meeting in November 2001, there was extraordinary Board attention to trade issues, with 12 informal meetings in 2002, 2003, and 2004. Initial quarterly meetings and accompanying trade progress reports and monthly meetings with the managing director responsible for trade issues are reduced to bi-annual meetings with briefing meetings beforehand as necessary. This schedule is still uncommon, because most informal Board meetings are ad hoc. The only other example of informal meetings held with such regularity is that of meetings held to discuss Poverty Reduction Strategy Progress Reports.

3. As stated in the first progress report of July 2001 (World Bank 2001a, p.3), at the global level, the Bank's work would focus on promoting development through international cooperation on trade-related issues with the WTO. At the Regional level, the focus would be on promoting efficient Regional integration schemes consistent with multilateral principles and overcom-

ing trade-related obstacles to growth at the Regional level. Finally, at the national level, the focus would be on policies and institutions needed for trade to be an instrument of pro-poor growth.

4. Although housed in PREM, the director of the Trade Department reports jointly to the vice presidents for DEC, PREM, and WBI, underscoring efforts to strengthen collaboration among the three units. In addition, the director is also director of the Prospects Group in the Development Economics Unit, which handles work on global commodity markets.

5. There appears to have been far less collaboration with academics in developing countries in Asia and Africa.

6. A standard way of assessing the quality of research is through number of publications in journals. By this criterion, the Bank's output is large compared with other policy-oriented institutions, though less so when the criteria of publications in established journals is used. De Melo (2005) argues that based on the volume of research in other policy-oriented institutions—arguably the more relevant comparison—the volume of Bank research in refereed journals is high. Anderson (2003) reports six to eight papers per capita in his review of research at the International Food Policy Research Institute. For the three-year period under review, De Melo (2005) estimates a per capita publication record of 12 for the 12 staff in the trade unit of the Research Group.

7. Most papers appear first in the World Bank Working Paper Series, and some have appeared in other working paper series produced both inside and outside the Bank (for example, the Center for Economic Policy Research).

8. De Melo (2005) defines "established journals" as those that are in the top quarter in either of two classifications, based on the *Journal of Citation Reports* (JCR). The JCR ranks journals based on the number of citations received. This "raw" count, however, does not take into account the age of the journal, adjustment to exclude self-citations, and adjustments for the number of pages. The ranking in Kalaitzidakis and others (2003) corrects for the above shortcomings for articles published during the period 1994–98 for 160 economics journals. Because new journals have been added in recent years, and because potential errors in the adjustment made, De Melo (2005) classifies as established or "top" journals the top quintile (that is., the top 40 journals) by either of the above criteria of the last year for which JCR has published its unadjusted rankings (2002). By this inclusive criterion, he obtains 61 journals for the top category.

9. The Bank's prodigious output over 2000–04 was achieved with the support of two bilateral donors. The Dutch (through the Bank-Netherlands Partnership Program (BNPP)), and the U.K. Department for International Development (DFID). These donors have maintained significant special programs targeted to trade. However, neither WBI nor DEC provided the requested trust fund data to enable an in-depth analysis.

10. This year's *Global Economic Prospects* is addressing migration.

11. The World Bank (Ellerman 2003) identifies the following areas of research: remittances; temporary movement of workers under the General Agreement on Trade Services (mode 4 negotiations), ties to the diaspora and return migration, and migration of skilled workers ("brain drain").

12. Three observations lead to this conclusion. First, agriculture became controversial as soon as a new round of trade talks was announced. Second, despite successful obfuscation by all participants in the move toward "greater" transparency, unlike other new areas of negotiation (such as services), assessing the efficiency and rent-transfer effects of agricultural policies (border and internal) could rely on relatively established methodologies (for example, on bananas and cotton). Third, reasonable amounts of data were available since the tariffication process was started under the Uruguay Round Agreement at least over the 1995-98 period. In sum, more work would have been expected in specialized agricultural journals. The four articles are: Hertel, Ivanic, Preckel, Cranfield, and Martin (2003); Martin (2000); Otsuki, Wilson, and Sewadeh (2001); and Anderson and Jackson (2003).

13. See, for example, speech by James Wolfensohn, Cancun Ministerial, Cancun, Mexico, September 2003.

14. While analyses undertaken in connection with the Uruguay Round and in subsequent *World Development Reports* highlighted inequities in the global trading system, there was no active attempt to disseminate these messages beyond the normal dissemination of research at the technical level. The Bank essentially assumed that the basic barriers were on the developing country side, not due to market access.

15. QUAD refers to Canada, the European Union, Japan, and the United States.

16. *Market Access for Developing Country Exports—Selected Issues*, September 2002, Joint paper prepared by the staff of the World Bank and IMF.

17. Oxfam's reach and influence are greater than may be commonly perceived. According to the Rushford Report, Oxfam spends $500 million annually and has approximately 4,000 employees worldwide. For comparison, the Bank's annual operating budget in 2004 was $1.5 billion and 9,300 employees worldwide.

18. See CUTS (2003) for statements and editorials by various parties in the run-up to Cancun, for example.

19. It is also instructive that the WTO members interviewed urged the Bank to be more pragmatic about regional trading arrangements, saying they were here to stay and that their rise was not unexpected, given the slowness of the Doha negotiating agenda.

20. Panagariya (2005) is more critical, arguing that over-simplification of the facts and analyses by donors and big NGOs such as Oxfam are misleading and risk distorting the facts.

21. UNCTAD (2004) traces the evolution of the terminology.

22. To give an idea of the importance of TCB, half of submissions at the "pre-negotiation" phase included in the Ministerial declaration at Seattle came from developing countries, yet because of research and capacity constraints a proactive constructive approach was beyond their reach, and their submissions were not included in the agenda largely because they were insufficiently developed. If the asymmetry in outcomes on the agenda was also partly the result of the strategy of developing countries (insisting on "special and differential treatment," which also suited industrialized countries by allowing them not to address issues of interest to the developing countries), much of it is due to lack of negotiation and research capacity as the above example suggests (see for example, Blackhurst, Lyakurwa, and Oyejide [2000]).

23. The dollar equivalents of TCB components need to be treated with caution as the components are not always associated with a specific dollar amount. The dollar amount has to be imputed from the component actions as a share of the overall loan.

24. The six are Bhutan, Cape Verde, Ethiopia, Lao PDR, Sudan, and Yemen. Since late 2004, the Bank has been assisting Ethiopia in its accession negotiations.

25. The Integrated Framework for Trade-Related Technical Assistance is a multi-agency and donor initiative to provide trade-related technical assistance to the 49 least developed countries. First established in 1996 following a meeting of high-level ministers, the initiative was significantly revamped in 2001. The partners in the initiative consist of the six core agencies: IMF, the International Trade Centre, UNCTAD, UNDP, World Bank, and the WTO. In addition, 17 donors have contributed to the initiative and are partners. The main elements of the initiative are a Diagnostic Trade Integration Study to assess constraints to trade and identify technical assistance needs, as well as coordinate and harmonize donor trade-related technical assistance. Each agency has a defined role in the initiative; the Bank, in collaboration with the six core agencies, leads the diagnostic work. The Bank has also contributed to the capacity building fund for the IF and contributed an average of two staff trade economists to each diagnostic study. For more information see www.integrated framework.org.

26. A third evaluation of the Integrated Framework initiative, carried out by the Netherlands as part of a broader assessment of the country's TRTA, was expected to be published in October 2005. Preliminary findings rated the efficiency, effectiveness and relevance of a two country sample of IF as poor to weak.

27. For example, Malawi proposed a project for trade policy advisory services. The content of the assignment is similar to the support being provided the country under the DFID Trade Policy and Poverty project.

28. By comparison, the Inter-American Development Bank, which focuses solely on the Americas, has staff members dedicated to external training activities in trade.

29. The chief economist also organized a roundtable of experts on *Informing the Doha Development Agenda* in May 2002 and in the run-up to Cancun the Bank organized a meeting for African trade policymakers.

30. See, for example, the March 2005 bi-annual progress report on trade.

31. The Country Assistance Strategy (CAS) is the World Bank's main instrument for defining country programs and investments. The CAS indicates how the Bank's objective of helping countries to reduce poverty and its sector objectives are incorporated into a strategy and reflected in the policy dialogue. Each CAS presents a comprehensive picture of a country's economic development, identifies the government's principal

concerns, and makes the case for new Bank services. CASs are usually undertaken every two to three years.

32. Country poverty reduction strategies are an indication of the extent to which client countries incorporate trade in their development strategies. A number of reviews (see for example, Hewitt and Gillson (2003); World Bank (2005b); Diop, Gust, and Khandelwal (2005)) suggest that trade issues (whether narrowly or broadly defined) have been incorporated only slowly by the countries, focused on a narrow set of trade issues and only poorly made the inter-linkages between trade and related complementary measures.

Chapter 6

1. Following a September 2004 report by the Bank's Debt Department on the volatility associated with exogenous shocks, the Bank is reviewing its instruments to see how it can better help low-income countries deal with external shocks in a timely objective manner, and facilitate their access to market-based instruments such as insurance facilities.

2. The first statement explicitly acknowledging the risk associated with the ambitious goals set for the Doha Development Agenda was stated by management at an Executive Board Meeting in March 2005, four years after the resurgence and three years after the publication of the trade strategy.

3. The institution is only now considering a policy note for operational staff on the Doha Development Agenda, three-and-a-half years since Doha.

4. Dani Rodrik put it best in the context of Africa: "There is actually a fair bit of consensus on what constitutes a reasonable trade strategy…The consensus can be crudely expressed in terms of a number of do's and don'ts: de-monopolize trade; streamline the import regime, reduce red tape and implement transparent customs procedures; replace quantitative restrictions with tariffs; avoid extreme variation in tariff rates and excessively high rates of effective protection; allow exporters duty-free access to imported inputs; refrain from large doses of anti-export bias; do not tax exports too highly." Rodrik (1998).

5. Management sees Poverty and Social Impact Analysis (PSIA) as being mainly a tool for use by client countries and most effective when led by the country itself, rather than imposed from the outside. IEG does not see encouragement of staff to systematically consider the use of PSIAs as equivalent to an imposition on the country. While in theory, country led PSIAs are ideal, in practice in many of the poorest countries, capacity to carry out PSIAs may be limited. It would seem that staff carrying out policy dialogue on these issues would benefit from having an empirical basis for the advice they give regarding the potential distributional impacts.

6. Management notes that an Operational Committee meeting held before the Cancun Ministerial, discussed and rejected the notion of a separate facility, concluding that the Bank possessed adequate existing instruments to address requests for trade-related adjustment shocks. However the Bank statement at Cancun is somewhat ambiguous and has been interpreted by some developing country clients as referring to a dedicated fund.

Appendix B1

1. As Stiglitz (1996, p. 173) found, "exports provided a performance-based criterion for allocating (preferential and subsidized) credit, encouraged the adoption of international standards, and accelerated the diffusion of technology."

2. The experience of the East Asian "tigers" that moved the furthest away from the import substitution model was simplified and generalized to support the export-led growth model. See Amsden (1989), Wade (1990), Lall (1992), Rodrik (1995), Leipziger (1997), and UNCTAD (2003) for differing and more nuanced interpretations of the East Asia experience.

3. Rodrik (1992, p. 88) argues that "common sense would suggest that the conventional benefits of (trade) liberalization become muted, if not completely offset, under conditions of macro instability characterized by high and variable inflation on the one hand, and fiscal and balance of payments crises on the other." Such a macroeconomic environment may not be hospitable for trade policy reform for several reasons. High and variable inflation could distort the price signals through trade policy to induce resource allocation. To the extent that macroeconomic instability leads to a general reduction in the level of domestic activity, the structural changes that trade policy reform would induce could become more painful as transitional costs of adjustment rise. Attempts to implement stabilization and trade liberalization simultaneously may create further problems as the policy instruments needed for both may conflict. In particular, restoring macroeconomic stability may require allowing the real exchange rate to appreciate, while trade liberal-

ization may be unsustainable unless the real exchange rate is depreciated. In addition, uncontrolled inflation tends to undermine an attempt to reduce the anti-export bias of a trade regime through real devaluation.

4. Anti-export bias arises from two sources (Milner 1990): the "input tax" source and the "exchange rate tax" source. In a restrictive trade regime, trade barriers effectively increase the domestic currency price of imports relative to exports. To the extent that the export sector uses imported inputs, its cost rises and its output declines. Trade barriers also raise the equilibrium exchange rate, which by depressing the domestic currency price of exports, further penalizes that sector. For these reasons, import barriers translate into a tax on exports.

5. The typical trade policy reform package consists, on the export side, of elimination of quantitative restrictions on exports; measures to offset anti-export bias of the trade regime, especially access of exporters to imported inputs at world market prices; export incentives; and trade facilitation including improved customs administration. On the import side, the reform package usually includes elimination of quantitative restrictions (with or without substitution of tariff equivalents), reduction of tariff dispersion, lowering of average tariffs, and moves to achieve uniform tariff rates.

6. It has been shown that unrestricted access for all exports of Sub-Saharan Africa to the markets of the European Union, United States, Canada, and Japan could generate a 14 percent increase in the region's non-oil exports as well as a 1.1 percent increase in welfare with very negligible costs to either other developing countries or the preference-granting countries (Ianchovichina and others 2001).

7. Anderson and others (2002, p. 248) show that "while the majority (60%) of the gains from such a reform would come from liberalization in the developing countries themselves, approximately 40% of the gains to developing countries would come from increases in market access in industrial countries."

8. The most relevant complementary policies concern effectively channeling market signals and those that address supply response constraints. The first group includes measures aimed at creating critical economic institutions generally, such as building missing markets, integrating segmented ones and ensuring that these institutions continue to develop and respond effectively to the evolving needs of economic agents. A second group of policies address supply response capacity constraints, such as policies aimed at establishing, developing, and maintaining a range of economic and social infrastructures. Both groups of policies aim to help reduce transactions costs and, thus, enhance productivity. The discussion in this chapter is not intended to be comprehensive. More panoramic surveys of the literature exist and are cited as appropriate.

9. See Amsden (1989), Wade (1990), Lall (1992), Rodrik (1995), Leipziger (1997), and UNCTAD (2003) for differing and more nuanced interpretations of the East Asia experience.

10. See, for example, the findings from the individual country studies from the Structural Adjustment Participatory Review Initiative http://www.saprin.org/SAPRI_Findings.pdf.

11. Hall and Jones (1999) and Rodrik and others (2004) suggest that institutions are an important determinant of growth while Acemoglu and Johnson (2003) delve more deeply into which institutions are most important.

12. Several studies carried out in the 1990s, such as Dollar (1992), Sachs and Warner (1995), Krueger (1998), Edwards (1998), and Frankel and Romer (1999), suggested that countries that are more open grow faster. These studies typically measured openness to trade with what is more accurately described as a trade intensity index—defined as the ratio of trade (imports plus exports) to GDP. As Collier, Greenaway, and Gunning (1997) show, however, the trade intensity index may not be an appropriate indicator of a country's trade policy stance. The index may instead reflect an increase in aid flows or an improvement in a country's terms of trade rather than the extent of trade liberalization. Rodriguez and Rodrik (2000) criticize this literature, arguing that methodological problems with the empirical strategies used make interpreting results more ambiguous than the various authors assert. In particular, they criticize the use of the "openness" dummy variable in Sachs and Warner (1995) and used by several researchers subsequently. In their view, the dummy variable that aims to characterize the restrictiveness of a trade policy regime is often correlated with other measures of poor economic performance. Additional challenges to a simple link between growth and openness have come from Stiglitz (2002).

13. Tybout (2003) and Amiti and Konings (2005) provide good surveys of the literature.

14. The Tokyo (1973-79) and Kennedy (1964-67) Rounds immediately preceded the Uruguay Round negotiations.

15. Finger and Schuler (2000) estimate that implementing three of the new areas—SPS, intellectual property rights and customs valuation—would cost the average developing country $150 million.

16. The "hangover" analogy is due to Bernard Hoekman.

17. See, for example, Van der Mensbrugghe 2005.

18. As De Melo (2005) notes, divergences in the perception of the world trading system run deep and are probably growing. The position of the critics of the single undertaking is well summarized in the following passage from Wade (2003) who argues that because of GATS, TRIMS, and TRIPS "…the 'development space' for diversification and upgrading policies is being shrunk behind the rhetorical commitment to universal liberalization and privatization. The rules being written into multilateral and bilateral agreements actively prevent developing countries from pursuing the kinds of industrial and technology policies adopted by the newly developing countries of East Asia and by the older developed countries when they were developing, policies aimed at accelerating the 'internal' articulation of the economy." He continues: "All this constitutes a shrinkage not only of development space, but also of 'self-determination' pace. It ties the hands of developing country governments 'forever' to the *North's interpretation* of a market opening agenda ('you open your markets and remove restrictions on incoming investment, in return for [promises of] improved access to our markets')," as cited in De Melo (2005).

19. Also U.S. negotiating power ends in 2007.

20. These can be either bilateral or plurilateral.

21. Global Economic Prospects (2005) provides an up-to-date and comprehensive overview of current RTAs. Pomfret (2001) provides a good overview of the economic, historical, and political factors underlying the rise of regional trading arrangements.

22. The theoretical literature on preferential trade agreements is reviewed in Baldwin and Venables (1996), Bhagwati and Panagariya (1997), and Panagariya (2000). Schiff and Winters (2003) and World Bank (2000, 2004a) review the empirical literature and place it in a development context.

23. World Bank (2004b).

24. Finger (1997); Martin and Ng (2004) "A Note on Sources of Tariff Reductions in Developing Countries, 1983-2003," background note prepared for Global Economic Prospects 2005.

Appendix C3

1. Conditions refers to both legally binding conditions and "desired" conditions as spelled out in the President's Report of the project.

REFERENCES

Acemoglu, Daron, and Simon Johnson. 2003. "Unbundling Institutions." NBER Working Paper Series No. 934. Cambridge, MA.

Agarwal, Manmohan, and Jozefina Cutura. 2004. "Integrated Framework for Trade-Related Technical Assistance." Case Study, IEG Study of Global Programs. IEG Working Paper Series. Washington, DC.

Agosin, Manuel. 2002. "Export Performance in Chile: Lessons for Africa." In Gerald K. Helleiner, ed., *Non-Traditional Export Promotion in Africa: Experience and Issues*. New York: Palgrave Macmillan.

Aksoy, M. Ataman, and John C. Beghin. 2005. *Global Agricultural Trade and Developing Countries*. Washington, DC: The World Bank.

Alavi, Hamid. 1993. *International Competitiveness of the Private Industry and the Constraints to its Development: The Case of Morocco*. Middle East and North Africa Region Discussion Paper Series No. 6. Washington, DC: The World Bank.

Alcala, Francisco, and Antonio Ciccone. 2004. "Trade and Productivity." *Quarterly Journal of Economics* 119(2): 613–46.

Amiti, Mary, and Jozef Konings. 2005. "Trade Liberalization, Intermediate Inputs and Productivity: Evidence from Indonesia." IMF Working Paper No. WP/05/146. Washington, DC.

Amsden, Alice H. 1989. *Asia's Next Giant: South Korea and Late Industrialization*. New York: Oxford University Press.

Amsden, Alice H., and Takashi Hikino. 2000. "The Bark is Worse Than the Bite: New WTO Law and Late Industrialization." *Annals of the American Academy of Political and Social Science* 570: 104–14.

Anderson, Kym. 2003. *Impact Assessment of IFPRI's Research and Related Activities Based on Economy Wide Modelling*, Impact Assessment Discussion Paper No. 21. Washington, DC: IFPRI.

Anderson, Kym, and Lee Ann Jackson. 2003. "Why Are U.S. and EU Policies toward GMOs So Different?" *AgBioForum* 6(3): 95–100.

Anderson, Kym, Betina Dimaranan, Joe Francois, Tom Hertel, Bernard Hoekman, and Will Martin. 2002. "The Cost of Rich (and Poor) Country Protection to Developing Countries." *Journal of African Economies* 10(3): 227–57.

Anderson, Simon P., and Nicolas Schmitt. 2003. "Nontariff Barriers and Trade Liberalization." *Economic Inquiry* 41(1): 80-97.

Balassa, Bela and Associates. 1982. *Development Strategies in Semi-Industrial Economies*, Baltimore: The Johns Hopkins University Press.

———. 1971. *The Structure of Protection in Developing Countries*. Baltimore and London: The Johns Hopkins University Press.

Baldwin, Richard E., and Anthony Venables. 1996. "Regional Economic Integration." In Gene M. Grossman and Kenneth Rogoff, eds., *Handbook of International Economics*. Volume 3. Amsterdam: North-Holland.

Ben-David, Dan, and L. Alan Winters. 2000. *Trade, Income Disparity and Poverty*. WTO Special Studies No. 5. Geneva.

Berg, Andrew, and Anne O. Krueger. *2003*. "Trade, Growth, and Poverty: A Selective Survey." IMF Working Paper No. 03/30. Washington, DC.

Bhagwati, Jagdish N. 2002. *Going Alone: The Case for Relaxed Reciprocity in Freeing Trade*. Cambridge, MA: MIT Press.

———. 1991. *The World Trading System at Risk*. Princeton, N.J.: Princeton University Press.

———. 1988. "Export-Promoting Trade Strategy: Issues and Evidence." *World Bank Research Observer* 3(1): 27-57.

———. 1978. *Foreign Exchange Regimes and Economic Development: Anatomy and Consequences of Exchange Control Regimes*. Cambridge, MA: Ballinger.

———. (ed.). 1982. *Import Competition and Response.* Chicago: University of Chicago Press.

Bhagwati, Jagdish N., and Arvind Panagariya. 1997. *The Economics of Preferential Trade Agreements*. Washington, DC: American Enterprise Institute for Public Policy Research.

Bhagwati, Jagdish N, and T. N. Srinivasan. 2001. "Trade and Poverty in the Poor Countries." Columbia University. Photocopy.

Blackhurst, Richard, and William Lyakurwa. 2005. "Markets and Market Access for African Exports: Past, Present and Future Directions." In Ademola Oyejide, ed., *Selected Issues of the Doha Agenda. Volume 1.* Trenton, N.J.: Africa World Press.

Blackhurst, Richard, William Lyakurwa, and Ademola Oyejide. 2000. "Options for Improving Africa's Participation in the WTO." *World Economy* 23 (4): 491-510.

Botchwey, Kwesi, Paul Collier, Jan Willem Gunning, and Koichi Hamada. 1998. *Report of the Group of Independent Persons Appointed to Conduct an Evaluation of Certain Aspects of the Enhanced Structural Adjustment Facility*. Washington, DC : IMF.

Bourguignon, François, and Chor-ching Goh. 2004. "Trade and Labor Market Vulnerability in Indonesia, Korea and Thailand." In Kathie Krumm and Homi Kharas, eds., *East Asia Integrates: A Trade Policy Agenda for Shared Growth*. Washington, DC: The World Bank and Oxford University Press.

Bourguignon, François, and Luiz A. Pereira da Silva. 2003. *The Impact of Economic Policies on Poverty and Income Distribution: Evaluation Techniques and Tools.* New York: Oxford University Press.

Boyenge, Jean-Pierre Singa. 2003. " ILO Database on Export Processing Zones." Sector Activities Department. Geneva: ILO.

Caballero, Ricardo J., and Vittorio Corbo. 1989. "How Does Uncertainty about the Real Exchange Rate Affect Exports?" World Bank Policy, Planning, and Research Working Paper 221. Washington, DC.

Cadot, Olivier, Jaime de Melo, and Marcelo Olarreaga. 2003. "Can Duty Drawbacks Have a Protectionist Bias? Evidence from MERCOSUR." *Journal of International Economics* 59(1): 161-82.

Capra International Inc. and Trade Facilitation Office Canada (CAPRA-TFOC) Consortium. 2003. "Evaluation of the Revamped Integrated Framework for Trade-related Technical Assistance to the Least-Developed Countries." Geneva: WTO.

Cavallo, Domingo F. 1991. "Argentina: Trade Reform, 1976-1982." In Geoffrey Shepherd and Carlos G. Langoni, eds., *Trade Reform: Lessons from Eight Countries*. San Francisco, CA.: ICS.

Chang, Ha-Joon. 2004. "Institutional Foundations for Effective Design and Implementation of Trade and Industrial Policies in Least Development Economies." In Charles Soludo, Osita Ogbu, and Ha-Joon Chang, eds., *The Politics of Trade and Industrial Policy in Africa, Forced Consensus?* Nairobi: World Press.

Chang, Roberto, Linda Kaltani, and Norman Loayza. 2005. "Openness Can Be Good for Growth: The Role of Policy Complementarities." World Bank Policy Research Working Paper No. 3763. Washington, DC.

Chenery, Hollis Burnley. 1979. *Structural Change and Development Policy.* New York, N.Y.: Oxford University Press.

Choi, E. Kwan, and James Harrigan. 2003. *Handbook of International Trade.* Oxford, United Kingdom: Blackwell Publishing.

Choksi, Armeane, and Demetriou Papageorgiou. 1986. (eds.) *Economic Liberalization in Developing Countries.* Oxford: Blackwell.

Clarkson, Stephen. 2002. *Uncle Sam and Us: Globalization, Neoconservatism, and the Canadian State*. Toronto: University of Toronto Press.

Cline, William R. 1989. "Can the East Asian Model of Development Be Generalized?" *World Development* 10(2): 81-90.

Coes, D. 1991. "Brazil: Precedents and Prospects in Foreign Trade." In Geoffrey Shepherd and Carlos Geraldo Langoni (eds.), *Trade Reform: Lessons from Eight Countries.* San Francisco, CA: ICS Press.

Collier, Paul. 2000. *Policy for Post-Conflict Societies: Reducing the Risks of Civil War.* Policy

Research Working Paper No. 28135. Washington, DC: The World Bank

———. 1993. "Higgledy-Piggledy Liberalization." *The World Economy* 16(4): 503–12.

———. 1991. "Africa's External Economic Relations, 1960-90." *African Affairs* 90(360): 339–56.

Collier, Paul, and Jan Willem Gunning. 1992. "Aid and Exchange Rate Adjustment in African Trade Liberalizations." *Economic Journal* 102(413): 925-39.

Collier, Paul, and Anke Hoeffler. 2002. *Greed and Grievance in Civil War.* World Bank Policy Research Working Paper No. 2355. Washington, DC.

Collier, Paul, David Greenaway, and Jan Willem Gunning. 1997. "Evaluating Trade Liberalization: A Methodological Framework." In T. Ademola Oyejide, Ibrahim Elbadawi, and Paul Collier, eds., *Regional Integration and Trade Liberalization in Sub-Saharan Africa. Vol. 1: Framework, Issues and Methodological Perspectives.* Basingstoke and London: Macmillan; New York: St Martin's.

Conway, Patrick. 2005. "Evaluation of World Bank Trade-Related Assistance in Morocco—Country Case Study. " Background Paper prepared for the Trade Assistance Evaluation, Independent Evaluation Group, World Bank. Washington, DC.

Cooper, Richard, Max Corden, and Sarath Rajapatirana. 1993. *Boom, Crisis and Adjustment*. Oxford, U.K.: Oxford University Press.

Corden, Max W. 1989. "Macroeconomic Adjustment in Developing Countries" *World Bank Research Observer* 4(1): 51-64.

Currie, Dan, and Ann Harrison. 1997. "Sharing the Costs: The Impact of Trade Reform on Capital and Labor in Morocco." *Journal of Labor Economics* 15(3) Part 2.

CUTS (Centre for International Trade, Economics & Environment). 2003. *We've Been Here before: Perspectives on the Cancun Ministerial*. Jaipur, India.

Dasgupta, Dipak, and Mustapha Kamel Nabli. 2003. *Trade, Investment and Development in the Middle East and North Africa: Engaging with the World*. Washington, DC: The World Bank.

De Ferranti, David M., Guillermo E. Perry, Daniel Lederman, and William F. Maloney. 2002. *From Natural Resources to the Knowledge Economy: Trade and Job Quality.* World Bank Latin American and Caribbean Studies. Washington, DC: The World Bank.

De Melo, Jaime. 2005. "Leveraging Trade for Development." Background paper prepared for the Trade Assistance Evaluation, Independent Evaluation Group, World Bank. Washington, DC.

De Melo, Jaime, and Sherman Robinson. 1980. "Trade Adjustment Policies and Income Distribution in Three Archetype Developing Economies. " World Bank Staff Working Paper No. 442. Washington, DC.

De Wulf, Luc, and José B. Sokol. 2005. *Customs Modernization Handbook*. Washington, DC: The World Bank.

Dean, Judith M., Seema Desai, and James Riedel. 1994. *Trade Policy Reform in Developing Countries since 1985: A Review of the Evidence.* World Bank Discussion Paper No. 267. Washington, DC.

Diaz-Alejandro, Carlos F. 1984. "Exchange Rates and Terms of Trade in the Argentine Republic: 1913–76." In Moises Syrquin and Simon Teitel, eds., *Trade, Stability, Technology and Equity in Latin America.* New York, N.Y.: Academic.

Diop, Ndiame, Charleen Gust, and Padamja Khandelwal. 2005. "Critical Review of Trade and Growth in PRSPs." The World Bank and the IMF, Washington, DC. Photocopy.

Dollar, David. 2001. "Globalization, Inequality, and Poverty since 1980." The World Bank, Washington, DC. Photocopy.

———. 1992. "Outward-Oriented Developing Economies Really Do Grow More Rapidly: Evidence from 95 LDCs, 1976-85." *Economic Development and Cultural Change* 40(3): 523–44.

Dollar, David, and Aart Kray. 2002. "Growth Is Good for the Poor." *Journal of Economic Growth.* 7(3): 195–225.

Dornbusch, Rudiger. 1992. "The Case for Trade Liberalization in Developing Countries." *Journal of Economic Perspectives* 6(1): 69–85.

ECLAC (Economic Commission for Latin America and the Caribbean). 2003. *Globalisation and Development*. Santiago, Chile.

Edwards, Sebastian. 1998. "Openness, Productivity and Growth: What Do We Really Know?" *The Economic Journal* 108(447): 383–98.

———. 1997. "Exchange Rate Issues in Developing and Transitional Economies." *Journal of African Economies* 6(3): 37-73.

———. 1994. "Trade Liberalization Reforms in Latin America." In Graham R. Bird and Ann Helwege, eds., *Latin America's Economic Future*. London: Academic.

———. 1993. "Openness, Trade Liberalization, and Growth in Developing Countries." *Journal of Economics Literature* 31(3): 1358–93.

Elbadawi, Ibrahim A., and Raimundo Soto. 1997. "Real Exchange Rates and Macroeconomic Adjustment in Sub-Saharan Africa and Other Developing Countries." *Journal of African Economies* 6(3): 74–120.

Ellerman, David. 2003. "Policy Research on Migration and Development." World Bank Policy Research Working Paper No. 3117. Washington, DC.

Erzan, Refik, and Christopher Holmes. 1992. *The Restrictiveness of the Multi-Fibre Arrangement on Eastern European Trade.* World Bank Policy Research Working Paper No. 860. Washington, DC.

Falvey, Rodney E., and Norman Gemmell. 1990. "Compensatory Financial and Fiscal Incentives to Exports." In Christopher R. Milner, ed., *Export Promotion Strategies: Theory and Evidence from Developing Countries.* Brighton: Harvester-Wheatsheaf.

Falvey, Rodney, and Cha-Dong Kim. 1992. "Timing and Sequencing Issues in Trade Liberalization." *The Economic Journal* 102: 908–24.

Feldstein, Martin S. 1998. "Refocusing the IMF." *Foreign Affairs* 77(2).

Finger, J. Michael. 2002. "The Doha Agenda and Development: A View from the Uruguay Round." ERD Working Paper No. 21, Economics and Research Department. Manila: Asian Development Bank.

———. 2001. "Implementing the Uruguay Round Agreements: Problems for Developing Countries." *The World Economy* 24(9): 1097–108.

———. 1997. "Trade Policy Reforms in Adjustment Operations." Paper prepared for the U.S. Executive Director. Photocopy.

———. 1991. "The Meaning of 'Unfair' in U.S. Import Policy." World Bank Policy, Research, and External Affairs Working Paper No. WPS 745. Washington, DC.

Finger, J. Michael, and Andrzej Olechowski. 1987. *The Uruguay Round: A Handbook for the Multilateral Trade Negotiations.* Washington, DC: The World Bank.

Finger, J. Michael, and Patrick A. Messerlin. 1989. *The Effects of Industrial Countries' Policies on Developing Countries.* Policy and Research Series No. 3. Washington, DC: The World Bank.

Finger, J. Michael, and Julio J. Nogués. 2002. "The Unbalanced Uruguay Round Outcome: The New Areas in Future WTO Negotiations." *The World Economy* 25(3): 321–40.

Finger, J. Michael, and Philip Schuler. 2000. "Implementation of Uruguay Round Commitments: The Development Challenge." *The World Economy* 23(4): 511–26.

Flatters, Frank. 2005. "Evaluation of World Bank Trade-Related Assistance in Indonesia—Country Case Study." Background Paper prepared for the Trade Assistance Evaluation, Independent Evaluation Group, World Bank. Washington, DC.

Frankel, Jeffrey A. 1997. *Regional Trading Blocs in the World Economic System*. Washington DC: Institute for International Economics.

Frankel, Jeffrey A., and David Romer. 1999. "Does Trade Cause Growth?" *American Economic Review* 89(3): 379–99.

Freund, Caroline. 2003. "Reciprocity in Free Trade Agreements." World Bank Policy Research Working Paper No. WPS 3061. Washington, DC.

Freund, Caroline, and Bineswaree Bolaky. 2004. "Trade, Regulations and Growth." World Bank Policy Research Working Paper No. WPS 3255. Washington, DC.

Ganuza, Enrique, Samuel Morley, Sherman Robinson, Valeria Pineiro, and Rob Vox. 2004. "Are Export Promotion and Trade Liberalization Good for Latin America's Poor? A Comparative Macro-Micro CGE Analysis." In Sherman Robinson and Rob Vos , eds., *Is Trade Liberalization Good for Latin America's Poor?* New York: UNDP.

GATT (General Agreement on Tariffs and Trade). 1966. *International Trade, 1965.* Geneva: GATT.

Gelb, Alan H. 2000. *Can Africa Claim the 21st Century?* Report prepared jointly by the African Development Bank, African Economic Research Consortium, Global Coalition for Africa, Economic Commission for Africa and the World Bank, Washington , DC: The World Bank.

Ghosh, J. 1992. "Can World Markets Continue to Absorb Export-led Strategies of Developing Countries? The Export Pessimist's Case." In H. Hughes, ed., *The Danger of Export Pessimism: Developing Countries and Industrial Markets.* San Francisco, CA: ICS.

Got'o, Jun'ichi. 1990. "A Formal Estimation of the Effect of the MFA on Clothing Exports from LDCs." World Bank Policy, Research Working Paper No. WPS 455. Washington, DC.

Greenaway, David. 1993. "Liberalizing Foreign Trade Through Rose-Tinted Glasses." *The Economic Journal* 103: 208–22.

Greenaway, David, and M. E. Haque. 2005. "Trade Liberalisation and Productivity Growth." In H. Görg, D. Greenaway and R. Kneller, eds., *Globalisation, Productivity and Technology*. London: Palgrave.

Greenaway, David, Wyn Morgan, and Peter W. Wright. 2002. "Trade Liberalisation and Growth in Developing Countries." *Journal of Development Economics* 67: 229–36.

Greenaway, David, Wyn Morgan, and Peter W. Wright. 1998. "Trade Reform, Adjustment and Growth: What Does the Evidence Tell Us?" *The Economic Journal* 108(450): 1547–61.

Hachette, Dominique. 1991. "Chile: Trade Liberalization since 1974." In Geoffrey Shepherd and Carlos S. Langoni, eds., *Trade Reform: Lessons from Eight Countries.* San Francisco, C.A.: ICS.

Haque, Nadeem Ul, and Mohsin S. Khan. 1998. "Do IMF-Supported Programs Work? A Survey of the Cross-Country Empirical Evidence." IMF Working Paper No. WP/98/169. Washington, DC.

Hall, Robert, and Charles I. Jones. 1999. "Why Do Some Countries Produce So Much More Output Per Worker than Others?" *Quarterly Journal of Economics* 114(1): 83–116.

Harrigan, Jane, and Paul Mosley. 1991. "Evaluating the Impact of World Bank Structural Adjustment Lending: 1980—1987." *Journal of Development Studies* 27(3): 63–94.

Helleiner, Gerald K. 2002a. "Marginalization and/or Participation: Africa in Today's Global Economy." *Canadian Journal of African Studies* 36(3).

Helleiner, Gerald K., ed. 2002b. *Non-Traditional Exports in Sub-Saharan Africa: Issues and Experience.* Basingstoke, Palgrave.

Helleiner, Gerald K. 1993. "Trade, Trade Policy and Economic Development in Very Low Income Countries." In Machiko K. Nissanke and Adrian Hewitt, eds., *Overcoming Economic Crisis in Developing Countries.* London: Pinter.

Helleiner, Gerald. K. , ed. 1992. *Trade Policy, Industrialization, and Development: New Perspectives.* New York: Oxford University Press.

Hertel, Thomas W., and Jeffrey J. Reimer. 2004. "Predicting the Poverty Impacts of Trade Reform." World Bank Policy Research Working Paper No. 3444. Washington, DC.

Hertel, Thomas W., Maros Ivanic, Paul V. Preckel, John A. L. Cranfield, and Will Martin. 2003. "Short- Versus Long-Run Implications of Trade Liberalization for Poverty in Three Developing Countries." *American Journal of Agricultural Economics* 85(5): 1299–306.

Hewitt, Adrian, and Ian Gillson. 2003. *A Review of the Trade and Poverty Content in PRSPs and Loan-Related Documents.* London: Overseas Development Institute.

Hill, Catharine B. 1994. "Trade Policies and the Promotion of Manufactured Exports." In David L. Lindauer and Michael Roemer, eds., *Asia and Africa: Legacies and Opportunities in Development*. San Francisco, CA: ICS.

Hill, Catharine B., and Malcolm F. McPherson, eds. 2004. *Promoting and Sustaining Economic Reform in Zambia.* Cambridge, MA: Harvard University Press.

Hinkle, Lawrence, and Maurice Schiff. 2004. "Economic Partnership Agreements Between Sub-Saharan Africa and the EU: A Development Perspective." *The World Economy* 27(9): 1321–33.

Hinkle, Lawrence E., Alberto Herrou-Aragon, and Keiko Kubota. 2003. *How Far Did Africa's*

First Generation Trade Reforms Go? World Bank Africa Region Working Paper Series No. 58b (Volume II). Washington, DC.

Hoekman, Bernard M., ed. 2000. *World Economy* 23(4).

Hoekman, Bernard M., Aaditya Mattoo, and Philip English, eds. 2002. *Development, Trade, and the WTO: A Handbook*. Washington, DC: The World Bank.

Hoekman, Bernard, Costas Michalopoulos, L. Alan Winters, Mari Pangestu, Kamal Saggi, and James Tybout. 2003. "Special and Differential Treatment for Developing Countries: Objectives, Instruments and Options for the WTO." Trade Department, The World Bank, Washington, DC. Photocopy.

Hofman, Bert, Ella Rodrick-Jones, and Kian Wie Thee. 2004. "Indonesia: Rapid Growth and Weak Institutions." Paper prepared for World Bank Shanghai Conference, http://www.worldbank.org/wbi/reducing poverty/case-Indonesia-PovertyReduction.html.

Hughes, Helen, ed. 1992. *The Dangers of Export Pessimism: Developing Countries and Industrial Markets.* San Francisco, CA: ICS.

Ianchovichina, Elena, Aaditya Mattoo, and Marcelo Olarreaga. 2001. "Unrestricted Market Access for Sub-Saharan Africa: How Much Is It Worth and Who Pays?" *Journal of African Economies* 10(4): 410–32.

IEG (Independent Evaluation Group, The World Bank). 2005. *OED Review of Bank Lending for Lines of Credit.* Washington, DC: The World Bank.

———. 2004a. *Addressing the Challenges of Globalization: An Independent Evaluation of the World Bank's Approach to Global Programs.* Washington, DC: The World Bank.

———. 2004b. *An Evaluation of World Bank Investment Climate Activities.* Washington, DC: The World Bank.

———. 2004c. "Trade Assistance Evaluation, Approach Paper." Washington, DC.

———. 2003. "Project Performance Assessment Report: Indonesia – Banking Reform Assistance, Policy Reform Support Loans I and II." Washington, DC.

———. 1999. *1999 Annual Review of Development Effectiveness.* Washington, DC: The World Bank.

———. 1997. *Adjustment Lending in Sub-Saharan Africa: An Update.* Washington, DC: The World Bank.

———. 1996a. *Reforming Agriculture: The World Bank Goes to Market.* Washington, DC: The World Bank.

———. 1996b. *Ports.* Lessons and Practices No. 9. Washington, DC.

———. 1996c. *Zambia: Country Assistance Review.* Washington, DC: The World Bank.

———. 1995. *Industrial Restructuring: A Review of World Bank Operations.* Washington, DC: The World Bank

———. 1993. *Adjustment in Sub-Saharan Africa: Selected Findings from OED Evaluations.* Washington, DC: The World Bank.

———. 1992a. *Trade Policy Reforms under Adjustment Programs.* Washington, DC: The World Bank.

———. 1992b. *World Bank Structural and Sectoral Adjustment Operations: The Second OED Overview.* Washington, DC: The World Bank.

———. 1991a. *World Bank Support for Trade Policy Reform.* Washington, DC: The World Bank.

———. 1991b. *OED Study of Bank Support of Industrialization in Newly Industrializing Countries: Case Studies of Korea, India and Indonesia.* Washington, DC: The World Bank.

IMF (International Monetary Fund). 2005. *Trade Conditionality under Fund-Supported Programs, 1990–2004. Background paper to the Review of Fund Work on Trade.* Washington, DC: IMF.

IMF and World Bank. 2002. "Market Access for Developing Country Exports—Selected Issues." Washington, DC, IMF and The World Bank.

Jinjarak, Yothin, Gonzalo Salinas, and Yvonne Tsikata. 2005. *Trade Adjustment Lending: Is the Glass Half-Full or Half-Empty?* Background paper prepared for the Trade Assistance Evaluation, Independent Evaluaiton Group. Washington, DC: The World Bank.

Kalaitzidakis, Pantelis, Theofanis P. Mamuneas, and Thanasis Stengos. 2003. "Rankings of Academic Journals and Institutions in Economics." *Journal of the European Economic Association* 1(6): 1346–66.

Kaminski, Bartlomiej, Zhen Kun Wang, and L. Alan Winters. 1996. *Foreign Trade in the Transition: The International Environment and Domestic Policy.* Studies of Economies in Transformation. Washington, D.C: The World Bank.

Krueger, Anne O. 1999. "Are Preferential Trading Arrangements Trade-Liberalizing or Protectionist?" *Journal of Economic Perspectives* 13(4): 105–24.

———. 1998. "Why Trade Liberalisation is Good for Growth." *The Economic Journal* 108(450): 1513-22.

———. 1997. "Trade Policy and Economic Development: How We Learn." *American Economic Review* 87(1): 1-22.

———. 1980. "Trade Policy as an Input to Development." *American Economic Review* 70(2): 288-92.

———. 1978. *Foreign Trade Regimes and Economic Development: Liberalization Attempts and Consequences.* Cambridge, MA: Ballinger.

Krueger, Anne O., and Andrew Berg. 2002. "Trade, Growth, and Poverty." Annual Bank Conference on Development Economics, Washington, DC, April 29-30.

Krueger, Anne O., and Sarath Rajapatirana. 1999. "The World Bank Policies Towards Trade and Trade Policy Reform." *The World Economy* 22(6): 717–40.

Krueger, Anne, Maurice Schiff, and Alberto Valdes. 1991. *The Political Economy of Agricultural Pricing Policy*. Baltimore : Johns Hopkins University Press for the World Bank.

Krumm, Kathie, and Homi Kharas, eds. 2004. *East Asia Integrates: A Trade Policy Agenda for Shared Growth.*. Washington, DC: The World Bank and Oxford University Press.

Lal, Deepak. 1995. "India and China: Contrasts in Economic Liberalization?" *World Development* 23(9): 1475–94.

Lall, Sanjaya. 2004. "Selective Trade and Industrial Policies in Developing Countries: Theoretical and Empirical Issues." In Charles Soludo, Osita Ogbu, and Ha-Joon Chang, eds., *The Politics of Trade and Industrial Policy in Africa, Forced Consensus?* Nairobi: Africa World Press.

———. 1992. "Technological Capabilities and Industrialization." *World Development* 20(2): 165-86.

Lambert, Andrew. 2005. "Evaluation of World Bank Trade-Related Assistance in Mozambique—Country Case Study. Background Paper prepared for the Trade Assistance Evaluation, Independent Evaluation Group. Washington, DC: The World Bank.

Laursen, Keld. 1996. "The Impact of Technological Opportunity on the Dynamics of Trade Performance." DRUID Working Paper, No. 96-12. Aalborg: Danish Research Unit for Industrial Dynamics.

Leipziger, Danny M. 2005. "What's Old and What's New in Development Policy." Address at the PREM Week Conference 2005, April 19, 2005, Washington, DC, The World Bank.

———, ed. 1997. *Lessons From East Asia*. Ann Arbor: University of Michigan Press.

Limäo, Nuno. 2005. "Preferential Trade Agreements as Stumbling Blocks for Multilateral Trade Liberalization: Evidence for the U.S." CEPR Discussion Paper 4884. http://www.cepr.org/pubs/dps/DP4884.asp. Also, forthcoming in *American Economic Review.*

Lindahl, Claes. 2004. "Evaluation of World Bank Assistance to Selected Export Development Instruments FY81–03." Background paper prepared for the Trade Assistance Evaluation, Independent Evaluation Group. Washington, DC: The World Bank.

Little, Ian M.D., Tibor Scitovsky, and Morris Scott. 1970. *Industry and Trade in Some Developing Countries.* Oxford, U.K.: Oxford University Press.

Little, Ian M.D., Richard N. Cooper, W. Max Corden, and Sarath Rajapatirana. 1993. *Boom, Crisis and Adjustment: The Macroeconomic Experience of Developing Countries.* New York: Oxford University Press.

Lopez, Ramon, and Vinod Thomas. 1998. "Growth in Imports and Income: Consideration for Africa." World Bank PRE Working Paper Series, WPS No. 20. Washington, DC.

Madani, Dorsati. 1999. "A Review of the Role and Impact of Export Processing Zones." World Bank Policy Research Working Paper No. WPS 2238. Washington, DC.

Martin, Will. 2000. "What Has the GATT/WTO Agricultural Agreement Actually Done?: Discussion." *American Journal of Agricultural Economics* 82(3): 729–30.

Martin, Will, and Alan Winters, eds. 1996. *The Uruguay Round and the Developing Countries*. Cambridge, U.K. and New York: Cambridge University Press.

Matusz, Steven J., and David Tarr. 1999. *Adjusting to Trade Policy Reform.* World Bank Policy Research Working Paper No. 2142. Washington, DC.

McCulloch, Neil, L. Alan Winters, and Xavier Cicera. 2002. *Trade Liberalization and Poverty: A Handbook.* London: DFID and CEPR.

McMillan, Margaret, Dani Rodrik, and Karen Horn Welch. 2002. "When Economic Reform Goes Wrong: Cashews in Mozambique." NBER Working Paper No. 9117. Cambridge, MA, National Bureau of Economic Research.

Michaely, Michael. 1991. "The Lessons of Experience: An Overview." In Geoffrey Shepherd and Carlos G. Langoni, eds., *Trade Reform: Lessons from Eight Countries*. San Francisco, CA: ICS.

Michaely, Michael, Demetris Papageorgiou, and Armeane Choksi, eds. 1991. *Liberalizing Foreign Trade: Lessons of Experience in the Developing World.*. Oxford, U.K.: Basil Blackwell.

Michalopoulos, Constantine, and David G. Tarr. 1994. *Trade in the New Independent States.* Studies of Economies in Transformation. Washington, DC: The World Bank.

Milner, Christopher Robert, ed. 1990. *Export Promotion Strategies: Theory and Evidence from Developing Countries*. London: Harvester Wheatsheaf.

Mosley, Paul, Turan Subasat, and John Weeks. 1995. "Assessing Adjustment in Africa." *World Development* 23(9): 1459–73.

Muendler, Marc-Andreas. 2004. "Trade, Technology and Productivity: A Study of Brazilian Manufacturers 1986–1998." CESifo Working Paper Series No. 1148. San Diego, CA: Center for Economic Studies and Ifo Institute for Economic Research, University of California.

Nash, John. 1993. *Implementation of Trade Reform in Sub-Saharan Africa: How Much Heat and How Much Light?* World Bank Policy Research Working Paper No. 1218. Washington, DC.

———. 1992. "An Overview of Trade Policy Reform, with Implications for Sub-Saharan Africa." In Jean Marc Fontaine, ed., *Foreign Trade Reforms and Development Strategy*. London: Routledge.

Nash, John, and Wendy Takacs, eds. 1998. *Trade Policy Reform: Lessons and Implications*. Washington, DC: The World Bank.

Ng, Francis, and Alexander Yeats. 2005. "Kenya: Export Prospects and Problems." World Bank Africa Region Working Paper Series No. 90. Washington, DC.

———. 2003. "Major Trade Trends in East Asia: What Are Their Implications for Regional Cooperation and Growth?" World Bank Policy Research Working Paper No. 3084. Washington, DC.

———. 2002. "What Can Africa Expect from Its Traditional Exports?" World Bank Africa Region Working Paper No. 26. Washington, DC.

Nogues, Julio, and Sunil Gulati. 1992. *Economic Policies and Performance under Alterrnative Trade Regimes: Latin America During the 80s.* LAC Regional Studies Program. Washington, DC: The World Bank.

O'Connell, Stephen A. 1997. "Macroeconomic Harmonization, Trade Reform and Regional Trade in Sub-Saharan Africa." In T. Ademola Oyejide, Ibrahim Elbadawi, and Paul Collier, eds., *Regional Integration and Trade Liberalization in Sub-Saharan Africa—Volume 1. Framework, Issues and Methodological Perspectives.* London: Macmillan.

OECD-DAC (Organisation for Economic Co-operation and Development–Development Assistance Committee). 2001. *DAC Guidelines on Strengthening Trade Capacity for Development*. Paris: OECD.

OED (Operations Evaluation Department, The World Bank). See IEG.

Olarreaga, Marcelo, Isidro Soloaga, and L. Alan Winters. 1999. "What's Behind Mercosur's Common External Tariff?" Centre for Economic Policy Research Discussion Paper Series, Number 2310. London.

Olechowski, Andrzej, and J. Michael Finger, eds. 1987. *The Uruguay Round: A Handbook for Multilateral Negotiations*. Washington DC: The World Bank.

Otsuki, Tsunehiro, John S. Wilson, and Mirvat Sewadeh. 2001. "Saving Two in a Billion: Quantifying the Trade Effect of European Food Safety Standards on African Exports." *Food Policy* 26(5): 495–514.

Oyejide, T. Ademola. 2004. "The Mechanics of Trade Policy Reform in Developing Countries: A Literature Survey." Background paper prepared for the Trade Assistance Evaluation, Independent Evaluation Group. Washington, DC.

———. 1999. "Options for Future Trade Liberalization in Sub-Saharan Africa." In T. Ademola Oyejide, Benno Ndulu, and David Greenaway (eds.), *Regional Integration and Trade Liberalization in Sub-Saharan Africa, Volume 4—Synthesis and Review*. London: Macmillan Press.

———. 1998. "Trade Policy and Regional Integration in the Development Context: Emerging Patterns, Issues and Lessons for Sub-Saharan Africa." *Journal of African Economies* 7(Suppl. 1): 108–45.

Oyejide, T. Ademola, Benno Ndulu, and Jan Willem Gunning, eds. 1999. *Regional Integration and Trade Liberalization in Sub-Saharan Africa, Volume 2—Country Case Studies.* London: Macmillan.

Pack, Howard. 2000. "Industrial Policy: Growth Elixir or Poison?" *The World Bank Research Observer* 15(1): 47–67.

Page, Sheila, and Adrian Hewitt. 2001. *World Commodity Prices: Still A Problem for Developing Countries?* ODI Special Report. London: Overseas Development Institute.

Panagariya, Arvind. 2005. "Evaluation of World Bank Trade-Related Assistance in India: Country Case Study." Background paper prepared for the Trade Assistance Evaluation, Independent Evaluation Group. Washington, DC: The World Bank.

———. 2004. "Miracles and Debacles: In Defense of Trade Openness." *The World Economy* 27(8): 1149–71.

———. 2000. "Preferential Trade Liberalization: The Traditional Theory and New Developments." *Journal of Economic Literature* 38(2): 287–331.

Papageorgiou, Demetris, Michael Michaely, and Armeane Choksi, eds. 1991. *Liberalizing Foreign Trade: Lessons of Experience in the Developing World*. Oxford, U.K.: Basil Blackwell.

Paredes, Carlos. 1988. "Nominal Exchange Rate Regimes, the Real Exchange Rate and Export Performance in Latin America." Washington, DC: The Brookings Institution.

Paus, Eva, Nola Reinhardt, and Michael Robinson. 2003. "Trade Liberalization and Productivity Growth in Latin American Manufacturing, 1970–98." *Policy Reform* 6(1): 1-15.

Pomfret, Richard. 2001. *The Economics of Regional Trading Arrangements*. Oxford Scholarship Online. Oxford University Press. http://www.oxfordscholarship.com/oso/public/content/economicsfinance/0199248877/toc.html

Primo Braga, Carlos Alberto, and Simão Davi Silber. 1991. "Brazilian Frozen Concentrated Orange Juice: The Folly of Unfair Trade Cases." World Bank Policy, Research, and External Affairs Working Paper No. WPS 687. Washington, DC.

Pritchett, Lant. 1996. "Measuring Outward Orientation in LDCs: Can It Be Done?" *Journal of Development Economics* 49(2): 307-35.

Pursell, Garry, and Ashok Gulati. 1993. "Liberalizing Indian Agriculture: An Agenda for Reform." World Bank Policy Research Working Paper No. WPS 1172. Washington, DC.

Rajapatirana, Sarath. 2003. "World Bank Advocacy Role in Trade vis-à-vis OECD Countries: An Evaluation." Background Paper prepared for the Trade Assistance Evaluation, Independent Evaluation Group. Washington, DC.

Rakner, Lise, Nicolas van de Walle, and Dominic Mulaisho. 1999. "Aid and Reform: Zambia." In Shantayanan Devarajan, David R. Dollar, and Torgny Holmgren, eds., *Aid and Reform in Africa: Lessons from Ten Case Studies.* Washington, DC: The World Bank.

Revenga, Ana. 1995. "Employment and Wage Effects of Trade Liberalization: The Case of Mexican Manufacturing." World Bank PRE Working Paper Series, No. 1524. Washington, DC.

Robinson, Peter B. 2004. 'Evaluation of World Bank Trade-Related Assistance in Zambia (1987–2002)—Country Case Study." Background Paper prepared for the Trade Assistance Evaluation, Independent Evaluation Group. Washington, DC.

Rodriguez, Francisco, and Dani Rodrik. 2000. "Trade Policy and Economic Growth: A Skeptic's Guide to the Cross-National Evidence." In Ben S. Bernanke and Kenneth Rogoff, eds., *NBER Macroeconomics Annual 2000.* Cambridge, MA: MIT Press for NBER.

Rodrik, Dani. 2003. *Growth Strategies.* NBER Working Paper Series No. 10050. Cambridge, MA.

———. 2001. "Globalization, Growth and Poverty: Is the World Bank Beginning to Get It?" Harvard University, Cambridge, MA. Photocopy.

———. 1999. *The New Global Economy and Developing Countries: Making Openness Work.* Washington, DC: Overseas Development Council.

———. 1998. "Why Is Trade Reform So Difficult in Africa?" In Zubair Iqbal and Mohsin S. Khan, eds., *Trade Reform and Regional Integration in Africa.* Washington, DC: IMF.

———. 1997. *Has Globalization Gone Too Far?* Washington, DC: Institute for International Economics.

———. 1995. "Trade and Industrial Policy Reform." In T.N. Srinivasan and Jere Behrman, eds., *Handbook of Development Economics.* Amsterdam: Elsevier Science.

———. 1993. "Trade and Industrial Policy Reform in Developing Countries: A Review of Recent Theory and Evidence. " NBER Working Paper No. 4417. Cambridge, MA: National Bureau of Economic Research.

———. 1992. "The Limits of Trade Policy Reform in Developing Countries." *Journal of Economic Perspectives* 6(1): 87-105.

Rodrik, Dani, and Francisco Rodriguez. 2001. "Trade Policy and Economic Growth: A Skeptic's Guide to the Cross-National Evidence." In Ben Bernanke and Kenneth S. Rogoff , eds., *NBER Macroeconomic Annual.* Cambridge, MA: MIT Press.

Rodrik, Dani, Arvind Subramanian, and F. Trebbi. 2004. "Institutions Rule: The Primacy of Institutions over Geography and Integration in Economic Development." *Journal of Economic Growth* 9(2).

Roemer, Michael. 1994. "Industrial Strategies: Outward Bound." In David L. Lindauer and Michael Roemer, eds., *Asia and Africa: Legacies and Opportunities in Development.* Cambridge, M.A.: International Center for Economic Growth.

Rose, Andrew K. 2004. "Do We Really Know That the WTO Increases Trade?" *The American Economic Review* 94(1): 98-114.

Sachs, Jeffrey, and Andrew Warner. 1995. "Economic Reform and the Process of Global Integration." *Brookings Papers on Economic Activity* 1: 1-118.

Safadi, Raed, and Sam Laird. 1996. "The Uruguay Round Agreements: Impact on Developing Countries." *World Development* 24(7): 1223–42.

Salinas, Gonzalo. 2003. "Internal Evaluations of World Bank-Supported Trade Activities." Background paper prepared for the Trade Assistance Evaluation, Independent Evaluation Group. Washington, DC.

Salinger, Lynn. 2005. "Evaluation of World Bank Trade-Related Assistance in Senegal—Country Case Study." Background Paper prepared for the Trade Assistance Evaluation, Independent Evaluation Group. Washington, DC.

Salvatore, Dominick, and Thomas Hatcher. 1991. "Inward-Oriented and Outward-Oriented Trade Strategies." *The Journal of Development Studies* 27(3): 7-25.

Schiff, Maurice. 2002. "Regional Integration and Development in Small States." Volume 1. World Bank Policy Working Paper No. WPS 2797. Washington, DC.

Schiff, Maurice, and L. Alan Winters. 2003. *Regional Integration and Development.* Washington, DC: The World Bank and Oxford University Press.

Shafaeddin, S. Mehdi. 1995. "The Impact of Trade Liberalization on Export and GDP Growth in Least Developed Countries." *UNCTAD Review.* Geneva.

Stiglitz, Joseph E. 2002. *Globalization and its Discontents.* New York, N.Y.: W.W. Norton.

———. 1996. "Some Lessons from the East Asian Miracle." *World Bank Research Observer* 11(2): 151–77.

Stiglitz, Joseph E., and Shahid Yusuf, eds. 2001. *Rethinking the East Asian Miracle.* New York, N.Y.: Oxford University Press.

SAPRIN (Structural Adjustment Participatory Review International Network). 2002. *The Policy Roots of Economic Crisis and Poverty.* Washington, DC: SAPRIN Secretariat.

Subramanian, Arvind, and Shang-Jin Wei. 2003. "The WTO Promotes Trade, Strongly But Unevenly" NBER Working Paper No. 10024. Cambridge, MA, National Bureau of Economic Research.

Swamy, Gurushri. 2004. "The Impact of International Trade on Gender Equality." PREMnotes No. 86. Washington, DC: The World Bank.

Takacs, Wendy. 1990. "Options for Dismantling Trade Restrictions in Developing Countries." *World Bank Research Observer* 5(1): 25-46.

Thomas, Vinod, and John Nash. 1991. "Reform of Trade Policy: Recent Evidence from Theory and Practice." *World Bank Research Observer* 6(2): 219–40.

Thomas, Vinod, and John Nash, with Sebastian Edwards, Thomas Hutcheson, Donald Keesing, Kazi Martin, Garry Pursell, and Alexander Yeats. 1991. *Best Practices in Trade Policy Reform*. New York, N.Y.: Oxford University Press.

Topalova, Petia. 2004. "Trade Liberalization and Firm Productivity: The Case of India." IMF Working Paper No. 04/28. Washington, DC.

Tsikata, Yvonne. 2005. "Trade Conditionality in World Bank Adjustment Lending." Background paper prepared for the Trade Assistance Evaluation, Independent Evaluation Group. Washington, DC.

Tybout, James R. 2003. "Plant- and Firm-Level Evidence on "New" Trade Theories." In E. Kwan Choi and James Harrigan, eds., *Handbook of International Trade*. Malden, MA: Blackwell.

———. 2000. "Manufacturing Firms in Developing Countries: How Well Do They Do, and Why? *Journal of Economic Literature* 38(1): 11–44.

UNCTAD (United Nations Conference on Trade and Development). 2005. *UNCTAD Handbook of Statistics 2004*. New York, N.Y.: United Nations.

———. 2004. *Trade and Development Review 2004: Linking International Trade with Poverty Reduction*. Least-Developed Countries Report Series. New York, N.Y.: United Nations.

———. 2003. *Trade and Development Review 2003: Capital Accumulation, Growth and Structural Change*. New York, N.Y.: United Nations.

Van Briesbock J. 2005. "Exporting Raises Productivity in Sub-Saharan African Manufacturing Firms." *Journal of International Economics* 67: 373–91.

Wacziarg, Romain, and Karen Horn Welch. 2003. "Trade Liberalization and Growth: New Evidence." NBER Working Paper No. 10152. Cambridge, MA, National Bureau of Economic Research.

Wade, Robert H. 2003. "What Strategies Are Viable for Developing Countries Today? The WTO and the Shrinking of Development Space." *Review of International Political Economy* 10(4).

———. 1990, 1992, 2004. *Governing the Market: Economic Theory and the Role of Government in East Asian Industrialization*. 2004 edition. Princeton, NJ: Princeton University Press.

Whalley, John. 1996. "Why do Countries Seek Regional Trade Agreements?" In Jeffrey A. Frankel, ed., *The Regionalization of the World Economy.* Chicago: University of Chicago Press.

———. 1991. "Recent Trade Liberalization in the Developing World: What is behind It and Where is it Headed?" In David Greenaway, Robert C. Hine, Anthony P. O'Brien, and Robert J. Thornton, eds., *Global Protectionism,* Hampshire, U.K.: Palgrave Macmillan.

Williamson, John. 1997. "Exchange Rate Policy and Development Strategy." *Journal of African Economies* 6(3): 17–36.

Winters, L. Alan. 2000. "Trade and Poverty: Is There a Connection?" In Dan Ben-David, Håkan Nordström, and L. Alan Winters, eds., *Trade, Income Disparity and Poverty*. WTO Special Studies No. 5. Geneva: WTO.

Winters, L. Alan, and Won Chang. 2002. "How Regional Blocs Affect Excluded Countries: The Price Effects of MERCOSUR." World Bank Policy Research Working Paper Series, No. 2157. Washington, DC.

———. 2000. "Regional Integration and Import Prices: An Empirical Investigation." *Journal of International Economics* 51(2): 363–77.

Winters, L. Alan, Neil McCulloch, and Andrew McKay. 2004. "Trade Liberalization and Poverty:

The Evidence So Far." *Journal of Economic Literature* 42(1): 72–115.

Wood, Adrian. 1997. "Openness and Wage Inequality in Developing Countries: The Latin American Challenge to East Asian Conventional Wisdom." *The World Bank Economic Review* 11(1): 33–57.

———. 1995. *North-South Trade, Employment and Inequality: Changing Fortunes in a Skill-Driven World.* Oxford, U.K.: Oxford University Press.

World Bank. 2005a. *Managing the Debt Risk of Exogenous Shocks in Low-Income Countries.* Report No. 31759. Washington, DC.

———. 2005b. *2005 Review of the PRS Approach: Balancing Accountabilities and Scaling Up Results.* Washington, DC.

———. 2005c. *Customs Modernization Handbook.* Washington, DC.

———. 2004a. *Global Economic Prospects 2004: Realizing the Development Promise of the Doha Agenda.* Washington, DC.

———. 2004b. *Global Economic Prospects 2005: Trade, Regionalism, and Development.* Washington, DC.

———. 2003. "Leveraging Trade for Development: The World Bank Agenda, September 2003 Progress Report." Report to the Board. Washington, DC.

———. 2002a. *Development, Trade, and the WTO: A Handbook.* Washington, DC.

———. 2002b. *Global Economic Prospects and the Developing Countries 2002: Making Trade Work for the World's Poor.* Washington, DC.

———. 2002c. *Globalization, Growth, and Poverty: Building an Inclusive World Economy.* New York: Oxford University Press for the World Bank.

———. 2002d. "Leveraging Trade for Development: The World Bank Agenda, September 2002 Progress Report." Report to the Board. Washington, DC.

———. 2002e. *Proposed Priorities for Trade Work at the Bank. 2002-2005.* Washington, DC.

———. 2001a. "Leveraging Trade for Development: The World Bank Group's Agenda—Progress Report." Report to the Board. Washington, DC.

———. 2001b. *World Development Report 2000/2001: Attacking Poverty.* New York, N.Y.: Oxford University Press for the World Bank.

———. 2000. *Trade Blocs.* New York, N.Y.: Oxford University Press for the World Bank.

———. 1994. *Adjustment in Africa: Reforms, Results, and the Road Ahead.* New York, N.Y.: Oxford University Press for the World Bank.

———. 1990. *World Development Report 1990: Poverty.* New York, N.Y.: Oxford University Press for the World Bank.

———. 1987a. *World Development Report 1987: Industrialization and Foreign Trade.* New York, N.Y.: Oxford University Press for the World Bank.

———. 1987b. "President's Report on a Proposed Second Trade Policy Loan to Mexico." Washington, DC.

———. 1986. *World Development Report 1986: Trade and Pricing Policies in World Agriculture.* New York, N.Y.: Oxford University Press for the World Bank.

Yang, Yongzheng and Sanjeev Gupta. 2005. "Regional Trade Arrangements in Africa: Past Performance and the Way Forward." IMF Working Paper WP/05/36. Washington, DC.